Endorsements

Finally, a strategy for *victory* in the battle for life. Read *A Heartbeat Away* and enlist in the special forces who will bring the killing to an end.

—General Jerry Boykin

Janet Porter is a frontline warrior whom I respect highly. She has done as much to protect the sanctity of human life as anyone I know. I'm also pleased to call her my friend.

—James Dobson Ph.D.
Founder and President
James Dobson Family Institute

When we one day (hopefully soon) look back on what I pray will be the end of the scourge of abortion on our civilization, there will be a short roster of the key people who led the efforts to stop the insanity of killing unborn babies. That list will surely include Janet Porter, whose long-time leadership in the pro-life world was made most prominent when she launched the effort for the Heartbeat Bill in Ohio and in numerous other states. Her fight was not only against the usual suspects of Planned Parenthood and the far left who have made the killing of a baby a religious ritual, but she was even opposed by other elements in the pro-life movement that have never made sense to me and still don't. I consider Janet Porter one of the most important figures in our culture today. You will too!

—Mike Huckabee
Governor of AR, 1996–2007
TBN host, best-selling author, Fox News contributor

Janet Porter's *A Heartbeat Away* is an inspirational history of the greatest defensive weapon envisioned so far for protecting lives of the unborn, while at the same time it can be a "how-to" book on getting harmful laws changed for the sake of our nation. We should literally thank God for Janet, for the team she assembled, and for His amazing mercy that has allowed America to continue despite the tens of millions of our most innocent being killed. It is a story worth reading, remembering, and emulating for the life of our country and the lives of our precious unborn.

—Congressman Louie Gohmert (TX-01)

Janet Porter has been a rare and special gift to the pro-life movement. What comes through powerfully in these pages is Janet's fierce determination and unwavering persistence in developing and then implementing such an inspired weapon in the battle for life, the Heartbeat Bill. Janet's book not only forcefully and colorfully details the battles already fought, but also serves as a useful guidebook for the battles to come. On that day, which we pray comes soon, when the killing of babies in the womb is not only illegal in this country but unthinkable, Janet will be among those most to be thanked.

—Abby Johnson
Author of *Unplanned* and *The Walls Are Talking*
Founder, And Then There Were None and Prolove Ministries

Janet Porter is the William Wilberforce of our time. I do not know of anyone more relentless and resolute in their cause or with a more important cause for America at this time. In Scripture, the "shedding of innocent blood" brings a curse upon the land. What could be more innocent than a child who has not yet been born? God has raised up a great champion in Janet for the most helpless and innocent among us, and I have no doubt that the Heartbeat Bill will soon be the celebrated law of the land. This powerful book will be oxygen for the fire that is now burning to rid our country of this scourge of death and help us to esteem all life as the great treasure that it is.

—Rick Joyner
Chairman, The Oak Initiative

A
Heartbeat
Away

A Heartbeat Away

How the Heartbeat Bill Will Pierce the Heart of *Roe v. Wade* and the Shocking Betrayal No One Saw Coming

JANET PORTER

DESTINY IMAGE® PUBLISHERS, INC.
P.O. Box 310, Shippensburg, PA 17257-0310
"Promoting Inspired Lives."

This book and all other Destiny Image and Destiny Image Fiction books are available at Christian bookstores and distributors worldwide.

Cover design by: Lisa Rae McClure

For more information on foreign distributors, call 717-532-3040.

Reach us on the Internet: www.destinyimage.com.

ISBN 13 TP: 978-0-7684-5589-2

ISBN 13 eBook: 978-0-7684-5603-5

ISBN 13 HC: 978-0-7684-5605-9

For Worldwide Distribution, Printed in the U.S.A.

2 3 4 5 6 7 8 / 24 23 22 21

Dedicated to President Donald J. Trump

Our leader with the courage to stand for life and liberty in the face of monumental adversity, refusing to cower to establishment politicians, fake news, and constant pressure in order to do what's right. If there was ever a leader who could keep hearts beating, it is President Donald J. Trump.

"Unborn children have never had a stronger defender in the White House.... They are coming after me because I am fighting for you and we are fighting for those who have no voice.... And **we will win because we know how to win.**"

—PRESIDENT DONALD J. TRUMP
The first President to speak at the
March for Life in Washington, D.C.
January 24, 2020

THE HEARTBEAT BILL
IS THE WAY TO WIN.

*"Let this be recorded for future generations,
so that a people not yet born will praise the Lord."*

Psalm 102:18 NLT

Contents

Foreword

By Tom DeLay, Former Majority Leader,
U.S. House of Representatives

I regret that while I had the position and power, I didn't end abortion. Thanks to God and Janet Porter, I got another opportunity. I repented to God and the public and went to work to save babies from the evil of abortion.

I served in the U.S. House of Representatives for 22 years, 12 of those years in leadership of the majority, where I became the Majority Leader of the House. I have always been pro-life. I believe life begins at conception. I believe *Roe v. Wade* is an unconstitutional, illegitimate decision by a Supreme Court that believed it had the right to legislate.

The foundation for my entire political career had always been God and the Constitution. Protecting life was built on that foundation. I tried to advance the pro-life movement but bought into the lie of incrementalism as the political strategy advocated by the pro-life movement. The movement thought that if we just regulate abortion we will save babies. We saved some but lost millions. It has been 47 years and more than 60 million babies suffered horrible deaths while pro-life leaders brag that there are now "only" a million abortions a year. I am ashamed I was part of that.

Then God sent Janet Porter. Out of the blue, Janet called in February 2017. She was working to pass the Heartbeat Bill in Ohio and needed help for the federal bill. She explained the Heartbeat Bill is very simple with profound implications. "If the child's heartbeat is detected, the child is protected." *That was it!* The child will be treated as a living human being, protected by God and the Constitution!

It hit me like a bolt of lightning! God gave me another chance to save babies and stop the culture of death destroying America. Janet worked with Congressman Steve King to introduce the Heartbeat Bill in January 2017; now they needed help to pass it. We went to work. We designed a strategy to secure the 218 votes needed to pass it in the House. I discovered as Majority Leader, God gave me a unique talent to count votes. We traveled to D.C. and went office to office in the House making the case to keep hearts beating. The reception from members of Congress was exciting! We garnered 174 cosponsors on the Heartbeat Bill in just a few months, more than any pro-life bill in Congress.

Then National Right to Life and the pro-life establishment influenced House leadership to oppose our efforts. They had a chance to pass the Heartbeat Bill but chose to regulate abortion instead. Then the window of opportunity closed with the 2018 election. Republicans lost majority control of the House. In Texas, Rep. Briscoe Cain (R-Deer Park) introduced the Heartbeat Bill, but, like in Congress, the Texas Republican leadership killed it in the House. These are merely temporary setbacks.

Rest assured we will not give up. We will prevail because God is at the center of all we do.

The states are building the momentum we need to challenge the Supreme Court. After two vetoes from Governor John Kasich, Janet and her supporters passed the Heartbeat Bill in Ohio for the third time, and this time a new governor signed it into law. Other states are passing the bill, nine so far. Thank God for Janet Porter.

The momentum to keep hearts beating is now unstoppable. Ending abortion was thought to be impossible. It is now inevitable.

My hope and prayer is that we elect more people who will save babies as their top priority; that God will continue to protect Janet Porter as He uses her to end abortion in the United States and beyond. I also pray that this nation will repent and turn from its wicked ways so God can bless us, heal our land, and use us for His purpose.

The Heartbeat Bill will end abortion!

Introduction

Behold, I will do a new thing. —Isaiah 43:19 NKJV

When speaking at a conference in Arizona recently, I held up my Bible and asked, "How many of you believe this book?" Every hand went up. I then asked, "How many believe that God is everything He claims to be?" Again, every hand was enthusiastically raised. That was nice, but as I told them that day, *actions* are what you believe. Everything else is religious talk.

That's because faith is an act. It is *acting* like the word of God is true, even when everything we see, hear, and feel is screaming "it's impossible." Francis Schaeffer said, "Faith is not a leap in the dark. It is ceasing to call God a liar."[1] In order to see the impossible, we must first believe Jesus meant it when He said "with God all things are possible." We've been told that ending abortion was impossible. But if with God *all things* are possible, then that includes ending abortion. What remains for us is to take God at His word and step out and *do* it.

As Christians, we have an obligation to demonstrate to a watching world that the impossible is no match for the name of Jesus. But that doesn't mean victory will be easy or automatic. But when God puts a dream in our heart, it's because He intends for us to do it. The dream He put in my heart is to end abortion. But before we step out to fulfil any dream, we must first make sure the dream is from God. It begins with the checklist in Second Chronicles that itemizes what to do if we want God to hear, forgive, and heal us as a nation. We know the first three prerequisites of 2 Chronicles 7:14 well: humble ourselves, pray, and seek God's face, but most Christians stop there. The final item required for God to heal a nation is for us to "turn from our wicked ways." What's more wicked than the shedding of innocent blood? And what are we supposed to do about it?

What Does the Bible Say?

Several years ago, I testified for a bill introduced by Rep. Tom Brinkman (R-Cincinnati) to protect babies from the moment of conception. Before I could speak, there was a Democrat woman who felt the need to "set me straight." She took the position many Christians take today: that we should "stay out" out of the issue and the culture.

"Christians should stay out of politics" is a lie that has kept Christians sidelined in disobedience for decades. To say you're "not interested in politics" is to say you're not interested in life, freedom, your rights, your health, or your future. We are called to obey God in *every* arena—including the political arena—where the decisions that affect us are made.

As I began to testify before the committee, the hostile state representative couldn't wait to question me. "Where do you come off saying that to be a Christian, you need to be pro-life?" she snarled, declaring, "The Bible is a book about tolerance, and Jesus never used the word abortion."

I replied, "Well, if you open the Bible you'll find that 'Thou shalt not kill' made the top Ten *Commandments*—not suggestions. And Jesus said that 'if you love me, you'll keep my commandments.' If you read a little further you'll find that in Proverbs 31:8 we are *commanded* to be 'a voice for those appointed to die,' and in Proverbs 24:11, we are *commanded* to 'rescue those who are being carried away to death.'" She didn't ask any more questions.

While people like to pick and choose what they want out of the Bible, it's not a buffet. You can't live off the dessert; you also need the meat and potatoes. To defend life is to obey God.

More and more Christians are coming to understand that the God of the Bible hasn't changed from when He intervened in battles to deliver the victory, raise the dead, and heal the sick. But most Christians stop there. We think too small and we pray too limited. That's because if God can heal a person, He can heal a *nation*. As stated, for our nation to be healed, we must first turn from our wicked ways—something God wouldn't have told us to do if it couldn't be done. But how?

To get to where we need to go, first let's step back and take a look at where we are and how we got here. For nearly two centuries, innocent children on their way to birth were legally protected across America with few exceptions. Growing babies were safe and warm inside their mother's wombs until a surprise attack from the highest court on January 22, 1973. The attack of *Roe v. Wade* started a war. A war which, up until now, we had been losing.

December 7, 1941 is "a date which will live in infamy."[2] On that day 2,403 innocent Americans were killed by a sudden and deliberate attack on Pearl Harbor.[3] But the following year, the groundwork was laid for an even greater attack on Americans, one unlike anything ever witnessed before or since.[4] This enemy attack was designed to annihilate nearly half the population of the United States at that time.

That attack is now being executed, and the casualties are staggering. This war has already wiped out almost half the number of people who lived in the United States in 1942. That is the year the war began; it is the year Planned Parenthood, America's largest abortion mill, was formed.[5] January 22, 1973 is also a date which will live in infamy. But the sudden and deliberate attack of *Roe v. Wade* had actually been in the works for decades.

We thought it couldn't get much worse when the bar graph depicting the war on the unborn was three stories high.

America's greatest enemy is abortion. It is the biggest threat to American lives[6] and the leading cause of death in the world.[7] Abortion has massacred more than 60 million innocent Americans—far more than all the casualties of all our wars *combined* and every terrorist attack on our nation since its birth.

I have fought against abortion since I first learned about it in the tenth grade, and in 1986, as an undergraduate at Cleveland State University, I became president of Students for Life. In order to display the catastrophic consequences of abortion, our group constructed a bar graph to compare American war casualties—including the war waged on innocent lives in the womb.

We displayed the graph in our favorite spot—the open area in the middle of the University Center, where everyone would see. One inch represented fifty thousand lives, and the bar graph for the Revolutionary War was half an inch high. The Civil War was nearly ten inches. The casualties of World War I were depicted on the bar graph at just over two inches, World War II was eight inches, and Vietnam's causalities were just over an inch.

Using that same scale, we depicted the lives lost in the war on the unborn. At the time, statistics showed seventeen million American babies had been killed through abortion. The bar graph representing it extended off the chart for three stories, suspended with helium balloons.

We thought that with seventeen million lives lost, the carnage couldn't get much worse. But since we've been talking and marching and regulating abortion, another forty-four million lives have been lost. *It's staggering.* But unlike our war casualties, these Americans didn't die for a noble cause. They were killed merely because someone wanted them dead, and someone else was hired to kill them for profit.

Using this scale, all the casualties of all our wars can be depicted by twenty inches[8]—less than a yardstick—while the bar graph depicting US abortions today would be over ten stories high—higher than the building![9] Even worse, the attack against innocent Americans has gone virtually unchecked for nearly half a century.

But all that changed with two simple words: "Detectable heartbeat."

With those words came the ammunition needed to launch a counterattack against the enemy of life, to move us from defense to offense, from marching about abortion to *ending* it.

After decades of looking for an answer, what we needed to do was *listen* for one. The child in the womb is sending a signal. Each beat of their heart is a sign of life, a cry for help—an SOS we can no longer ignore.

Armed with a bill to ensure "if a heartbeat's detected, the baby's protected," legislators are listening. Heartbeat Bills have been heard in twenty-nine states and passed in nine *and counting*—with more on the verge of passing bills to keep hearts beating.

As Heartbeat laws race through the legislatures, others are racing through the courts to their final destination: the U.S. Supreme Court, where the war will be won. But to get to the Court, we first have to get to the legislative finish line—something critics said was impossible.

Today I stand on the other side of the finish line, where the word *impossible* is just an opinion—one that has been overruled. I am here to tell you we no longer have to settle for merely regulating around the edges of abortion. We can *end* it. Even against enormous obstacles and insurmountable odds—against double agents posing as pro-lifers and RINOs (Republicans in Name Only) posing as Republicans, against death-loving Democrats and a maligning media—the truth will prevail and victory will come.

We will stand up to those who stand in the way of ending abortion. No matter the threat. No matter the slander. No matter the cost. And we will win.

I invite you to step into this kairos moment—when the sound of a beating heart will prevail against the propaganda and win the war that's been waged against innocent lives. A moment when the enemy over-played its hand and America is repulsed by the glimpse it was given into the pro-abortion plan, which unashamedly includes infanticide.

This book is not for the half-hearted establishment, content with a million casualties each year, patting themselves on the back for their great "progress." If you think the death of a million innocent lives each year is something to be celebrated, you have either set the bar far too low or... you're a *terrorist*.

This book is for those who don't want to build another display depicting millions more lives lost because we kept doing what didn't work. This book is for whole-hearted warriors willing to get off defense and fight in a new way—to *win*.

This book is for everyone who has marched, worked, or prayed to end abortion and meant it. No matter your background, your age or experience, *you* can become the answer to those pro-life prayers and proclamations.

America's greatest enemy will be defeated—it is no longer a question of "if" but of "when." What has been missing until now is "how."

You'll find out how we are closer to the finish line than ever before—and what you can do to help turn the tide. If a purple state like Ohio can overcome insurmountable obstacles to pass a Heartbeat law, it can pass most anywhere. You will learn from our experience how to overcome "insurmountable" opposition with creative ideas and unwavering faith.

With every Heartbeat Bill that passes, another message is sent to the Supreme Court that the will of the people is to protect children from the moment we can hear their heartbeat. Whether your state or nation is red, purple, or deepest blue, lives will be saved just from Heartbeat Bill publicity. How do I know? Because I have seen it happen. Introducing a Heartbeat Bill is like plastering a billboard across your state and nation: "Abortion stops a beating heart." But instead of abortion stopping a beating heart, a beating heart will stop abortion.

True victory is within our reach, and this book will equip you with the strategy to end abortion instead of merely regulating it. The arrow to pierce the heart of *Roe v. Wade* has been crafted and is yours for the taking (see Faith2Action.org or HeartbeatBill.com). All you have to do is place the Heartbeat Bill in the hands of a pro-life champion—a legislator in your state or your nation—and this book will show you how.

But the effort to end abortion is not for the faint of heart. Those who kill babies will oppose you. People you thought were allies will oppose you. Those you thought were your friends will oppose you. But every one of them can be overcome. How do I know? Because I have experienced and witnessed it firsthand.

Ending abortion doesn't take an army. It takes lion-hearted leaders who enlist in the Special Forces to launch a counterattack against abortion with one goal: victory. It takes courageous leaders who won't back down to the bullies, who aren't afraid to fight. If only a small band of warriors are willing to do "whatever it takes" to keep hearts beating—to take heart and fight to the finish—we will win. The impossible will bow to the name of Jesus just as He said it would.

When we succeed, the question will be asked: "Where were you when they were killing babies?" When our history is written that question will be answered by those willing to stand and act in this hour: "We were the ones who brought the killing to an *end*."

Step into your destiny because the end of abortion is a heartbeat away.

CHAPTER 1

The Spark
That Ignited the
Heartbeat Revolution

"Rescue those who are unjustly sentenced to die."

—Proverbs 24:11 NLT

Why don't you outlaw abortion while you're here?"

Those eight words were spoken by my husband, David Porter, in October, 2010. That was the spark that ignited the Heartbeat revolution—when America went from regulating abortion to *ending* it.

We had just moved from Florida to my home state of Ohio—a state whose motto is, "With God all things are possible." At my husband's "impossible" suggestion, I did what a lot of people would have done: *I laughed.*

"Sure (looking at my watch), I have a few minutes, let me just knock that out while I'm here."

I dismissed the idea. It seemed impossible. But less than a month later, I realized my husband's charge had taken root in my heart.

I've never shared this publicly until now, but at least twenty-five years ago I pitched the idea for a bill to protect babies from the point of heartbeat (or brainwaves) to my former boss and a group of leaders while at a pro-life legislative conference in Chicago in the early 1990s. I was sternly dismissed for my naïve idea they said would "never work." When I wasn't convinced, reinforcements were called into this post-session social gathering. Legislators and leaders circled around me emphatically repeating the predominant presumption "we can only *regulate* abortion," listing the reasons anything more was certain to fail. While some all but patted me on the head, others were red in the face, but they all shared the same sentiment: Who did I think I was to challenge their "well-thought-out" strategy? Another reiterated the "incremental" party line while citing his impressive credentials and vast experience, reminding me that I was just a kid out of college with much to learn.

What I learned is that merely regulating abortion for fifty years has cost more than sixty million children their lives. I'm guessing there were many others who encountered the very same resistance. But victory belongs to those who push past the overpowering obstruction in order to act. It belongs to those with the courage to stand against the crowd even if they stand alone. I am ashamed that was not me. I let the naysayers kill the dream God put in my heart decades ago. It is ironic that the forgotten idea that had been beaten out of me resurfaced at the wake of my former boss, a staunch "incrementalist."

On Tuesday, November 30, 2010, I drove to Columbus to attend the wake of my friend and former boss, Mark Lally, legislative counsel for Ohio Right to Life, never recalling my rejected idea from the nineties, which had been berated and dismissed by the pro-life powers that be.

As I looked at the body of my friend lying in the casket it occurred to me, "He worked his entire life to end abortion but never got to see it." My heart was still broken from losing my father three months earlier, and it dawned on me just how short life really is. That was the moment a spark ignited like a lightning bolt to my heart: "We need to end abortion now! Not just march about it. Not just regulate it. We need to *end* it—*now!*"

In an instant, my mind replayed all our failed attempts of the past. I had been a part of the ballot initiative to protect children from conception just four years earlier in South Dakota. It failed not once, but twice. I testified for bills to protect babies from conception that never made it out of committee. Personhood amendments, to put full protection of children to a vote on the ballot, had not yet succeeded even in the most conservative states.

We've been passing "incremental laws"—moving a millimeter down the field for decades. That noble but failed approach has left us with a body count of 60 million and another million children who continue to be brutally killed each year.

As legislative director of Ohio Right to Life for nearly a decade, I worked to pass many of those incremental laws, including bills supporting the "Woman's Right to Know"; informed consent with a 24 hour waiting period; legal protection from fetal homicide; and parental consent, as well as initiatives to defund and regulate abortion. I even successfully lobbied to pass the nation's first ban on partial-birth abortion. But as the late Dr. Jack Willke, cofounder of the National Right to Life Committee, said, that incremental approach "didn't get us far enough fast enough." *He was right.*

I was accustomed to the string of victories from passing the millimeter incremental bills. After all, we were told that's *the best* we could do. Over and over...*and over.* Every time a suggestion was made to the contrary, we were given the incremental party line again

John Kasich speaking at my campaign fundraiser back when I was merely regulating abortion

until everyone marched in lockstep, a millimeter at a time. Introducing bill after bill, year after year, barely impacting the colossal casualties suffered every day, every year, *every decade.*

Each of those incremental victories were celebrated with cheers from the pro-life crowds and even the Republican establishment. After all, I was one of them, toeing the party line. I had open door access to state and congressional leaders as well as the governor; I was invited to all the receptions, bill signings, and Republican conventions. I had photo ops with U.S. presidents, vice presidents, and was even given an audience with the pope. We were well-liked—and why wouldn't we be? We were working our tails off to elect pro-life candidates while asking almost nothing in return.

It was fun to dance at the gubernatorial and presidential balls. It's nice when all the "cool kids" want you on their team. John Kasich, then chairman of the U.S. House Budget Committee, asked me to be his campaign spokesperson and trusted me to debate his Congressional opponent in his stead. When I ran against the Secretary of the Ohio Republican Party for State Central Committee, Kasich campaigned to help me unseat her. He even invited me on Bill O'Reilly's show when he was a guest host.

I was on the "inside." But the moment we set out to do more than regulate abortion all that changed.

John Kasich, who ran on making pro-life promises, betrayed us and the babies with not one, but two vetoes of the pro-life Heartbeat Bill costing more than 150,000 babies their lives.

Suddenly, I was on the outside of the establishment and the outside of political favor that comes with asking those who represent us to merely manage abortion. But you know what's better than having everyone like you? Better than all the accolades, photo ops, and balls? That's easy—ending abortion.

We in the pro-life movement spent decades patting ourselves on the back for all our "achievements." It's not that we didn't work hard to get them. And yes, add them all up and they saved some lives. But the fact remains that each year nearly a million babies are aborted in the United States. That's the official abortion rate, but *many* more abortions are unreported[1]—including the entire state of California.[2] If *any other* organization fought for almost half a century and suffered more than sixty million casualties[3] and lost *a million more* innocent lives each year, we could use a lot of words to describe it, but "successful" would not be one of them.

To win the war, we needed a paradigm shift. One that would take us off defense and incremental regulation. To quit playing safe, defensive ball like we're the ones winning. To quit punting when a touchdown is required. To play to *win the game* rather than merely putting a few points on a lopsided scoreboard.

So how could we actually *win*? Outright bans had not worked. Incremental bills were woefully inadequate. We needed a scientific step that would get us as close to the finish line as possible. I knew a baby's heartbeat began within eighteen to twenty-one days of gestation, and brain waves were measurable at about six weeks. But the idea to protect babies using those indicators of life had been so obliterated that I didn't even make the connection to my long-forgotten idea from the nineties, which the pro-life establishment had refused and rejected. Yet, there was something about heartbeat that resonated in my heart—it just made sense.

That's when I turned to some friends at Mark Lally's wake and told them what I had been thinking, "If we can't rescue every child just yet, let's protect as many as we can." I pitched the idea for a Heartbeat Bill, and unlike in the past, hearts were now open, and the idea for a Heartbeat Bill was born—*again*.

After all, a heartbeat is the universally recognized indicator of life. Everybody gets that. If there's any doubt about whether someone's alive, we instinctively check for a pulse. We *all* know the heart monitors in hospitals aren't there for decoration. It's why we've never been to a funeral of someone with a beating heart. So, why would we ignore this scientific yardstick? Arkansas State Senator Jason Rapert, who passed the nation's first Heartbeat law in 2013, stated the case very simply, "If there's a heartbeat, there's life." Louisiana Heartbeat Bill joint sponsor Rep. Valarie Hodges put it this way, "Nothing is more precious to any of us than the heartbeat."[4] Without it we're dead.

With the Heartbeat Bill, we would no longer discriminate against the youngest members of our human family by ignoring the SOS they'd been sending with each beat of their heart.

Janet Porter presenting the Hero for Life Award to Arkansas Senator Jason Rapert.

After the wake, I asked a group of people to dinner and called my best friend Lori Viars on the way to the restaurant to discuss the idea. Three days later, Lori was among those who came to our housewarming party on Friday, December 3, 2010. No, it wasn't a "slumber party" as was widely reported in the news. But Lori lived several hours away and, like four or five others, spent the night rather than driving home. The next morning I greeted our guests with breakfast and a whiteboard. On it I wrote two words no one had ever heard before: "Heartbeat Bill." It would ensure that instead of abortion stopping a beating heart, a beating heart would stop abortion.

A Scientific Solution to Abortion

That afternoon, we made a phone call and got our bill sponsor, the chairman of the House Health Committee, a legislator I knew from my days at Ohio Right to Life. Ten days later, we had a first draft of the bill, thanks to my friend John Jakubczyk, past president of Arizona Right to Life and president of the Southwest Life and Law Center. The next day, December 15, 2010, I hosted a conference call with about twenty pro-life attorneys from around the country and medical experts—including pro-life hero Dr. Jack Willke—to discuss the nation's first Heartbeat Bill.

I remember the discussion. Lawyers talked of "measurable heartbeat," doctors talked about "cardiac activity," but by the end of the call, the two words that everyone agreed upon were "detectable heartbeat." At the time, we didn't know just how profoundly important those two words would be.

Gregory J. Roden was the guy who told us the significance of that language. In his *Issues in Law & Medicine* article, he noted a shift evident in the 2007 Supreme Court case *Gonzales v. Carhart*.[5] Roden explained that nearly four decades of cases viewed the child in the womb as "potential life." He then provided me with three pages of thirty-four years of court citations that referred to the child in the womb as "potential life" or a "potentially living" fetus.

Brace yourself for what came next: In *Gonzales v. Carhart*, the Supreme Court, for the first time, admitted—as a "finding of fact"—that instead of a "potentially living" fetus, a "*living* fetus" is recognized from the time of..."*detectable heartbeat*."[6]

Not only was it a finding of fact; it was an *undisputed* finding of fact. Even those in favor of legal abortion on demand agreed with this fact, now recognized for the first time since 1973 by the U.S. Supreme Court. There is a *living fetus* from the point of "detectable heartbeat"—the exact wording used in our Heartbeat Bill and in Heartbeat *laws* that are making their way to the U.S. Supreme Court!

As North Dakota Governor Jack Dalrymple said when he signed the Heartbeat Bill into law in 2013, the Supreme Court "has never considered this precise restriction."[7] But that's about to change when the same court that said there is a "living fetus" from the point of "detectable heartbeat" makes a ruling on that very thing.

Don't let the word "fetus" throw you; it's just a Latin word for the young human being. *Black's Law Dictionary* defines fetus as "an unborn child."[8] *Merriam-Webster* defines it as "a developing human,"[9] while the *Cambridge English Dictionary* defines fetus as "a young human being... after the organs have started to develop."[10]

The abortion movement has used the Latin term "fetus" to clinically dehumanize the unborn child in the minds of the public for fifty years. But it doesn't make someone less human when we use Latin to describe them any more than it makes someone less pregnant by using the Latin word for pregnant woman and talk about the "gravida."[11] But since most people aren't fluent in Latin, I prefer English, especially when talking about the rights of a fellow human being.

With forty-six human chromosomes, *of course* it's a human being, no matter how loudly the science deniers protest. It's not a rabbit or a carrot or a tumor or a ferret. And once there's a detectable heartbeat, even the Supreme Court admits that "young human being" is *alive.*

The issue is no longer contested. If there's a detectable heartbeat, we are legally talking about a living human being. *Period.* That matters because *all* human beings are created equal and endowed by our Creator with the inalienable right to life, as our nation's birth certificate, the Declaration of Independence, declares.

Legislators around the country are agreeing with the Supreme Court—once there is a detectable heartbeat, we are talking about a living human being *worthy of protection.* Pennsylvania Heartbeat Bill sponsor Senator Doug Mastriano stated, "If a heartbeat denotes the end of life, obviously, logically, scientifically, it denotes, clearly, the beginning of life."[12] *Obviously.*

When speaking about the Mississippi Heartbeat Bill, sponsor Senator Matt Castlen stated it plainly, "That child in her womb is a living human being. And all living human beings have a right to life."[13]

Heartbeat is a scientific approach to replace the outdated standard of "viability," which is merely a measure of our ever-changing technology. The Heartbeat Law will present the opportunity for the Supreme Court to simply move the line of allowable protection from the arbitrary marker of viability to the scientific marker of heartbeat—something which is no longer in conflict with Supreme Court abortion jurisprudence.

It's a scientific step everyone can recognize. As Texas Heartbeat Bill cosponsor Rep. Steve Toth said, "It doesn't get any more basic than this." Toth added, "The Heartbeat marks the beginning and the end of life...It's the easiest thing to help people understand how basic our fight is for the right to live."

While we who are pro-life want to protect babies from conception, the pro-abortion movement applauds killing them until birth as New York has done—and beyond birth as Virginia Governor Ralph Northam publicly declared. But we can all agree that we should *at least* protect a fellow human being who has a detectable heartbeat. It's common sense.

It should be common ground. In fact, it is.

A 2017 Barna poll asked, "If a doctor is able to detect the heartbeat of an unborn baby, that baby should be legally protected." Guess what? Seven out of ten Americans (69%) agree! That includes 86% of Republicans, 61% of Independents, and even a majority—55%—of Democrats.[14] *What do you know?* The Democrats are out of step with even their own base if they oppose a Heartbeat Bill. Maybe that's why we're seeing some Democrats willing to take the lead like Senator John Milkovich, the Democrat Heartbeat Bill sponsor in Louisiana, and Louisiana Governor John

Edwards, a Democrat, who signed it into law, and just won reelection in a state where President Trump won by 20%.[15] Shocked commentators declared, "Louisiana is a ruby-red state that has no business being led by a Democrat."[16] That's what happens when Democrats vote in step with their constituents to keep hearts beating—they *win*.

The Heartbeat Bill is the scientific solution to abortion upon which America agrees. It doesn't take us all the way to the finish line, but gets us within inches. As Mark Minck, who is spearheading the Heartbeat initiative in Florida stated, "The majority of people are quick to realize that anyone who has a beating heart should have their lives protected." The Heartbeat Bill will ensure that "if a heartbeat is detected the baby is protected." Simple. Scientific. Certain.

To deny a heartbeat is to deny science. To ignore it is heartless.

Rep. Stephanie Borowicz, who sponsored the House version of the Pennsylvania Heartbeat Bill, put it this way, "If you can be declared dead when the heart stops why not declared alive when it starts?"[17] It makes perfect sense.

In his committee testimony, Georgia Heartbeat Bill sponsor state Rep. Ed Setzler called the Heartbeat Bill "medically sound and legally sound."[18] He is right.

Because the Heartbeat Bill refers to detecting a heartbeat using "standard medical practice," as technology improves, more babies will be protected with the very same law. And, as the pro-abortion side testified in committee, "This will end all abortion!" It may very well be that abortionists, who are motivated by money, won't stay open if they'll only earn a fraction of their business. I can't wait.

At the 2011 Heartbeat rally in the Ohio Statehouse, pro-life hero Joe Scheidler, founder of the Pro-Life Action League, said, "When I first heard about this bill, my heart beat faster! I love this bill. It's not vague... Heartbeat is the strongest anybody has come up with."[19]

When signing the Mississippi Heartbeat Bill, Governor Phil Bryant said, "The Heartbeat has been the universal hallmark of life since man's very beginning."[20] Bryant added, "I can remember the exciting moments both with my children and grandchildren when the first sonograms were taken and that heartbeat could be heard."[21] Everyone has seen the sonograms. Everyone understands the significance of heartbeat, and it is changing the way America sees the child in the womb.

There has been a shift. In addition to Alabama, which passed a law to protect babies from conception in 2019, as of this writing, Heartbeat Bills have been introduced in twenty-nine states and passed in nine (and counting): Arkansas (2013), North Dakota (2013), Iowa (2018), Mississippi, Kentucky, Georgia , Missouri, Louisiana, and Ohio, where it all began (2019). Six Heartbeat Laws passed in the first five months of 2019 and there will be more.

The federal Heartbeat Bill (H.R. 490) was introduced in January 2017. It had 174 cosponsors—more than any other pro-life bill in Congress. It was reintroduced in the U.S. House (with the same bill number) in January 2019.

Heartbeat Bills crafted from our Ohio bill are spreading like wildfire across the country. South Carolina, Tennessee, and Oklahoma are closing in on the finish line, while Michigan furiously collects signatures for their Heartbeat initiative to bypass their pro-abortion governor. California is looking to put it on the ballot, as is Florida, already gathering signatures to bypass their legislature who refused to act. Heartbeat Bills have also been introduced in Alabama, Alaska, Idaho, Indiana, Illinois, Kansas, Maryland, Minnesota, New Hampshire, New York, Pennsylvania, Rhode Island, Texas, West Virginia, and Wyoming. The momentum is unstoppable, rapidly approaching the tipping point.

The Heartbeat Bill gives the pro-life movement what it has been missing for decades—a clear pathway to victory, where babies with beating hearts will live and not die. Missouri Rep. Nick Schroer said, "It's the most sound, comprehensive, pro-life bill in the entire U.S."[22] While opponents claim it's unconstitutional, they have lost sight of the fact that it is *Roe v. Wade* that is unconstitutional. It also doesn't take a constitutional scholar to count to five—the current pro-life majority on the Supreme Court, which will likely increase in the coming months.

This fresh, bold, commonsense bill to protect nearly every child facing abortion is on the way to our goal of protecting them all. It is the scientific step that even the Supreme Court can't ignore, especially since they too recognize a living human being from the point of "detectable heartbeat."

In her video testimony for the Michigan Heartbeat Bill, Abby Johnson, former Planned Parenthood clinic director, spoke of the hope of the Heartbeat Bills—they are our best chance of overturning *Roe v. Wade.*

I did work in politics for Planned Parenthood. They are not concerned about a particular type of abortion procedure being banned.... They are concerned about the pro-life movement coming up with a bill that will actually scientifically and medically challenge *Roe,* because that, in the law, that is what is absolutely required in order for *Roe* to be overturned.... And I believe that the Heartbeat Bill is our very best chance of making that happen.

> The Supreme Court, their job is to look at the will of the states. So if the will of let's say half of the states of the United States is to make abortion illegal at the moment of a detectable heartbeat, they have to take that into consideration—they must take it into consideration. I believe absolutely Heartbeat Bills are the very best chance we have right now of overturning *Roe*.[23]

She is right. When the Heartbeat Bill is upheld, it will protect more babies than all the bills we have passed in the last 50 years—*combined*.

Pro-lifers are realizing the same thing across the nation and around the world. I met with pro-life leaders in Singapore and Israel in 2019, including a member of the Knesset, and with leaders from New Zealand and Panama. Our team just spent a day with leaders interested in bringing a Heartbeat Bill to Japan. The Heartbeat Bill wildfire is not only spreading across our country; it will soon ignite around the world!

Don't let the court battles discourage you. That is the process, and that is the plan. In order to deliver the fatal blow to abortion on demand, we must first get to the Supreme Court. When these judges enjoin heartbeat laws, they are really doing us a favor. That temporary setback is really a setup. Keep in mind an arrow can only be shot by pulling it backward. These courts are just launching our arrow where it must go—to the heart of *Roe v. Wade*.

Kentucky Governor Matt Bevin stayed past midnight to sign their Heartbeat Bill into law. He didn't lose his enthusiasm with the legal challenge, exclaiming, "Bring it![24] Kentucky will always fight for life... always!"[25] The legal battles must be fought in order for the Heartbeat Bill to pierce the heart of *Roe v. Wade*.

Our constitutional experts crafted the bill with the court challenge in mind. The Supreme Court has always been its destiny. When lower and appellate judges strike our laws down, they are setting up the challenge to go over their heads to the place where abortion ends. The arrows are launched while others are loading. There is no stopping it. The end of abortion has already begun.

I spent a few weeks in Michigan helping launch their Heartbeat Bill and was asked, "How can you be so sure the Heartbeat Bill can pass?" That's easy. Now that the dust has settled, the view from *this side* of the finish line is clear. I know the Heartbeat Bill will pass because I have already seen it done—in state after state.

Experience trumps every discouraging argument a person can make. Once you have seen Goliath fall, *no one* can tell you it can't happen. More giants are about to fall, just as they did after David brought his rock to a sword fight (see 2 Sam. 21:22).

Missouri Rep. Sonya Anderson (R-Mo) stated, "I am proud that Missouri, the Show-Me State is showing the rest of the country that we will stick up for the unborn."[26] And she is not alone. Pennsylvania Heartbeat Bill sponsor Senator Doug Mastriano (R-Gettysburg) stated, "So anytime there's a heartbeat up until death, that baby needs to be left alone."[27]

Even Miss Universe Philippines 2019, Gazini Ganados, was asked about the Heartbeat Bill. She responded, "It's just not an option at all for me...I just think it's inhumane to do that."[28] She is right. But "inhumane" doesn't begin to describe what abortionists do to innocent human beings with beating hearts. And we're going to stop them.

I knew the Heartbeat Bill was an idea from God. And I knew the state of Ohio motto—"With God all things are possible"—was true, because Jesus was the one who said it. That's how I knew the Heartbeat Bill would

From left to right: Lori Viars, Janet Porter, Fmr. Rep. Christina Hagan, and Beth Folger, Janet's mom. Janet is holding Christina's twins Wyatt and Colton Nemeth moments after the final victory for the Ohio Heartbeat Bill in the Ohio Senate on April 10, 2019.

pass. What I didn't know was how hard it would be or how long it would take.

We in the pro-life movement were used to being praised for incremental victories, but I've learned that *true* leadership is willing to go where immediate success is not guaranteed. To obey God without knowing the outcome in advance. Winston Churchill said, "Great success always comes at the risk of enormous failure."[29] True leadership can't be swayed by doubters or defeatists, by credit or by criticism.

When you step out and challenge a losing strategy, don't expect the welcome mat. Some politicians and establishment "pro-life" groups aren't going to like you stepping on their turf or challenging them to do more than merely regulate abortion. The organizations we built for decades are now being used against us. You'll also need to overcome the hand-wringers who are worried about offending our "friends" in public office. But if our "friends" aren't willing to do what we elected them to do, then they aren't really our friends.

True leaders are not satisfied with marching about abortion, talking about abortion, or regulating around the edges of abortion. Because now we have a way to *end* it. And we can do it *now*. We are running for the finish line and, regardless of what the "pro-life" establishment says, we won't go back to crawling.

I promised God that when He gave us the victory, I would give Him the credit. Before our Ohio Heartbeat Bill passed, I already had the press statement written. I sent it out the moment the Senate vote was cast from the Statehouse chamber, knowing with a promised signature from the new governor, it would soon become law. The statement read: "All the credit—all the glory—goes to Jesus Christ, the author and giver of life."

If the media wanted a quote from me, that's what they had to use, because it was the only thing I said. I wanted to see the name of Jesus honored when the victory came, and it was.

You see, this really is a testimony of Jesus. Revelation 19:10b states: "For the testimony of Jesus is the spirit of prophecy." If you will take the baton and run this race, our testimony of what Jesus did is your prophecy. Our victory will soon become *yours*.

Babies will live and the God of the impossible will be glorified. Then you can join your voice to others including Louisiana Heartbeat Bill sponsor Democrat John Milkovich who said, "We give God the thanks for this victory."[30]

At the January 24, 2020 March for Life in Washington, D.C., President Trump said, "We are fighting for those who have no voice…And we will win because we know how to win."[31]

The Heartbeat Bill is the way to win.

So whether you are reading this book as a pro-lifer seeking a roadmap to victory, an uninvolved spectator, or a pro-abortion operative doing opposition research, I have the same message for you. It's the message inspired by my husband in October, 2010. It's a message I have been declaring across Congress and in state legislatures throughout our nation and beyond. It's a message that even the skeptics are beginning to believe. Write it down: We're gonna *end* abortion.

And one more thing: Ending abortion is *just the beginning.*

CHAPTER 2

The Enemy Has Overplayed His Hand

"Never yield to the apparently overwhelming might of the enemy." —Winston Churchill[1]

On January 22, 2019, the forty-sixth anniversary of *Roe v. Wade*, New York Governor Andrew Cuomo signed the "Reproductive Health Act" into law, which allows abortion until the moment of birth. He then directed the One World Trade Center to be lit pink to celebrate this "achievement" and shine a "bright light forward for the rest of the nation to follow."[2]

Isaiah said it best: "Woe to those who call evil good, and good evil; who put darkness for light, and light for darkness" (Isa. 5:20).

When Governor Cuomo called "evil good" and "put darkness for light," he didn't realize that he and the abortion movement also overplayed their hand. They displayed their insatiable thirst for the blood of infants for all the world to see, and the world was sickened, outraged, and repulsed. President Donald Trump said it well in his 2019 State of the Union Address:

> Lawmakers in New York cheered with delight upon the passage of legislation that would allow a baby to be ripped from the mother's womb moments from birth. These are living, feeling, beautiful babies who will never get the chance to share their love and their dreams with the world.[3]

Georgia Heartbeat Bill supporter Senator Renee Unterman said, "We are not like New York or Virginia," she said. "We will not throw away children who aren't perfect because all children are perfect in the eyes of God."[4]

No matter what abortion proponents say, abortion is not about "terminating a pregnancy"—*birth* terminates a pregnancy. New York's abortion legislation proved it is not a decision "between a woman and her doctor," because the law eliminated the physician requirement and invites nondoctors to kill children through all nine months.

It's not about "choice," as the law strips the fetal homicide protection from women who choose life for their babies but have that choice taken from them by an outside assailant. *No choice. No justice.* It also strips protections from babies who survive abortion. New York's abortion law makes it clear; the law is about guaranteeing what abortion proponents have always wanted: a dead baby. As Rep. Sandy Salmon said during the floor debate for the Iowa Heartbeat Bill, "A baby has become something we can throw away. This bill says it's time to change the way we think about unborn life."[5]

By the way, the same One World Trade Center that was lit pink to celebrate the "freedom" to kill unborn children also memorializes eleven unborn babies who died in the 9/11 terrorist attack.[6] Cuomo celebrated taking unborn life at the very place we memorialized unborn life—lighting a beacon to death *and* hypocrisy. What Governor Cuomo signed into law will kill far more innocent Americans than the Islamic terrorists ever dreamed of killing.

Speaking of hypocrisy, the New York death-until-birth law was signed the same month a bill was introduced in New Jersey—to protect unborn *cows*. Pro-abortion Democratic Assemblyman Benjie Wimberly said, "Cattle can't defend themselves on issues like this…It's animal rights. It's the right thing to do. It's the moral thing to do and you're protecting something that really can't protect itself."[7] Like New York, New Jersey allows abortion until birth for humans, but it's the unborn *cows* they're trying to protect.

And not only cows. In May 2019, New Jersey's Democratic governor, Phil Murphy, also "proudly" signed a bill to make it harder to euthanize dogs, just weeks after signing a bill allowing human beings to be killed by assisted suicide. He said, "I am proud to sign these bills that will protect animals in danger of abuse and treat our four-legged residents with the compassion they deserve."[8] Apparently, two-legged residents don't deserve such protection or compassion.

The pro-death movement is the embodiment of hypocrisy.

Fueling it all is the blood money behind the billion-dollar business of child killing. The more blood that flows, the more money they make and the more political contributions they can give to the pro-abortion candidates who enable them.[9] Planned Parenthood announced their plans to spend a record 45 million—not on healthcare for low-income women—but for the 2020 elections to support fringe candidates who want legal abortion through birth—so they can keep the blood and their money flowing.[10]

New York and New Jersey aren't the only states that permit abortion until birth. Prior to New York's law, Alaska, Colorado, New Hampshire, New Jersey, New Mexico, Oregon, Vermont, and Washington, D.C. already had no gestational limits on abortion whatsoever.[11] We've been trying to convince people of this—quite unsuccessfully—for decades. But now New York has made their radical pro-abortion brutality clear for all to see.

But even abortion until birth isn't enough for those who love death. What do they want to do if the infant they attempt to abort happens to survive?

On February 25, 2019, the U.S. Senate failed to pass the Born-Alive Abortion Survivors Protection Act by a vote of 53–44 (hiding behind their self-imposed sixty-vote supermajority rule). In an op-ed on *Fox News'* website, Republican Senator Ben Sasse of Nebraska stated:

> Let's speak plainly: This is barbaric. The Born-Alive Abortion Survivors Protection Act would do nothing more than require that health care providers offer to a baby who survives an abortion the same level of medical care they would give to any other baby at the same gestational age.... If my colleagues can't say that it's wrong to leave a living, breathing baby, cold and alone on a table, to die of neglect, then they are not only tacitly endorsing infanticide. They are helping to create a society where some people count more than

others, and where the vulnerable are always at the mercy of the powerful.[12]

Among those who voted against the Born-Alive Abortion Survivors Protection Act were senators Bernie Sanders (I-VT), Elizabeth Warren (D-MA), and Amy Klobuchar (D-MN), denying legal protection to babies who are born.[13]

President Trump rightly stated, "This will be remembered as one of the most shocking votes in the history of Congress."[14] President Trump added in a tweet, "The Democrat position on abortion is now so extreme that they don't mind executing babies AFTER birth."[15]

Homosexual activist Pete Buttigieg jumped on the radical Democrat bandwagon to allow children to be legally killed even *after* birth. When asked about whether born-alive babies should be legally protected, he reiterated the radical position, "it shouldn't be up to a government official to draw the line."[16] Whether Buttigieg believes the government should "draw the line" to protect toddlers remains to be seen.

Instead of automatically giving an infant who survives an abortion a normal standard of care, Ralph Northam, the Democratic governor of Virginia, thinks the "physicians and mother" should decide what happens to the baby.[17] In other words, he wants to let the mother choose to kill the born-alive infant. That's something currently referred to as murder.

In a January 30, 2019 radio interview about the Repeal Act, Governor Northam defended H.B. 2491, a bill that its sponsor, Democratic Delegate Kathy Tran, testified would allow abortions even during labor.[18]

Republican Todd Gilbert, majority leader of the Virginia House of Delegates, asked Tran exactly how far her bill would go:

> **Gilbert**: How late in the third trimester could a physician perform an abortion if he indicated it would impair the mental health of the woman?
>
> **Tran**: Or physical health.
>
> **Gilbert**: Okay. I'm talking about the mental health.
>
> **Tran**: Through the third trimester. The third trimester goes all the way up to 40 weeks.
>
> **Gilbert**: Okay. But to the end of the third trimester?
>
> **Tran**: Yep. I don't think we have a limit in the bill.
>
> **Gilbert**: Where it's obvious a woman is about to give birth, that she has physical signs that she is about to give birth. Would that be a point at which she could still request an abortion if she was so certified? She's dilating.
>
> **Tran**: Mr. Chairman, that would be a decision that the doctor, the physician, and the woman would make at that point.
>
> **Gilbert**: I understand that. I'm asking if your bill allows that.
>
> **Tran**: My bill would allow that, yes.[19]

Yes, Tran admitted during the floor debate that her bill "would allow" for a woman to kill the baby as she is "about to give birth" because not killing the baby would affect her "mental health."

On the same day Tran introduced the bill to legally kill human babies as they're being born, she also introduced a bill to save the cankerworm—prohibiting spraying an insecticide that would take the precious life of a *worm*.[20] Kill the innocent babies; save the destructive worms. This is beyond hypocritical; it is psychotic.

> And then we heard the case of the Governor of Virginia, where he stated he would execute a baby after birth.
>
> —President Donald Trump
> State of the Union Address, February 5, 2019[21]

In a radio interview Governor Northam tried to justify the proposed infanticide since some of the babies being aborted at such a late stage in the pregnancy would be disabled and, apparently, not worthy of legal protection:

> When we talk about third-trimester abortions, these are done with the consent of obviously the mother, with the consent of the physicians, more than one physician, by the way. And it is done in cases where there may be severe deformities. ... The infant would be resuscitated if that's what the mother and the family desired.[22]

Only resuscitate a baby who's wanted, not one who has "deformities," of course. I wonder what Virginia's disabled citizens think about how little their governor values their lives.

In state after state, we have seen amendments to discriminate against the disabled—using the term "fetal anomaly." Killing children who aren't perfect isn't a new idea, but it's one that history has summarily rejected.

Even after the backlash, Governor "Blackface" Northam, who admitted to dressing in blackface[23] and appearing in a racist photo in his medical school yearbook wearing either blackface or a KKK costume,[24] said he doesn't have "any regrets" about his pro-infanticide position.[25]

By contrast, at his State of the Union address on February 4, 2020, President Trump featured Robin Schneider and her 2-year-old daughter Ellie, who was born at 21 weeks and 6 days.[26] President Trump stated, "Through the skill of her doctors—and the prayers of her parents—little Ellie kept on winning the battle for life."[27] President Trump welcomed them in the gallery and declared, "Every child is a miracle of life."[28] Maybe that's why Speaker Nancy Pelosi ripped up his State of the Union speech.

Louisiana Democrat Heartbeat Bill sponsor Senator John Milkovich said at the passage, "This is another victory in defense of the lives of the unborn and another blow upon the abortion cartel's effort to assault the next generation with infanticide."[29]

While Alabama's law to protect every child in the womb and six heartbeat laws all passed in the first five months of 2019, states like Illinois, Vermont, Maine, Nevada, and Rhode Island joined New York in the effort to legally and officially expand the killing.[30] Rhode Island's Reproductive Health Care Act also allows abortions until birth for any reason and repeals the state's ban on partial-birth abortion "in its entirety."[31] That means it would allow living, kicking, half-born babies to have their skulls punctured with scissors and their brains sucked out.

In 1993 "ethicist" Peter Singer stated that newborn babies shouldn't be considered a person until thirty days after birth and that the attending physician should kill disabled babies on the spot. Five years after making such an outrageous statement, he was appointed the Ira W. Decamp Professor of Bioethics at Princeton University.[32] He also said, "The life of a newborn is of less value than the life of a pig, a dog, or a chimpanzee."[33] *Just the kind of guy you want teaching ethics to our students at Princeton.*

The pro-abortion camp used to claim they wanted abortions to be "rare" and would hide their grisly agenda behind slogan-bearing banners. Not anymore. Speaking against the Alabama bill to protect children from conception, Democratic State Senator John Rogers put it this way, "So you kill them now or you kill them later. You bring them in the world unwanted, unloved; you send them to the electric chair. So you kill them now or you kill them later."[34] Think of how this direct approach would "solve" the discipline problem in today's public schools, homelessness, and prison overpopulation. *Just kill them all now.*

The Masks Are Off

I noticed just how blatant this new approach had become during the hearings for Ohio's Heartbeat Bill. Abortion proponents were no longer cryptic about their desire for death. All slogans aside, they want to kill any child who gets in their way. One man testified that his unborn child stood in the way of the "big wedding" he and his girlfriend had planned—*a capital offense.*

The father wanted to finish school on "his own" timetable. So they aborted their child and, oh, what a great decision that was for them (and their subsequent "wanted" children who fit into their schedule). I'll bet their first child would have liked to go to school and have a big wedding too. Too bad the innocent child got in the way of their plans. Even a legislator on the committee couldn't keep from saying out loud what we were all thinking—how "selfish."

Rep. Christina Hagan pushing her babies into the House Chamber through a hostile group of pro-abortion protesters.

One day I was standing near Rep. Christina Hagan, one of the Heartbeat Bill sponsors, who had her beautiful twin babies in a stroller. A pro-abortion woman looked down at the babies and literally said, "Yuck!" The masks are off, and their display is repugnant.

Women testified that if they were to become pregnant they would "absolutely" have an abortion, with one woman saying that having a baby "sucks!" If a baby doesn't fit into their plan, their timetable, their desires, he or she will be dead. It is ironic that before I left for the committee hearing that morning, I was in my hotel room giving myself shots to increase the likelihood that my husband and I will conceive babies we desperately want. Here I was doing everything I could to have babies while those working against us bragged about killing them and any others who might get in their way.

Sadly, there were amendments to the Ohio bill to allow exceptions so disabled babies with detectable heartbeats could be killed. Sure, give the disabled a parking place up close for the hearing, but if you can kill them before they're born, all the better.

I once had Jack Kevorkian on my radio show and asked him if he would be willing to help me kill myself because I was upset about being dumped by my boyfriend. His answer at the time was no. I then asked him if he would help someone with a disability kill themselves who was upset for *the very same reason*. His answer was an emphatic yes.

Kevorkian, Governor Northam, and the Democrats who sponsored and voted for the death-for-the-disabled amendments all believe the same thing: that being disabled makes someone deserving of death. *Now* how do you feel about the government deciding who gets healthcare and who doesn't?

There was even an amendment to kill *just* the black babies with detectable heartbeats. *I'm not kidding.* Democratic Representative Janine Boyd proposed an amendment to exempt African-American women from the Heartbeat Bill, ensuring that while Hispanic, white, and Asian babies with detectable heartbeats were protected, black babies with detectable beating hearts would be singled out for death.[35] This was the most lethally racist amendment I have ever seen. Prenatal lynching—surely the Ku Klux Klan would be proud. They would also be right at home in New York City, where more African-American babies are killed by abortion than are born alive.[36]

Even the witches came out with their "PRO ABORT WITCH" T-shirts accessorized by pentagram earrings the size of saucers. On the day of the vote, their constant shrieking outside the chamber was described by legislators as "demonic."

The parable of the wheat and the tares in Matthew 13 describes exactly what we are now seeing. The seeds that have been growing together are coming to maturity—making it a lot easier to tell them apart. The wheat—or "sons of the kingdom"—are looking a lot more like wheat, while the tares—or the "sons of the wicked one"—are, likewise, becoming the picture of their parent. This is true for even the most proficient pretenders—"pro-life" groups that claim to want to end abortion but frantically oppose the efforts to do so. The Heartbeat Bill serves as an excellent wheat/tare litmus test.

Abortion until birth, during birth, and after birth—you would think those running for president would run from this obsession with death, but quite the contrary. The Democratic presidential candidates are standing on the backs of aborted babies—tripping over themselves to see who can have the most radical position.

President Trump speaking at the 2020 March for Life stated, "Nearly every top Democrat in Congress now supports taxpayer-funded abortion all the way up until the moment of birth."[37] That is also the case for every Democrat candidate running for President—they want unrestricted abortion until birth and they want us to pay for it. So much for "choice" and "getting the government out of the issue."

Former mayor Mike Bloomberg, whose foundation gave 13.9 million dollars to baby-killing giant Planned Parenthood, joined the Democrat pack of candidates who all want to force us to pay for killing children. But abortion extremist Mike Bloomberg also wants to force doctors to become trained executioners. When running for mayor, Bloomberg pledged to force every obstetrician and gynecologist to learn how to perform abortion as part of their training in New York City hospitals.[38]

Former presidential candidate Senator Cory Booker called Alabama's protecting of children in the womb "an assault on human rights."[39] That's like saying protecting endangered species is an "assault on animal rights." It's absurd.

And just when you thought it couldn't get any more extreme, former Democratic presidential candidate Julián Castro announced in the Miami presidential debate that he believes transsexual females—that is, men who identify as women—should also be funded for abortion. Let me translate: taxpayers should pay real money for men pretending to have a uterus and pretending to be pregnant.

He then said what he *meant* was taxpayers should pay for abortions for women pretending to be men.[40] When you're playing a game of pretend, it gets confusing. Sounds just like the Ohio circus act we endured as opponents of the Heartbeat Bill testified. One woman pretending to be a man (call it what you'd like) spoke about the need for "his" abortion. Every "man," apparently, should now have the right to choose to kill the child in "his" uterus.

Let me summarize the Democrats' positions on abortion: Evil is good. Darkness is light. Women are men.

Have the Democrats *really* become the party of butchery and bloodshed? Read their platform; the answer is yes. While there are still some pro-life Democrat champions like former Ohio representative Bill Patmon, Louisiana state senator John Milkovich, and Louisiana governor John Bel Edwards, who have the courage to stand against their party, they are the rare exception. The Democrat platform is the most pro-abortion platform in history[41]—with the possible exception of the platform on which people sacrificed children to the pagan god Molech.

The Democrat Party's platform not only promises taxpayer-funded abortion without limits and the overturning of "federal and state laws and policies that impede a woman's access to abortion," but promises to force taxpayers to fund abortion giant Planned Parenthood.[42] As far as I know, even Molech's child sacrifice wasn't taxpayer funded.

If you are one of the 21 million who identify as a "pro-life Democrat," the abortion extremists running for president don't even want you as part of their party.[43] In an MSNBC town hall on abortion, Senator Bernie Sanders said, "Being pro-choice is an absolutely essential part of being a Democrat."[44]

At a FOX News town hall meeting Kristen Day, director of Democrats of Life of America, asked Mayor Pete Buttigieg "Do you want the support of pro-life Democrats? And if so, would you support more moderate platform language in the Democratic Party to ensure the party of diversity and inclusion really does include everybody?"[45] Buttigieg responded by ignoring the question and doubling down on his radical pro-abortion position. Day summarized Buttigieg's answer as: "I'm not going to change, so deal with it."[46] Regarding whether he wants the support of pro-life Democrats, Day concluded, "I guess the answer is no."[47]

A note of clarification: when I referred to the Democratic Party as the "party of death," that's not entirely true—they want to abolish the death penalty. So they don't want death for those guilty of murder, only the death of the innocent. They don't want death for rapists, just death for the innocent children of rapists. I just want to be clear. If you think I'm letting Republicans off the hook, keep reading. It is *because* Republican actions don't match their platform and their campaign promises that abortion is still legal in America.

I watched in Ohio and in Congress as *Republicans* stood in the way of our Heartbeat Bills. The true blame belongs to those "Republicans In Name Only" (RINOs)—who ignore the pro-life Republican platform and the babies most of them promised to protect. (This is such a problem, I'm devoting a whole chapter to it.)

Cowardice is the tragic flaw of the Republican Party. Fear has turned Republicans into the "Do-Nothing Party." They are so worried about losing power that they forget why they worked so hard to get it in the first place. Instead of *using* the power they have to do what they were elected to do, their goal has become to do whatever it takes to *keep* the power. Their strategy? Do as little as possible. After all, they don't want negative headlines from a leftist press.

What they don't understand is that doing nothing is the very thing that gets them voted out of office. Voters have seen enough broken campaign promises to last a lifetime. It's the reason the Republicans lost the U.S. House in 2018. I only hope they will realize it before they ask for our votes again.

Too many Republicans think if they stay in the middle of the road they won't get run over. They think being lukewarm will enable them to appeal to everyone. Being lukewarm appeals to no one, least of all God.[48]

> *So then, because you are lukewarm, and neither cold nor hot, I will vomit you out of My mouth* (Revelation 3:16).

I have fought RINOs, I have recruited candidates to run against them, and even ran against one for the Ohio State Senate. Sometimes the only way they'll listen is if we threaten what they care about most—*their jobs*. Because whether it's at the hands of the "Democrat Death Party" or "do nothing" RINOs, the results are the same: *dead babies*.

Proverbs 16:25 applies to both: "There is a way that seems right to a man, but its end is the way of death."

If only there was a Republican at the national level who stood for the pro-life Republican Party platform, someone who would appoint pro-life judges to the courts, someone with the courage to fight against the establishment. Oh, wait—*there is*. His name is Donald Trump. He may be rough around the edges, but President Trump is God's answer to our cry for mercy.

You may not like things he has said or done in his past. I don't like everything I've said and done in the present. But one thing is certain: *without the election of President Trump, all hope of ending abortion in our lifetime would be gone.*

President Trump did what they said couldn't be done: he defunded Planned Parenthood! He took sixty million of our tax dollars out of their blood-stained hands! Congress wouldn't do it. So Trump changed the Title X rules that made them separate their baby killing from legitimate healthcare in order to receive taxpayer funds.[49] We need to cut the *rest* of our tax money from them, but it's a good start.[50]

Why would Planned Parenthood turn down $60 million rather than comply with President Trump's reasonable regulation? Because their "legitimate healthcare" is just smoke and mirrors to hide what they really do: kill babies.

Actions are what you believe. And President Trump's actions make him our most pro-life president in history. No wonder they hate him so much they want to remove him from office! As President Trump said at the 2020 March for Life, "Unborn children have never had a stronger defender in the White House...They are coming after me because I am fighting for you and we are fighting for those who have no voice."[51]

President Trump has already nominated two pro-life judges to the U.S. Supreme Court, and, when reelected, will nominate more. He also appointed 51 judges (in 3 years) to the circuit courts of appeal.[52] Tilting even the 9th Circuit Court (based in San Francisco) from its far-left position with 10 new judges, more than a third of the active judges on the court.[53]

President Trump also kept his word to the late conservative leader Phyllis Schlafly to keep the Republican Party platform strongly pro-life. And it is now the most pro-life party platform in our nation's history.[54]

In case you've never read it, here's an excerpt from the 2016 Republican Party platform. If you compare that to the Democrats' party platform, you'll see the difference is life and death.

> We support a human life amendment to the Constitution and legislation to make clear that the Fourteenth Amendment's protections apply to children before birth. We oppose the use of public funds to perform or promote abortion or to fund organizations, like Planned Parenthood, so long as they provide or refer for elective abortions or sell fetal body parts rather than provide healthcare.[55]

Here's what it says about judges and justices to the U.S. Supreme Court:

> We support the appointment of judges who respect traditional family values and the sanctity of innocent human life.[56]

Just that sentence alone should be enough to convince anyone claiming to be pro-life to vote to reelect President Trump.

A Brand-New Day

While RINOs run for cover and Democrats embrace abortion to the moment of birth and beyond, Heartbeat Bills have ignited the heart of America. A March 29, 2019 headline from *The Daily Beast* reads: "Heartbeat Abortion Bills Were Once a Fringe Idea. Could They Overturn *Roe v. Wade*?"[57]

Take a look at the overwhelming margins of passage of state Heartbeat Bills and Alabama's full-protection bill, all of which passed in 2019 in the states' House and Senate respectively:

- ♥ Alabama: 74–3 and 25–6
- ♥ Georgia: 92–78 and 34–18
- ♥ Kentucky: 71–19 and 31–6
- ♥ Mississippi: 78–37 and 34–14
- ♥ Ohio: 56–40 and 19–13
- ♥ Missouri: 110–44 and 24–10
- ♥ Louisiana 79–23 and 32–5

What do you know? Protecting our fellow human beings with beating hearts isn't such a "fringe idea" after all. Far from it. In fact, as the *National Review* reported, "Majorities this lopsided demonstrate...there is nothing 'extreme' about laws they passed."[58]

It's a brand-new day. Life-loving Americans are no longer satisfied with empty campaign promises and regulating around the edges of abortion. We will no longer ignore the universally recognized indicator of life—beating like an SOS from within the womb. We will not follow the science deniers or the establishment who tell us it can't be done.

I know for a fact that it can. The enemy has overplayed his hand, providing us with the greatest opportunity to end abortion we have ever had.

The answer to *The Daily Beast*'s headline: "Heartbeat Abortion Bills... Could They Overturn *Roe v. Wade*?"

In a word, "Yes."

Here's three more: "Count on it."

CHAPTER 3

From the Basics
to the Impossible

"Faith is not a leap in the dark. It is ceasing to
call God a liar..." —Francis Schaeffer[1]

After what happened in New York, I feel compelled to state the obvious. There is not an embryology, fetology, or biology book *in existence* that says life begins at any point *other* than the moment of conception. Once a woman is pregnant, the question before her isn't *whether* she will have a baby. If a woman is pregnant, she *already has* a baby—a separate, unique, individual human being who about half the time is male, has different DNA and a separate *beating heart*. Once a woman is pregnant, the "choice" before her is whether she will have a: 1) live baby or 2) dead baby.

And for those who are still grappling with which choice is the *right* one, let me clarify the entire abortion debate as simply as I can:

Live baby, good.

Dead baby, bad.

See? The abortion issue really isn't so complex, after all. That's all you really need to know to be a voice for the voiceless. I said this once in Oregon, and they turned it into bumper stickers. It's obvious. Like a sign I saw a teenager carrying: "Call me an extremist, but I think dismembering children is wrong."

Guess what? Biologists agree with us—life begins at fertilization. A 2019 survey of thousands of Americans and biologists found:[2]

1. Most Americans (93 percent) believe a human's life is worthy of legal protection once it begins.[3]

2. When asked "Which group is most qualified to answer the question, 'When does a human's life begin?'" 86 percent said biologists.[4]

3. When 5,577 biologists were asked, 96 percent admitted, "Life begins at fertilization."[5]

Nine out of ten Americans say life is worthy of legal protection once it begins. Those Americans trust biologists to give them the answer, and the answer from 9.6 out of 10 biologists is "Life begins at fertilization." We are on the side of science and the side of Americans.

You may have noticed I don't use the words "pro-choice." That's because it's a lie—the human being whom the "choice" most impacts *doesn't get one.* The slogan is just recycled rhetoric from the slavery debate. *Never use it.*

You remember Stephen Douglas from Lincoln–Douglas debates? Summarize Douglas's position on slavery, and you have something that sounds a whole lot like what we heard from our opponents in the Heartbeat Bill hearings: "I'm not pro-slavery—I just believe in the slave-owner's 'right to choose.'"

On July 9, 1858, Douglas stated:

> My object [citing the Kansas-Nebraska Act which he authored] was to secure the right of the people of each state... to decide the question for themselves, to have slavery or not, just as they chose.[6]

What a reasonable guy. Let the people *choose* whether or not to own a fellow human being. I wonder if their signs were like the ones we see about abortion—*"Against Slavery? Don't own one."*

As Benjamin Dierker wrote in "The Federalist":

> Those who advocate choice for others while remaining personally opposed to abortion are no better than the racist Douglas, who believed the people's choice for slavery was moral so long as the powerful chose it.[7]

Whether it's slavery or abortion, the "pro-choice" position is, "Yes, it's a human being, but that human being gets no rights." Just as that nice sounding slogan overlooked the rights of the slave, the very same slogan overlooks the rights of the child in the womb. History does not view well those who were "pro-choice" for slavery. History will not view well those who are "pro-choice" for the torture and death of defenseless children.

The Truth Isn't Complicated

The truth about abortion is plain for anyone willing to see. Several years ago, I spoke at the University of Cincinnati, and the communists, socialists, and pro-abortion clubs all joined together to greet me. It looked just like the Democrat primary debate stage—the socialists, communists, and pro-abortion gang all standing together.

The protestors welcomed me with some very open-minded and tolerant signs—the nicest of which was, "Janet, go home."

I was speaking outside on what was called "the Bridge," next to a pro-life table that displayed fetal models depicting the various stages of a baby's development. An angry woman with a three-year-old on her arm got in my face demanding that I no longer refer to the being in the womb as a "baby."

"It's a fetus!" she shouted.

I calmly explained that the word *fetus* was a Latin word that *means* unborn child, developing human, young one, and yes, *baby*. It's the very definition of the word.

"No!" she yelled. "It's not a baby! It's a *fetus!*"

Our little exchange was interrupted by her three-year-old daughter pointing to the fetal models displayed on the table. She excitedly exclaimed, "Look mommy! *Babies!*"

The truth is so simple even a child can see it. Even *their own* children. Sadly, that sweet little three-year-old was promptly yanked away—to reeducation camp, no doubt.

Like that little girl, once I saw a picture of the "products" of abortion I had no doubt about what I was seeing. This is the picture that settled the debate for me. I saw it in the tenth grade when pro-life speaker Tom Zabor came to my public high school. That was when I first learned what they were doing to babies. Once I saw this picture, there was no going back. No slogan, no argument, no judge could make a garbage bag full of dead babies OK.

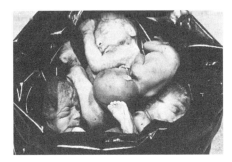

The "choice." This is the picture that got me into the pro-life movement. I have yet to hear a single argument that makes this OK.

Picture from "Why not love them both?: Questions & Answers about abortion," Dr. J.C. Willke, 2003, p. 147, Hayes Publishing Company.

While a lot of pro-lifers balk at showing the "choice" for which so many are chanting, I say *show them.* In fact, when the Ohio Senate continued to block our Heartbeat Bill vote, my friend Mark Harrington of Created Equal put the pictures of aborted children on a truck that circled the Ohio Statehouse during more than one of our outside rallies.

Every few minutes I would look up from the podium where I was introducing speakers and see Mark's truck with enormous pictures of dead babies and the prominent headline: "This is the price of Senate delays."

Another said, "What's more OFFENSIVE than abortion? A Republican Senate that won't stop it! Call Senate President Tom Niehaus...to end the killing." By the way, Niehaus refused. He would not even schedule a vote.

If a picture is worth a thousand words, the picture of the truth of abortion is worth at least a thousand *lives.* Every life I've been a part of saving began with seeing a picture of the truth of abortion.

When you are staring at the face of that tiny victim, the most common reaction of those who favor abortion is to shoot the messenger and pretend what they are seeing is not real. I just watched a few of Created Equal's videos, which reveal the reactions of students to signs that portray the graphic reality of abortion on college campuses.

What's more OFFENSIVE than abortion? A Republican Senate that won't stop it!

One pro-abortion woman punched the pro-life student in the face and the stomach screaming, "This is wrong! This is triggering!"

Another woman screamed, "You are absolutely f---ing lying! ...That is not what a fetus looks like! It's a clump of cells at twelve weeks! ...It does not look like that! It's a clump of mother f---ing cells! No hands are shown at that time! ...Racist f---ing male that doesn't stand for women's rights!" She then kicked the sign and assaulted the student.[8]

I can understand why people are going off the rails. They've been lied to. Keep in mind Planned Parenthood's first plan for your life was abortion. Why in the world would anyone listen to them now?

When I was president of Students for Life as an undergraduate at Cleveland State University, I would carry around an embryology book with me and challenge people to find out the truth for themselves. At the time, it had an image of an unborn baby on the front. In subsequent printings, a veil was put over the baby's picture, apparently after the publisher received complaints by people who were offended by the facts.

I remember getting a call from a student named Carol who belonged to Students for Choice. She asked me to meet her for coffee and told me how they used to make fun of us and our materials. She didn't believe that babies at six weeks had beating hearts.

Then she told me, "But I remembered one thing you said. 'Don't believe me—go to the library and pick out any biology, embryology, or fetology book and see for yourself. At six weeks, a baby has a beating heart and detectable brain waves.'"

Carol told me, "You were right. But I found out *too late*—I found out the truth *after* I aborted my baby at six weeks."

Even then I realized the significance of a heartbeat. If even the most ardent "student for choice" would have known, she would have chosen life. What would happen if *other* mothers found out about their baby's heartbeat before their abortion? We asked that question at the Heartbeat Bill hearings to demonstrate the answer to the representatives and senators on the committee. "How many women here would not have chosen abortion if you knew about your baby's beating heart?" Dozens of hands went up all over the room from heartbroken women who were denied the truth.

Sadly, Carol found out about her baby's beating heart too late. I hugged her and cried with her. She told me how she couldn't stand the sound of a vacuum and when she told her pro-abortion friends, they now made fun of *her*. Carol said she had the abortion so she could finish school and start a life with her boyfriend. She then told me how she and her boyfriend broke up. She dropped out of school and begged me to tell women this one thing: "Hard times pass, but *abortion lasts forever*."

Abortion stops a beating heart. Abortion also breaks a mother's heart. That is why we must stop it. But abortion has been legal for nearly fifty years—what can we do about it? The answer is easy: *end it*.

Stepping Out

Before you set out to do the impossible you need to be connected to the God of the impossible. But it's not just about what God will do for us; it's really all about Him. His kingdom and His plan. History is *His* Story. Pastor Bill Johnson stated, "If you'll make history with God, He'll make history through you."[9] He formed us and has a plan and purpose for our lives—already written:

> *And in Your book they all were written, The days fashioned for me, When as yet there were none of them* (Psalm 139:16).

God has a book—*about us*. I think of it more as a movie script, really. It's the movie of your life, and God is the producer. If we will also make God the Director of that movie—it will be "exceedingly abundantly above all that we ask or think" (Eph. 3:20). The New International version says, "immeasurably more than all we ask or imagine." I don't know about you, but I can imagine a lot. God's book about your life—like the script for your movie—is "immeasurably" more than Hollywood could ever dream up.

Is the movie of your life something anyone would want to watch? You see, being a Christian isn't really about the stuff we're not supposed to do. It's about the amazing destiny we were *created* to do! That's what happens when you make God the Director of the movie of your life and join the Father in the family business. Your life fits into God's purpose. I don't know about you, but I want to live every page—every scene God has in my movie. I want every purpose and destiny God has ordained for my life. As I said when I walked through the Billy Graham museum, "I want my life to count—*like this*."

It begins by acting like the word of God is true. Faith is being 100% sure of what God said and acting accordingly. Francis Schaeffer's statement bears repeating: "Faith is not a leap in the dark. It is ceasing to call God a liar...."[10] God's word is the check; faith takes it to the bank. As Henry Blackaby said, "When faith appropriates a promise from God, it is done; it is accomplished."[11]

Fear is also faith—in an inferior kingdom. If you want to do the impossible, you'll have to conquer fear. Fear is having a great big devil and a little bitty God. But Satan has already been defeated. The only power he has over a Christian is to get us to agree with him. To sign for the package he wants to deliver. He tries to get you to agree with the thoughts he throws into your mind or mistake them for your own:

"I can't speak."

"I will fail."

"I will be rejected."

There were many times I signed for those packages and agreed with those lies. You see, I was the girl who was afraid to give a speech. Fear holds people back from even trying; it almost silenced me despite God's command in Proverbs 31:8 to "Open your mouth for the speechless, in the cause of all who are appointed to die."

Whether it's fear of failure, fear of man, or fear of being outside your "comfort zone," we've been putting our inadequacies over God's adequacy. Pastor Jentezen Franklin said, "An idol is anything you make bigger than God." You can make safety and security your idol or cling to a label of "shy" or "introvert" instead of trusting God to make up for what's lacking. As Pastor Mark Batterson said, "Jesus didn't die just to keep you safe, he died to make you dangerous!"[12]

So I went through the pro-life speaker's training and I spoke. Not very well, but I spoke. And kept speaking. At one event, I was approached by the emcee preparing to introduce me. I will never forget her words of "encouragement": "I went through speaker's training with you and I have to tell you, I'm *really surprised you* ended up being our spokesperson!"

Me too. But it's not about us. It's not about our talent or what we lack. It's about obeying God and letting Him make up for all that is missing. If we want to fulfill the destiny God has for us, fear can't be our god and our comfort zone can't be our prison.

The most repeated command in the New Testament is to "Fear not."[13] It makes sense since fear kills more dreams than failure ever did. But the remedy isn't self-confidence. It's confidence in the one who can actually do what can't be done.

> *For the Lord will be your confidence, and will keep your foot from being caught* (Proverbs 3:26).
> *Forget about self-confidence; it's useless. Cultivate God-confidence* (1 Corinthians 10:12 MSG).

If you are a Christian, you have greatness in you—because "greater is he that is in you, than he that is in the world" (1 John 4:4 KJV). Every obstacle we face is measured against the almighty God who spoke the universe into existence. The supernatural is the natural for Him.

Fear can kill not only a dream, it can kill a country by keeping good men silent. Edmund Burke said, "The only thing necessary for the triumph of evil is for good men to do nothing." That is true, but so is what President Ronald Reagan said: "Evil is powerless if the good are unafraid."

Salvation Army founder William Booth, said, "God loves with a great love the man whose heart is bursting with a passion for the impossible."[14] Booth added, "I am not waiting for a move of God, I am a move of God!"[15]

Yes, with God all things are possible. But it is also true that without Him we can do nothing. The key is getting plugged in to the source.

> *I am the vine, you are the branches. He who abides in Me, and*
> *I in him, bears much fruit; for without Me you can do nothing*
> (John 15:5).

The late evangelist Reinhard Bonnke questioned those who found Christianity boring: "So is television if we don't plug in."[16]

For a watching world to see the impossible bow to the name of Jesus, we have to make sure we're on God's side. Then we must step out. But unless we are plugged in to the source of power and authority, we will lose. Every promise, every victory, every dream is found in Him: "For all the promises of God *in Him* are yes, and *in Him* Amen, to the glory of God through us" (2 Cor. 1:20).

We need to keep our eyes on the God of the impossible and not the voices screaming to the contrary. David didn't focus on Goliath. But it might have been a different story if he spent his evenings watching CNN (the *Canaanite News Network*):

> CNN Correspondents: "Have you seen the size of that sword?" "Goliath is absolutely undefeated." "He's enormous! I heard he eats shepherd boys for breakfast!" "He occupies the land and it's Trump's fault." (Oh, sorry, wrong CNN.)

Isaiah 40:22 tells us God "sits above the circle of the earth, and its inhabitants are like grasshoppers." Goliath was like a grasshopper to the God who sits above the *circle* of the earth. David knew that God trumps giants.

By the way, contrary to what you've likely been taught in government schools, it was *God's word* that was accurate from the beginning, even when "science" taught that the earth was flat. Much like today's science books which teach the very same thing as we read in fairy tales: "Once upon a time there lived a frog who became a handsome prince." And people ridicule the story of creation? No, everything with a design had a designer. His name is God, and it is *His word* which remains true.

David said, "The Lord, who delivered me from the paw of the lion and from the paw of the bear, He will deliver me from the hand of this Philistine." To face the impossible, you have to remember that God is everything He claims to be, and recall the miraculous things you've already seen Him do. Not just in the Bible, but in your life. Before I set out to introduce the nation's first Heartbeat Bill, like David, I remembered when the Lord delivered me from the paw of the lion and the paw of the bear. I remembered the times when I had seen God do the impossible.

A Presidential Debate

In 2007, I complained to a friend about how biased and unfair the presidential debates were. My friend's response was, "Why don't you have *your own* presidential debate?"

Our Values Voter Debate at the Broward Center for the Performing Arts.

I laughed. Just like I did when my husband suggested that I "outlaw abortion" while I'm here.

If what you set out to do is something that doesn't make you laugh, chances are it's too small.

What presidential candidates would come because I invited them? But here's something I've learned. It's not about *us*—our abilities, our connections, our gifts. It's about the one in whom we trust—not the dollar, but the God of our national motto on the dollar.

And so, I set out to do what seemed impossible.

I was living in Florida at the time and looked at the magnificent Broward Center for the Performing Arts on the Intracoastal. It cost $8,000 just to reserve the date. And, well, I had nothing.

Phyllis Schlafly and Janet Porter at the Values Voter Presidential Debate September 17, 2007.

From Governor Mike Huckabee (left) to Ambassador Alan Keys (right), CNN canceled their debate while our Values Voter Debate took place.

Our Values Voter Debate podiums. Green (left) and red (right) lights for yes/no answers on the top, yellow lights on the bottom for more time.

So I also checked the War Memorial, which I could rent for $2,000 dollars. That's when my friend Greg Darby said to me, "If you're going to do something for God, do it right."

Why not? It's not like I had $2,000, either.

I was speaking at an event in South Carolina and mentioned in my speech, "Why should we take the crumbs that fall from MSNBC and CNN? Why don't we have a debate of our own?" I didn't ask for money. It's never been my strength.

But on that day God moved in the heart of a family who approached me with a check for $3,000. Then another who donated $5,000.

At lunch, I met John and Kristi Collins, who had distributed "clicker" keypads for conference participants to interact with the speakers. I thought they would be perfect for delegates to use when casting a vote in a presidential debate. "How much would something like that cost?" They said, "free." We've been friends ever since.

I called my mother that night and told her we got the money, "Looks like there is going to be a Presidential debate!"

Her reply? "Oh, I knew that *before* you got the money." That's my mom, Beth Folger, a faith-filled walking pep talk.

But that wasn't the only money we would need and that wasn't the only obstacle we would face.

The first thing I did was reach out to my heroes of the faith to assemble a steering committee: Phyllis Schlafly, founder of Eagle Forum; Don Wildmon, founder of the American Family Association; Paul Weyrich, cofounder of the Heritage Foundation, Free Congress, and the "Weyrich Lunch"; Rick Scarborough, founder of Vision America; and Mat Staver,

The table to the left is where Phillis Schlafly, Buddy Smith (AFA), and I asked questions, while the podium to the right was used by the 50 groups for the yes/no questions.

founder of Liberty Counsel. I invited 50 pro-family groups to participate and to ask questions of the candidates.

I wanted to ask a lot of questions and put everyone on record about the issues we care about, but that takes a lot of time. So, I had a dozen podiums with lights on them built to my design. The candidates could hit a button for "yes" and a green light would appear for all to see or a "no" button which would display red on their podiums—all at once. I called this the "speed round." If the candidates needed extra time, they hit one of two yellow lights which gave them an additional two minutes to explain an answer.

In one meeting of pro-family leaders in Washington I was publicly ridiculed, "There's not a campaign manager in America who would sign off on your 'game show' of a debate." I responded, "We'll see."

The RSVPs came in. While none of the Democrats responded, we had eight Republican candidates who agreed to come. This was really going to happen; on September 17, 2007, there was going to be a "Values Voters Presidential Debate." That was when I got a call from one of our key leaders who said he was backing out—and taking critical funds with him. I remember the call; it was a few minutes before I went on the air with

Phyllis Schlafly receives the Key to the City from Ft. Lauderdale Mayor Jim Naugle at the Values Voter Debate.

my daily radio program. I told him that we had eight Republican candidates already committed to come...and pro-family groups from around the country who agreed to participate. The hall was rented, the questions were being written.

There seemed to be no convincing him. Moments later, another leader threatened to quit. And, as the theme music began to play on my headphones, I said, "I'm going to follow the lead of my friend Phyllis Schlafly. I'm going to host this debate even if I have to do it *alone*." Then, I went on the air and talked about the debate as if everything was fine.

The decision to lead where God is directing isn't based on who is willing to follow. The debate was moving forward with or without these key leaders, who both stayed on board when they saw I wasn't about to quit.

Then, I needed to come up with an additional $8,000 for a "ticketing fee." When I asked the fifty groups for help in paying for it, it was like the sound of crickets. *Nothing.* Not a single dime—which was about what I had to my name.

I asked a friend from church to go with me to the meeting with the Broward Center officials. She had helped to coordinate stadium events and was familiar with what it took to pull off something of this magnitude. She informed me that such a fee was "standard," and that there was no way around it, I would just have to pay it, "That's all there is to it."

Before the meeting, I pulled her aside and said, "Look, I'm going to ask her to waive the 'ticketing fee,' and if you can't back me up, then I need you to stay quiet." She looked at me like I was crazy and walked into the meeting even though I'm sure she was embarrassed to do so.

In the meeting, the woman from the Broward Center brought up the mandatory $8,000 ticketing fee, expecting me to write her a check.

I replied, "Yeah, what would it take to waive that fee?"

My friend wanted to disappear from the room. How could I be so naïve? So embarrassingly stupid?

The Broward Center rep's response was, "Oh, I'm not able to waive it unless you ask. But, since you asked, I'll go ahead and waive it."

I've learned when God puts something in your heart, He overcomes the obstacles that stand in the way.

That was about the time my mother called to inform me that, "CNN scheduled their Republican Presidential Debate for the same day as yours!" They, apparently, had been promoting it on air and on their website for weeks. I didn't know, because I don't typically watch fake news.

So, I went on my radio show and called for a three day fast. I remember saying, "I know that God is mightier than the media—but maybe some others need to find that out for themselves." Three days later, CNN backed down and changed their date, and our debate went forward.

I didn't even have the money to rent a shuttle to take the candidates from the hotel to the debate venue. That was about the time I got a call from a man asking to transport the candidates on his *catered yacht* from their hotel, down the Intracoastal to the Broward Center for the Performing Arts. A catered yacht? "Yes, that would be fine."

Mike Huckabee, who won that debate, said it, along with winning the Iowa Primary, was what led to his "Huckaboom." In his book *Do the Right Thing,* he described our Values Voter Debate as: "the fairest and most objective of any of the debates we ever had in the entire campaign."

And the guy who said no one would come to my "game show" of a debate called to apologize.

I look to the Values Voters Presidential Debate as the paw of the lion. God did the impossible, He can do it again. Here's the paw of a bear.

Yes, I Believe in God

I was National Director at the Center for Reclaiming America, when the 1999 Columbine shootings happened. Cassie Bernall and Rachel Scott were Columbine High School students who faced a gun and a question from shooters on a killing spree. That question: "Do you believe in God?" was met with a courageous "Yes," and it cost them their lives.

I gathered my staff and told them we were going to assemble "Yes, I Believe in God Kits" to empower students to stand for their faith in schools even in the face of adversity and persecution. We included 10 Commandment book covers (similar covers were being ripped off books by public school teachers who didn't like them), a Bible, a T-shirt with a "Student Bill of Rights" on the back, and organizations like Liberty Counsel, the American Center for Law and Justice, and the Alliance Defending Freedom they could call should those rights be

The number two song on the Christian Contemporary Music chart began on a piano phone.

violated. My plan was to offer it on Dr. D. James Kennedy's Coral Ridge Hour television broadcast.

Then I told my staff, "We need a 'Yes, I believe in God' song!" with a well-known Christian artist to record and release it. No one in the room believed it could be done.

Of course, I told them the motto of my home state: "With God *all things* are possible." They weren't impressed. I reminded them that Jesus was the one who said it. But what I found was a group of people who didn't actually believe those words. Because actions are what you believe, everything else is just religious talk.

Perhaps that's why I started an organization called Faith2*ACTION*. As James 2:17 states, "Faith by itself, if it is not accompanied by action, is *dead*" (NIV).

There was a time in my life when I saw the impossible happen so much that I actually *loved* to hear the word. When I heard it, something in me rose up and said, *"Oh yeah? Just watch what God can do!"* This was one of those times.

And so I set out to put my faith to action. I was told I needed a prototype song to pitch the idea, so I set out to write one with the only instrument I had available at the time—a piano phone. It was a phone with a keyboard made of notes that sounded like a toy piano when you dialed it. You can't really find one at most music stores, but I'm pretty sure Beethoven used one to write his symphonies.

Allison and Romeo DeMarco were friends of mine who happened to be talented musicians. I invited them to my office at 7:00 a.m. to discuss my idea. I still remember Romeo's face when I said, "I was thinking something like this" while proceeding to play the "notes" on the piano phone. He was both shocked and insulted. Not only did he wake up early, drive to my office to meet me at 7:00 a.m., he, apparently, did it all for nothing.

His "don't embarrass yourself speech" began with something like, "Look Jan, I'm a serious musician...." He was interrupted by his wife Allison, who said, "Come on Rome, for the refrain, we can just hit redial!"

I told them I was going to have a song. It was either going to be a lousy song that I write on my own or a much better song if they decided to help me. They helped me. As did my friend Lisa Velazquez, who also sang our prototype "Yes, I Believe in God" song.

One of my interns saw a guy walking in the church with a guitar. I told him, "Go get him!" He played the music for us to record it on our lunch hour.

Barry Kase from my staff arranged a meeting with the former president of the Gospel Music Association and another big wig from Nashville. There, with my boss, Clark Hollingsworth, the Executive Vice President

Barry Kase (top left), Rebecca
St. James in the middle, I'm to
the right of her, with some of the
Reclaiming America crew in our
"Yes I Believe in God T-shirts.

of Coral Ridge Ministries, Dan Scalf, the ministry consultant, and Barry,
I played our "Yes, I Believe in God" prototype song on a borrowed cas-
sette player.

Hoping to discourage me, the response was, "On a one-to-ten scale,
I'd give your little song a *seven*."

I was *thrilled* our piano phone song got a seven! Clearly their little
insult didn't have the desired effect of dissuading my enthusiasm.

That's when they stepped up their game to make sure everyone in the
room knew what an absolutely ridiculous idea this was, "Janet, your little
idea of getting an artist to record a song in your time frame is simply *not*
going to happen."

Seemed clear enough for everyone in the room. But, just in case I missed
it, the former president of the Gospel Music Association felt the need to
spell it out. Looking directly at me he stated, "Let me clarify this for you:
Short of God appearing here Himself, this is simply *not* going to happen."

All eyes were on me. Surely I *got it* this time.

I was already writing in my notebook. Reading his words back to him,
I said, "Short of God appearing here Himself, *what was that?*"

"This is simply not going to happen." I added, "When this happens, I just want to make sure that I quote you right."

I still remember the day my friend Mickey called and said, "Turn your radio to 88.1" because my "Yes, I believe in God" song, recorded by Grammy award-winner Rebecca St. James, just hit number one (in Florida)! It only reached number two nationally, probably because if it hit number one, I planned to call the people who said it was "not going to happen" to make sure they knew about it.

So my name's on the Christian contemporary music chart as coauthor with Rebecca St. James; it didn't mention the piano phone. There's one addendum to this story that happened in 2009 when I cohosted a "Take Back America" conference with Phyllis Schlafly in St. Louis. We needed music and had no budget for it. So I prayed for God to provide it. That same week I got a call from the Grammy nominated, Dove Award-winning band "SonicFlood," famous for songs like "Here I am to Worship," and "I Could Sing of Your Love Forever."

They had read one of my columns and wanted to know if I had a need for a band. *Nice.* And, yes, they came to our conference for free.

In 2010, I hosted a "May Day" rally at the Lincoln Memorial where leaders from around the country prayed for our nation—for about seven hours (broadcast on God TV). I asked SonicFlood to join us and told them we needed a "May Day" song. They invited us to their home studio in Nashville to help them write it.

As my husband and I approached the bed and breakfast in Nashville where we would be staying, we heard worship music from some people on the front porch. I told my husband, "We're staying at the *right place.*" The next morning the owner warned us in hushed tones that we "might not want to eat breakfast with *those people*" since "they're kind of '*churchy.*'"

I replied, "Oh, those are *exactly* the kind of people we want to have breakfast with, *make sure* we have breakfast with them."

And so we did. The young woman told about how she and her musician friend, who was playing the guitar when we arrived, had become worship leaders for their church. Then, they got around to asking us why we were in town.

I responded, "Did you ever hear of the band SonicFlood?"

The young woman oozed, "Oh! I *love* SonicFlood! We sing *all* their songs! They are amazing! You *know* them?"

"Well, we spent the day in their home studio with them working on a song."

She couldn't believe it. This was her dream. She was sitting at the table with people who were living her dream.

She asked us, "Do you sing?"

Both of us smiled and said, "No."

She persisted, "Are you guys musicians—do you play any instruments?"

Again, "No."

"Then, how in the world did you get to write a song with SonicFlood?"

I told her, "I prayed for a band and they called us."

Then I remembered. "Well, there was one other time when I wrote a song...on a piano phone." I told her how it wasn't going to happen unless "God appeared Himself." When she heard the name "Yes, I Believe in God," she almost fell to the floor.

"*What!?*" She was clearly in shock.

"'Yes, I Believe in God' was the song I sang in the pageant—it's what lead to my becoming a worship leader!"

We owe it to the world to exhibit the impossible bowing the knee to the name of Jesus. And there's nothing better than a front row seat when it happens. It's not about talent; it's about faith that's put into action. SonicFlood's Rick Heil then wrote a song for the Heartbeat Bill and came and performed it on the steps of the Ohio Statehouse—*thank you, Rick!*

When you are plugged in to the source you can step out to host a presidential debate or help write a chart-topping song with a piano phone. You see, it's not about us; it's about the God in whom we trust.

Commentators on the national news tried to figure out how Heartbeat Bills were sweeping the nation. It wasn't the big donors. It was a big God. He also happens to be mightier than the media, bigger than the billionaires, and more powerful than the political pundits. Don't believe me? Search for "Snowflake meltdown Trump election" and watch the news coverage from the (first) victory for President Trump. I predict they'll be just as shocked and incensed the night of his *second* victory.

That leads me to the moment when I *knew* we were going to end abortion in America. On Wednesday, November 1, 2017, I stood with our team outside the hearing room in Washington, D.C. for the House Judiciary Committee's Subcommittee on the Constitution and Civil Justice hearing on H.R. 490, the federal Heartbeat Bill.

I asked Arkansas State Senator Jason Rapert, who passed the nation's first Heartbeat law, to join us. We were all praying in the hallway when Senator Rapert pulled out an "Appeal to Heaven" flag. It's a white flag with an evergreen tree and the words "An Appeal to Heaven" on it. We had used it at many of our Statehouse rallies and prayer events. Most don't know that was our nation's first flag commissioned by George Washington to fly over our first Navy ships as we entered into the Revolutionary War. As Pastor Dutch sheets stated in my documentary, *Light*

Wins, "This is the banner we were born under."

Our founders knew that we didn't stand an earthly chance against the most powerful nation on earth, but the words of English philosopher John Locke (1632–1704) inspired them. In his "Second Treatise of Government," Locke stated:

We made an Appeal to Heaven outside the U.S. Judiciary Committee.

Where the body of the people, or any single man, is deprived of their right, or is under the exercise of a power without right, and have no appeal on earth, then they have a liberty to appeal to heaven, whenever they judge the cause of sufficient moment.[17]

The quote was part of Locke's justification for the 1688 overthrow of Britain's King James II. Locke argued that rebellion, which became known as the "Glorious Revolution," was justified in order to defend the rights of the people against a tyrannical government. The American colonists were facing a similar tyranny and were inspired to make an appeal to Heaven in an American Revolution.[18]

A ragtag band of patriots against the most powerful nation on earth. We shouldn't even be a nation, and yet we are—*Americans.* As I held the "Appeal to Heaven" flag and prayed outside the Judiciary Committee room, it dawned on me. Not only did God answer our "Appeal to Heaven" to become a country, He answered our "Appeal to Heaven" in the last presidential election. God gave us mercy with the election of President Trump despite every poll and political pundit who said it was impossible.

I knew that day that God not only heard our "appeal to Heaven" for the Heartbeat Bill but would answer us just as He had done before. After all, as the flag we held reminded us, His power to do the impossible is *proven*. God answered our appeal to Heaven to become the land of the free. Then He answered our cry for mercy—to *remain* the land of the free. He gave our nation another chance, and it's up to us to take it.

If we are standing on His word, doing His will, plugged in to His power, we will see His victory. What impossibility will you see bow to the name of Jesus? For starters, let's outlaw abortion while we're here.

CHAPTER 4

Crafting the Arrow

"You will make ready your arrows on your string."
—Psalm 21:12

The Heartbeat Bill was crafted to be the arrow to deliver the fatal blow to the heart of *Roe v. Wade*. In order to craft the arrow, we needed to recruit the best and the brightest legal minds in the country. We had about twenty of them on the first conference call, but this was a task that required a specialized legal strategist.

Mat Staver, the founder of Liberty Counsel, and Wendy Wright, a former president of Concerned Women for America, both used the same words to describe Walter Weber: "He's the best there is." That was all I needed to hear.

Weber is the senior counsel for the American Center for Law and Justice (ACLJ). He received his bachelor's from Princeton and his JD from Yale Law School. He has specialized in constitutional law for more than thirty years, has assisted with numerous abortion cases, and has written over one hundred briefs for the U.S. Supreme Court. He is brilliant.

I called him, and he said, "Yes," the same thing he has said to state after state that asked him for help drafting (and reviewing) their Heartbeat Bills. Walter co-drafted the first Heartbeat Bill and became our co-counsel. He testified for the Ohio, Kansas, and Kentucky Heartbeat Bills and took countless calls from me at various stages of multiple state and federal battles.

But there was someone else we also needed: the rock star attorney who testified back in 1995 as we worked to pass the nation's first ban on partial-birth abortion. I remember the reaction of my boss Mark Lally, the man whose wake I was attending when I got the idea for the Heartbeat Bill. Mark was a very steady, even-keeled kind of guy who wasn't easily excitable. He would give his legislative reports to the board with painstaking legal detail that caused more than a few eyes to glaze over. But when I told Mark that I recruited law professor David Forte to testify in support of the partial-birth abortion ban, he couldn't contain himself. "You don't *even know* who you just got to testify!" He was right. I didn't know. Mark was practically doing cartwheels, which is perhaps the reason I remembered Professor Forte's name fifteen years later.

I knew I had to get him. So I called. And I emailed. And I called again. Finally, I went to Cleveland-Marshall College of Law at Cleveland State University to find his office. After all, it's a lot harder to ignore someone in person. He wasn't there.

I didn't have paper with me, so I used the back of a flier I found nearby to write him a note, and I slid it under his door. I walked away thinking, "That was a mistake." I should have planned better. I should have typed out the critical case for him to help us and had it delivered in some professional portfolio.

Janet Porter with Professor David Forte and Walter Weber of the ACLJ while in Kansas to testify for the Kansas Heartbeat Bill.

But instead, I not only had a handwritten note, but one that contained what I'm sure was a *very compelling* "P.S." written around the edge and up the side of the paper like a crazy person would write. I wondered if I had just blown my chance at getting our rock star, so as I walked away I prayed.

God answered that prayer with Dr. Forte's call and the words, "Alright, you pro-life stalker, I'll help you." And he's been helping ever since.

Forte holds degrees from Harvard, the University of Manchester, England, the University of Toronto, and Columbia University. During the Reagan administration, Forte served as chief counsel to the U.S. delegation to the United Nations and alternate delegate to the Security Council. He has received numerous awards, including the Cleveland Bar Association's President's Award and the Cleveland State University Award for Distinguished Service. Forte was also consultor to the Pontifical Council for the Family under Pope John Paul II and Pope Benedict XVI. He was a senior visiting scholar at Princeton and a former judge, and just returned from teaching law in Warsaw, Poland.

When Dr. Forte and I met with Ohio attorney general Mike DeWine (now Ohio governor) to ask him to file a motion to rehear the *Obergefell v. Hodges* marriage decision, Forte admonished me not to praise his achievements. He said, however, that I "might want to mention" that he was quoted and cited by Chief Justice John Roberts in his *Obergefell* dissent. *Good to know.* I told you he was a rock star.

Forte has since written a law review article titled "Life, Heartbeat, Birth: A Medical Basis for Reform." He explained that the Supreme Court's current standard permits legal protection of the unborn child by the states when there is a likelihood of survival to live birth. But "viability," the Court's current standard, is based on an arbitrary guess—which can be up to 90% wrong.[1] The measurement isn't a measurement of the child's humanity, it is merely a determination of our current technology's ability to sustain life outside the womb. Viability is a line that is far less concrete since it changes with the year and hospital in which a child is born.

Fifty years ago, a child born at seven months may not have had much chance of survival while today it's a common occurrence. Does that mean babies born at seven months are more *human* or more worthy of protection today than they were fifty years ago? *Of course not.* The current viability standard is merely a measure of our ever-changing technology.

On the other hand, Forte reveals the medical findings that if there is a detectable heartbeat in an unborn child, there is a 95% to 98% likelihood that child will survive to live birth.[2] Heartbeat is a much better, and more scientific, marker than viability—the arbitrary measurement of technology the Supreme Court is currently using.

Simply put: Heartbeat is the new viability.

As I mentioned previously, Gregory J. Roden made a strong case in *Issues in Law & Medicine* that a heartbeat approach will work due to a "shift" in *Gonzales v. Carhart*. But I needed something short and easy to hand out to legislators, who wouldn't take the time to read his law review article. So Roden was kind enough to clarify his position about our Heartbeat Bill in a letter to me on March 24, 2011.

Quoting from *Gonzales v. Carhart,* which upheld the Partial-Birth Abortion Ban Act, Roden wrote:

> The [Partial-Birth Abortion Ban] Act does apply both previability and postviability because, by common understanding and scientific terminology, a fetus is a living organism while within the womb, whether or not it is viable outside the womb. See, e.g., Planned Parenthood, 320 F. Supp. 2d, at 971-972. We do not understand this point to be contested by the parties.[3]

Here the Supreme Court was referring to one of the cases it was reviewing, *Planned Parenthood Federation of America v. Ashcroft,* 320 F.Supp.2d 957 (2004). The specific portion of the case the Court was referring to was a "Finding of Fact," which reads:

> The fetus may still have a **detectable heartbeat** or pulsating umbilical cord...and **may be considered a "living fetus."**[4]

Roden clarified: Under our Federal Rules of Civil Procedure, the District Court's finding of fact in *Planned Parenthood v. Ashcroft* cannot "be set aside unless clearly erroneous" (Rule 52).[5] Furthermore, the Supreme Court in *Gonzales* went onto state, *"We do not understand this point to be contested by the parties."*[6] Under Rule 201 of the Federal Rules of Evidence, the Supreme Court has thereby given that finding of fact judicial notice; Rule 201(b) reads:

> The court may judicially notice a fact that is not subject to reasonable dispute because it: (1) is generally known within the trial court's territorial jurisdiction; or (2) can be accurately and readily determined from sources whose accuracy cannot reasonably be questioned.[7]

Let me translate: The courts have determined there is a living fetus from the point of a detectable heartbeat. It is a fact. It is an undisputed fact. And it is a fact upon which the courts can rely.

Roden continues:

> Having done so, as an integral principle of the Gonzales decision, all states and courts now may rely on this finding of fact under the doctrine of stare decisis. That is because courts "should rely only upon the facts that are contained in the record or that are properly subject to judicial notice" [Planned Parenthood of Southeastern Pa. v. Casey, 505 U.S. 833 (1992)].

Hence, all states and federal courts, *where a fetus has a detectable heartbeat* or pulsating umbilical cord, should take judicial notice of it being a "living fetus"; the issue is no longer a matter of legal controversy.

Roden stated, "This fresh, new approach has never before been tried before the Supreme Court and, based on *Gonzales v. Carhart*, there is a crack in the door right now that never before existed."

In fact, the Eighth Circuit Court of Appeals stated they were unable to uphold the Arkansas and North Dakota heartbeat laws "because United

States Supreme Court precedent does not permit us to reach a contrary result." However, the Eighth Circuit asked the Supreme Court to review it, stating that *heartbeat* is "a more consistent and certain marker than viability."

It's the reason the Iowa heartbeat law was challenged in *state* court. The pro-abortion movement didn't want to risk the Iowa law going back to the Eighth Circuit—which would have sent a similar request for review to the U.S. Supreme Court—with similar arguments to move the line of allowable protection from viability, which is miles away from our goal of conception, to heartbeat, which is inches away.

University of Georgia Law Professor Randy Beck, in his law review article "The Essential Holding of Casey: Rethinking Viability," not only questions the arbitrary notion of the viability standard, but reveals that members of the Supreme Court agreed. In their 1992 decision in *Planned Parenthood of Southeastern Pa. v. Casey*, Justices Sandra Day O'Connor, Anthony Kennedy, and David Souter wrote, "Legislatures may draw lines which appear arbitrary without the necessity of offering a justification. But courts may not. We must justify the lines we draw."[8]

The Supreme Court must "justify the lines" they draw. How about we quit ignoring the line science has already drawn to determine if someone's alive? For those who testified that heartbeat isn't such a line, I dare them to go to their local hospital and unplug all the heart monitors because whether someone's heart is beating *doesn't really matter*. They would be arrested.

The Heartbeat Bill was crafted to legally protect unborn children whose heartbeats can be detected by a doctor, except to save the life or physical health of the mother. Simply put: If a heartbeat is detected, the baby is protected. The language found in the model bill does three primary things:

1. Requires physicians to TEST (according to standard medical practice) to determine whether the unborn child has a detectable heartbeat.

2. INFORMS the mother of the results of that determination.

3. PROTECTS each unborn child with a detectable heartbeat except to save the life or physical health of the mother.[9]

The first requirement to test for the baby's heartbeat is according to "standard medical practice." This is important so the abortionist can't say, "I listened from across the room but couldn't hear anything." No, they have to use whatever technology is the current medical standard. This also means as technology improves, so will the standard to test for a heartbeat. Over time, we will be able to detect the baby's heartbeat earlier, protecting more children at younger ages without ever changing the law.

In the Ohio and fine-tuned model bill (available at Faith2Action.org and HeartbeatBill.com), we added a reporting requirement. This part is critical. It means if the abortionist claims to be unable to find heartbeats in children past six weeks in the womb, they are creating a red flag for the state health departments to charge them with violating the law. With that violation comes a felony. And with a felony comes an abortionist who is out of work.

Likewise, if the abortionist keeps killing babies with detectable heartbeats because of a disproportionate "life or physical health of the mother" exception, another red flag will alert the health department or government officials to investigate whether the law is being violated. If you are contemplating introducing a Heartbeat Bill in your state or nation, I *strongly* recommend the reporting requirement. Here's why:

♥ If the abortionist doesn't test for a heartbeat or doesn't inform the mother whether her baby's heartbeat is detected, she has a legal remedy.

♥ If the abortionist aborts a child with a detectable heartbeat (except to save the life or physical health of the mother), he is guilty of a felony—putting his medical license, and future child killing, in jeopardy.

♥ If the abortionist lies repeatedly about "not being able to find a heartbeat," or has a disproportionate number of "life/physical health of the mother exceptions," it will signal a red flag to the state health inspectors.

We know the abortionists don't much care about obeying the law, but they do care about putting themselves at risk. The more they violate the law, the bigger and brighter the red flag they wave, prompting an investigation.

For children to be protected, we must first ask for it. Professor Forte told our legislative committee in his testimony, "Courts never change their minds unless they are invited to."[10] Former Justice Antonin Scalia encouraged people to do just that. Scalia said:

> You want a right to abortion? There's nothing in the Constitution about that. But that doesn't mean you cannot prohibit it. Persuade your fellow citizens it's a good idea and pass a law. That's what democracy is all about. It's not about nine superannuated judges who have been there too long, imposing these demands on society.[11]

Georgia Heartbeat Bill sponsor Rep. Ed Setzler said, "If a legislature is not going to do this, why should we expect the Supreme Court to get out ahead?"[12]

He is right, but that is exactly what National Right to Life Committee Attorney Jim Bopp expects. When testifying against the Tennessee Heartbeat Bill on August 12, 2019, he said:

> It's not a matter of whether these judges are pro-life...It's the reality that they have an obligation to follow precedent. And there's simply no question that pre-viability prohibitions are unconstitutional...We have precedent we cannot avoid with a clever legal argument.[13]

So by Bopp's theory, we shouldn't challenge the court at all and just give up. Bopp suggests we not pass any law to challenge *Roe* and just wait for it to be magically overturned. But, again, as Professor Forte said, "Courts never change their minds unless they are invited to."[14]

Heartbeat Bills are being challenged in court, but that is to be expected. The bills must travel to the U.S. Supreme Court in order for change to occur. Congressman Steve King, sponsor of the federal Heartbeat Bill, said it is "legal malpractice to tell the public that we are defeated at the lower court level, and therefore we can't achieve an accomplishment of restoring this protection for life which actually is in the Fourteenth Amendment of the Constitution."[15]

King is right. The Fourteenth Amendment states, "Nor shall any State deprive any person of life, liberty, or property, without due process of law; nor deny to any person within its jurisdiction the equal protection of the laws."[16] Federal law already recognizes and protects unborn life in its earliest stages. As federal Heartbeat Bill team member Larry Cirignano explained to members of Congress, "Over a million frozen embryos are testament to America's belief that embryos are people. Some 65,000 babies were born after coming out of a freezer in 2016.[17] Recently a baby that was in a freezer for twenty four years was born."[18]

Louisiana's Fifth Circuit Court of Appeals has determined that embryos are people, and thus custody battles between parents are covered by family law.[19] The federal government has also recognized embryos for survivors' benefits for both Social Security and VA benefits.[20]

In addition, according to the National Conference of State Legislatures, at least thirty-eight states have fetal homicide laws that already recognize the personhood of an unborn child.[21] I worked to pass the fetal homicide statute in Ohio, which protects the unborn child from an outside assailant (except an abortionist) from the moment of conception. There are at least twenty-nine states that protect the unborn child from "any stage of gestation/development," "conception," "fertilization," or "post fertilization."[22] Yet if the abortionist is the one doing the killing, it's perfectly fine. This hypocritical double standard is yet another challenge that should be made to the current Court. *Roe* is a violation of the Fourteenth Amendment, and many state and federal laws fall on the side of protecting human life even at its earliest stage.

As attorney Andy Schlafly stated in *The Tennessee Star*, "How do we ever overturn *Roe v. Wade* if legislators don't want to vote for anything that will overturn *Roe v. Wade*?"[23]

I'm proud to call Andy Schlafly my friend. He is a lot like his mother, Phyllis Schlafly. In all the years I have known him, I have never seen him back down from a fight. Andy rightly pointed out in that interview, "The

Court is constantly reversing itself on prior rulings. The only way that can happen is if legislators do the right thing."[24]

Even Justice Harry Blackmun, the author of *Roe v. Wade*, knew his decision was on borrowed time. The State of Texas argued in *Roe* that the fetus is a "person" within the definition of the Fourteenth Amendment. Blackmun responded:

> If this suggestion of personhood is established, the appellant's case, of course, collapses, for the fetus' right to life would then be guaranteed specifically by the Amendment.[25]

You have it directly from the author of *Roe v. Wade* himself: If this human being (with forty-six human chromosomes) also has a detectable heartbeat—an undisputed indicator of life recognized by the U.S. Supreme Court—then *Roe v. Wade*, "*of course, collapses.*"

The Goliath of *Roe v. Wade* is about to collapse. "*Of course.*" The court just needs a case to challenge it. I say, let's give them one. As Abby Johnson stated, the Supreme Court has a duty to consider the will of the states. The more states that pass Heartbeat Laws, the better our chances of being heard and upheld.

The Supreme Court refused the Arkansas and North Dakota Heartbeat Laws, Iowa's Heartbeat Law went to the state court, but six other Heartbeat Laws (and counting) are working their way through the court system. We've given them nine so far, and the more heartbeat laws that pass, the better.

No Exceptions Needed—Punish Rapists, Not Babies

As a second victim of the abortion industry, the mother may not be prosecuted under the Heartbeat Law. When a mother learns about her baby's beating heart, lives are saved. That's what happened to a little boy named Duncan, who was spared by the informed consent provision of the Arkansas Heartbeat Law, which was passed in 2013. Even though the legal protection of babies with beating hearts was enjoined by the court, the informed consent provision went into effect.

Senator Jason Rapert, the sponsor of the Arkansas Heartbeat Law, told me about an encounter he had with a woman and a baby in a stroller. The adoptive mother ran over to Senator Rapert and introduced her baby boy to him. "His name is Duncan." She explained that his life was spared because his biological mother, who had been raped, found out about his beating heart because of the Heartbeat Law's informed consent provision.

Duncan's birth mother had already taken the morning-after pill, but it didn't work. So she went to the abortion mill to have little Duncan killed, but they had to comply with the law and inform her of Duncan's beating heart—the knowledge of which saved his life.

Senator Rapert is now friends with the adoptive mother on social media, which means he gets to watch little Duncan grow up—his birthday parties, his T-ball games, his first day of school. Senator Rapert wants to send a message to Duncan's biological mom, to thank her for realizing that one tragic situation is not a reason to *do* something tragic. He asked me to say, "Thank you for having the courage to save that little boy's life."

When drafting your Heartbeat Bill there is the question of whether or not to include a rape/incest exception. I strongly urge against it. The model bill, like the Ohio Heartbeat Law, has no exception for rape or incest. No pro-life law in the state of Ohio has ever had such an exception, and we weren't about to change that. A second act of violence against an innocent child and a woman's body can't erase the first one. That is also the case for heartbeat laws in Louisiana, Mississippi, and Missouri. There is no other law in the nation that allows an innocent child to be killed for the crime of the father.

As Rep. Alan Seabaugh (R-Shreveport) said during the floor debate for the Louisiana Heartbeat Bill, "We don't punish children in this country for the sins of their fathers."[26] Louisiana Rep. Beryl Amedee (R-Houma) added, "I want you to remember that having an abortion doesn't mean that you're no longer a mother, it means that now you are the mother of a deceased baby."[27]

Rebecca Kiessling is a beautiful wife, mother, attorney, and speaker. She was also conceived by rape. She testified powerfully that her heart beats too. She profoundly said, "We punish rapists, not babies."[28]

None of the abortion supporters asked her any questions. They pretended she didn't exist while discussing how horrible it would be for such a child to be born, as if she wasn't in the room. As I told you before, they are not for women's rights; they are for death.

Rebecca's birth mother told her that if abortion had been legal in the state of Michigan at that time, she would have aborted her. Rebecca points out that she is the "child of a rape *victim*" who is now very glad her daughter was born. She credits the pro-life legislators in the state of Michigan for passing the law that saved her life. She told them, "Today my birth mother and I are both thankful that we were both spared from the horror of abortion, just as you have the opportunity today to protect mothers and their children."[29]

Julie Makimaa, who was also conceived by an act of rape, rightly said, "It doesn't matter how I began. What matters is who I will become."[30]

None of us can control the circumstances of our conception. Imagine for a moment that your parents sat you down and told you that, contrary to what you had believed, you were not the product of their loving marriage, but instead were adopted. Loved, cherished, and chosen. But there's more. Imagine that, like Duncan, you found out that you were conceived when your biological mother was raped. The question is this, "Is your life any *less valuable* than it was ten minutes before you heard such news?" Is it any less worthy of protection? The answer, of course, is *no*.

Then, imagine after hearing this news that you were being summoned by a group of state legislators who just cast a vote that said your life had no worth. That, as a result of how you were conceived, you were going to be escorted by the state police to a facility where your life would be taken from you in one of a variety of brutal ways. That is what a rape/incest exception does—kill the innocent for the crime of the father.

Meet Isabella. She's is an adorable little girl who came to all the hearings with her baby doll. She, too, was conceived by rape. On the day of

Bella's "Thank You" heart given to a Heartbeat Sponsor Rep. Christina Hagan.

the committee vote, she handed out red hearts made from construction paper, like the one Representative Christina Hagan (pictured) is holding. It has the words "Thank You" on it. She gave one to each of the committee members on the day they were considering whether or not to gut the Heartbeat Bill with a "rape/incest" amendment.

As the amendment to take the lives of children like Bella was being proposed, members were literally holding her heart in their hands. They decided they would not sentence innocent children like Bella to death for the crime of their father.

None of us chose the manner in which we were conceived; it does not change our humanity. Pastor James Robison, whose LIFE Outreach organization helps feed over 400,000 children per month throughout Africa, was conceived through rape. There are a lot of children (and souls) saved because he was born. I'm glad he wasn't killed for the crime of his father.

I remember attending a pro-life concert in Cleveland. One of the musicians asked the audience how many believe in abortion for a twelve-year-old girl who is raped by her father. Hands went up all over the room. She then looked to all those who believed in abortion for that hard case and said, "You just killed me. And not only me, but all of my children, and all of their children." Abortion takes the lives of the most innocent and robs us of generations.

My good friend Rachelle Heidlebaugh is a champion for life. One night, while out with her friends, someone slipped a drug into her drink and subsequently raped her. She had an abortion that led to a downward spiral in her life that resulted in a second abortion. Rachelle joined our effort in Ohio to speak with legislators about her experience. Later, she organized our meetings with hundreds of members of Congress on Capitol Hill.

Rachelle Heidlebaugh dancing with the star of "Dancing with the Stars"—Fmr. Majority Leader Tom DeLay. There is joy in the battle for life!

She explained when a woman is facing an unplanned pregnancy, she feels a sense of panic, fear, and pressure that affects her ability to think clearly at that moment.

I watched as she asked members of Congress: "Would we hand a gun to a suicidal person and say here, 'Choose Life or Death?' Absolutely not, that would be cruel."[31] Yet that is what we are doing with desperate women in crisis who need our love and compassion to be talked down from the abortion ledge.

When Rachelle came with us in the early days in Ohio, I saw a woman whose head was down, carrying the weight of what she had done everywhere she went. By the time we were lobbying in Congress together, I saw a completely transformed woman. She was no longer carrying the guilt and weight of her abortions—she had given it to Jesus, who not only forgave her, but restored her joy and turned her into one of the most powerful voices on the side of life.

If you've had an abortion in your past, once you repent, God will forgive you and can use you in a powerful way. I can talk about abortion, but those who've actually experienced its horror can speak powerfully from firsthand experience. When Rachelle shares her testimony in legislative meetings, even staffers who are stridently against us begin to tear up.

Another woman who's been there is Kathleen DeZeeuw, who said:

> I, having lived through rape, and also having raised a child "conceived in rape," feel personally assaulted and insulted every time I hear that abortion should be legal because of rape and incest. I feel that we're being used by pro-abortionists to further the abortion issue, even though we've not been asked to tell our side.[32]

Rape is a violent act perpetrated against a woman for which she has no choice. The abortion is a second act of violence in which she participates. It does not erase the first act of violence; it compounds it with more violence and (fatally) harms yet another innocent victim.

While we oppose an amendment to kill children who, through no fault of their own, were conceived through rape or incest, an exception is completely unnecessary for Heartbeat Bills, even for those who may want one. As I explained to members of Congress who wanted such an exception, because the Heartbeat Bill protects from the point of a detectable heartbeat, abortions before that time, including those for rape and incest, are not prohibited. With the Heartbeat Bill all of the "hard cases" are removed, leaving us with our strongest argument—protecting every child with the medical yardstick used for everyone else—heartbeat.

To answer the claim that "the rape victim may not know she is pregnant," she *does* know if she was raped. It is in the best interest of a rape victim to be treated immediately following the assault—to prevent a human life from being conceived and to get treated for sexually transmitted diseases as well as trauma. A report made within seventy-two hours after an assault allows for the collection of forensic evidence, which makes the conviction of a rapist more likely, protecting other women from a similar assault.[33]

We heard many abortion activists testify that abortion is "needed" because of a woman's "mental health." Does killing children really prevent suicide in adults?

The *British Journal of Psychiatry* found:

> Women who aborted were 81 percent more likely to experience mental health problems compared to all other control groups, and 55 percent more likely to have problems compared to women who delivered an unplanned or unwanted pregnancy.[34]

Turns out when you protect children, their mothers are protected as well.

Researchers at the University of Minnesota found that a teenage girl who has had an abortion in the last six months is ten times more likely to attempt suicide than a comparable teenage girl who has not had an abortion.[35]

A large-scale study conducted in Finland found the suicide rate for women who had abortions the prior year was three times higher than women in the general population, and six times higher compared to women who gave birth.[36]

Officials in Australia are also alarmed. The 2013 Queensland Maternal and Perinatal Quality Council report stated:

> There appears to be a significant worldwide risk of maternal suicide following termination of pregnancy and, in fact, a higher risk than that following term delivery.[37]

A U.S. study of more than 173,000 low-income California women found that those who received "state-funded abortions were 2.6 times more likely to die from suicide compared to women who delivered their babies.... Giving birth...was shown to reduce women's suicide risk compared to the general population."[38] Abortion leads to the loss of women's lives as well as the lives of their children.

Allan Parker, President of the Justice Foundation in San Antonio, said the "facts and circumstances" around abortion have changed in ways that could make the High Court less wedded to its historical position.[39] Parker points to the safe haven laws in all fifty states (see NationalSafeHavenAlliance.org for the law in your state), which allows a mother within a set time after birth to drop off a child she doesn't want or can't care for with no questions asked. There are no child-abandonment charges, and unlike expensive abortions, there is no charge and no abortion related trauma for the mother. There is no longer the argument that a mother is stuck raising a child for eighteen years. A change in facts and circumstances justifies a change in a prior precedent like *Roe v. Wade* under the Law of Judicial Precedent.[40]

The Heartbeat Bill makes sense on so many levels. As the Eighth Circuit Court of Appeals stated, heartbeat is a "more consistent and certain marker than viability."[41] The Supreme Court's undisputed finding of fact recognizes a living (not potentially living) fetus from the point of "detectable heartbeat." The Heartbeat Bill doesn't discriminate based on the manner in which someone is conceived and protects women from a lifetime of regret and increased suicides associated with abortion. It truly is a scientific step that brings us within inches of our goal of protecting every child.

The Heartbeat Bill was crafted to be the arrow to pierce the heart of *Roe v. Wade* and deliver the fatal blow to abortion on demand. To again quote Justice Blackmun, the author of the decision that gave us abortion on demand:

> If this suggestion of personhood is established, the appellant's case, of course, collapses, for the fetus' right to life would then be guaranteed specifically by the Amendment.[12]

Roe v. Wade has been on borrowed time since 1973, but that time is about to expire. Arrows have been released while more are made ready. The sound of beating hearts will bring the collapse of *Roe v. Wade*.

CHAPTER 5

Creative Strategies

Once you've seen Goliath fall,
giants no longer intimidate you.

O nce you've seen Goliath fall, no one can tell you it can't be done. My first legislative "Goliath" was the nation's first ban on partial-birth abortion. After passing it, I never looked at passing a bill as impossible again.

On August 16, 1995, Ohio Governor George Voinovich signed the nation's first ban on partial-birth abortion into law. I was at that bill signing, along with Mark Lally and Dr. Jack Willke. But there wouldn't have been a bill signing if we didn't use creative ways to overcome the impossible and keep going when everyone said to quit.

Like virtually all bills I've been a part of passing, we had a majority of House members as cosponsors, providing proof we had the votes, lest anyone try and make a claim to the contrary. But we had a pro-abortion speaker (Jo Ann Davidson) who sent the bill to a bad committee. And when that committee was in recess, a pro-abortion Republican did what had never been done. She called her pro-abortion cronies on the committee and held a secret meeting to vote the bill down.

It was unprecedented. This kind of thing isn't done behind a chairman's back—behind everyone's back. But when you have a pro-abortion speaker, the pro-aborts can do what they please. The speaker ruled to allow the secret meeting to kill the nation's first ban on partial-birth abortion.

It looked like it was game over. I couldn't find anyone who didn't think so. But giving up isn't something that comes natural to me. Well, you know the Ohio motto by now—with God *all things* are possible.

You know when you watch a movie there's usually some seemingly insignificant piece of information that doesn't appear to matter at the moment, but you know it's going to be critical to the plot and the outcome? A few years earlier, I had a moment like that. A state representative by the name of Lou Blessing had been reading the rules of parliamentary procedure and told me about a thing called a "discharge petition." Something in me told me to remember that—that one day I would need it. Today was that day.

A group of legislators and I were meeting about what to do regarding the speaker's ruling on their clandestine killing of our bill. Seeing no way around it, our allied legislators had given up and were getting up to leave.

They were already patting me on the back, "We'll get 'em next time, Jan."

I told them, "Wait a minute—this isn't over." I could feel the resistance and even the sympathy from the discouraged legislators. When I told them about Rep. Blessing's discovery of a procedure to pull a bill out of a hostile committee, an elder statesman, Rep. Robert Netzley, responded. He had been in the legislature longer than I had been alive.

I can still see him rubbing his chin as he dredged up a distant memory, "*Discharge petition*—we tried that in the 1970s but could never get enough signatures."

I was not dissuaded. Somebody has to be first, why not us? Why not now?

The objections began to pile up,

It can't be done."

"We're out of time."

"It's impossible."

Oh, they said the wrong thing. I reminded the legislator of our state motto. They weren't impressed.

I followed with, "What do we have to lose? If we try and fail we're no worse off than we are right now."

Then came the objections about "perceived weakness" and "optics."

When you care about how something looks more than you care about doing what's right, it's time to find another line of work.

"Just give me the petition and let me try." They hesitantly agreed. They reluctantly signed, with what seemed like a pat on the head to the naïve little girl. If memory serves, we had about a day and a half to gather the names of fifty legislators on a petition no one had ever heard of to resurrect our bill.

No one offered to help me gather names...except one guy. His name was Representative Ron Hood. We were both in our twenties and crazy enough to try. He and I split up and started gathering signatures. But by the end of the day, we had only a handful. The prospect of getting to fifty was bleak. But we had to try.

You see, win or lose, at the end of the battle I want to lay my head down on the pillow with no regrets. If we didn't win, it wasn't going to be because we didn't try with everything we had. Ron and I chased people down the halls, down escalators, holding elevator doors, even finding legislators in nearby restaurants. No matter how hopeless it looked, we didn't stop.

It was just a few minutes before session the following day and we were one signature short. The bells were chiming signaling the beginning of session and I had one chance. If I could get to an elderly African-American pro-life Democrat named Representative Troy Lee James, we could do it! But he was being guarded by a female Democrat Representative wearing a large flamboyant hat. She didn't know my name, but she was pretty sure she knew I worked against abortion.

"What's your name?" she demanded.

Looking at Rep. James walking toward the chamber where I couldn't follow, "My name's Janet."

"Janet *what*?" she demanded.

I was trapped so I told her, extending my hand. "Folger (my maiden name, since I was not yet married), nice to meet you."

She ignored my hand and demanded to know, "Where do you work?"

I replied, "I work for a child-protection, women helping agency."

She wasn't having any of that. "Which *issss?*"

"Non-profit." As I ran past her I looked back and said, *"Great hat!"*

As Representative James was halfway into the chamber, I called to him. He told me he was heading to session, but would talk to me later. But later wouldn't work.

I explained that we needed his signature to bring the ban on partial-birth abortion to a floor vote.

He was surprised. No one had ever heard of this before, how could such a thing work?

"We can bring it to the floor?" he asked.

"With your signature we can." I showed him the other signatures to gain legitimacy.

The bells were ringing, session was beginning, the other Democrats were wondering what was going on—why was their liberal friend talking to *me*?

Representative Troy Lee James signed every letter of his name for what seemed like an eternity. But he signed it. And we did what had never been done before—gather a majority on a discharge petition to bring the ban on partial-birth abortion to a floor vote.

The fireworks began. The pro-abortion speaker tried to make a deal with our Democrat sponsor Jerry Luebbers, who lived in a Republican-leaning district. The speaker promised Luebbers that if he would back down they wouldn't run a Republican against him. I was afraid he might waver out of fear for his political life. Every battle worth fighting is one you have to fight to the end. I was sending the message to Jerry, in the closed-door meeting, that we would do whatever it took to help him keep his seat—including bussing people into his district to go door to door. He held firm.

Back on the floor, the left was throwing a fit. Many pro-aborts in the Democrat caucus were calling for the speaker to recognize their liberal buddy, Troy Lee James. It was becoming unruly, "Let Troy speak!" "Let Troy speak!" They thought he was on their side.

As Mark Lally and I sat in the gallery, he turned to me with an uncustomary sense of alarm. "Why are the pro-aborts motioning for Troy?"

I answered, "Don't worry, he's with us. He signed the discharge."

Mark was still worried, "Maybe they got to him."

But I knew something about Representative James that made me absolutely sure he would not flip. Even though he was a liberal Democrat, Representative James was also *the youngest of 18 siblings.*

When they motioned for him, I couldn't wait for him to speak. I don't have the exact words, but here's the scene as I remember it, from the script of the movie I'm going to make about it one day.

SPEAKER

The Speaker recognizes Representative Troy.

Mark Lally is visibly worried.

REPRESENTATIVE TROY LEE JAMES

What we're about to do right now has never been done in the history of our state. We are overruling a committee, and if there was ever a time to do it, this is it.

This issue cuts across labels and party lines. I've been called a "liberal Democrat" and there are some people who aren't going to be too happy with me, but I don't care. I didn't come to this legislature to make people happy. I came here to do what is right.

STATEHOUSE BALCONY—CONTINUOUS

Janet looks knowingly to Mark Lally who is relieved and exhilarated.

MARK LALLY

Wow.

STATEHOUSE CHAMBER—CONTINUOUS

REPRESENTATIVE TROY LEE JAMES

I'm really glad that my parents aren't alive to see this. They wouldn't believe what I am hearing today. Sucking out baby's brains? Is this really what we're debating?

STATEHOUSE BALCONY—CONTINUOUS

JANET

(to self) Tell 'em how many kids are in your family, Troy...

STATEHOUSE CHAMBER—CONTINUOUS

REPRESENTATIVE TROY LEE JAMES

We were so poor growing up that my parents sacrificed just to provide the next meal. I am the youngest of eighteen—and I am so very glad that my parents didn't shut the door on me!

The legislators in favor of partial-birth abortion look at each other in shock.

REPRESENTATIVE TROY LEE JAMES (CONT'D)

And I'm not going to shut the door on the children of our state. I urge my colleagues, Republicans and Democrats alike, to stop this horrific practice and vote for H.B. 135.

SPEAKER

(pounding gavel) The question is, shall the bill pass? The House will prepare and proceed to vote.

The lights on the voting board turn 82 green and 15 red.

Ohio Governor George Voinovich, who supported the Heartbeat Bill before he died, signing the nation's first partial-birth abortion ban. Left to right: Democrat sponsor Jerry Luebbers, Janet Porter, Dr. Jack Willke, Senate Sponsor Merle Kearns, and Mark Lally.

Janet Porter and Rep. Ron Hood on the steps of the Ohio Statehouse in the movie scene we already filmed. Rep. Hood helped circulate the partial birth abortion discharge petition that led to its passage and became the sponsor of the Ohio Heartbeat Bill.

I *told* you God had a movie of your life! We just need to live it in a way that's worth watching!

Everyone was in shock. The pats on the back weren't so condescending on that day.

We actually ended up with 51 signatures, when all we needed was 50. A guy who called himself "pro-choice," Rep. Mike Fox, wanted to sign, so I just drew an additional line and let him. *No one said I couldn't.*

Fifty-one people signed but only one Representative helped me gather names—Representative Ron Hood. If I was writing the movie for the Heartbeat Bill, I would cast Ron Hood as the sponsor of it. Oh yeah, that's what we did. When looking for a sponsor, find the one who will charge the hill to do what can't be done. That's who you want, and that's who we found in Ron Hood. Which is not to diminish the heavy lifting by many others, including Heartbeat Bill Champions former Rep. Christina Hagan and Rep. Candice Keller along with Senate Sponsor Kristina Roegner. What started with this law led to the ultimate Supreme Court victory in *Gonzales v. Carhart* in 2007. That was the same decision with the *undisputed* finding of fact where the Supreme Court of the United States recognized: there is a *living fetus* from the point of "detectable heartbeat"—the exact wording used in our Heartbeat Bill. *It's almost as if God had a plan!*

Of course, it was also a battle to get the Supreme Court victory. State Rep. Micah Van Huss, the sponsor of the Tennessee Heartbeat Bill, pointed out, "Forty-two times in the court system the partial-birth abortion ban failed. The 43rd time it passed, so the question for people voting on this: Is this a fight worth fighting? For me it is."[1] For me, too.

The Heartbeat Bill Begins to Beat

I have learned that sometimes what you lack in funds, you can make up for in creativity. Don't have it? Do what I do, just ask the Creator. And just because you're in the epic battle of our time doesn't mean that you can't have fun along the way.

Now, I don't despise the day of small beginnings, but I wanted the introduction of the nation's first Heartbeat Bill to be a bit more...*grand*.

February 2011. The Heartbeat Bill is announced to the press—with 4,000 red heart balloons as the backdrop.

99 Red Balloons Music Video that inspired orders for 4,000 red heart balloons to be delivered to State Reps.

Delivering 4,000 red-heart balloons to the Ohio state representatives following the press conference which announced the first Heartbeat Bill to the world.

We introduced the first Heartbeat Bill in the Ohio House just after Valentine's Day in 2011. It was launched with 4,000 red heart balloons, which we delivered to House members with notes attached from their constituents asking them to "Have a heart" and pass the Heartbeat Bill.

They were sent by people from across the state and the nation who saw our "Heartbeat Bill Music Video" (to the tune of "99 Red Balloons") and ordered through our Faith2Action.org website.[2]

The press surrounded by hearts at the launch of the nation's first Heartbeat Bill in Ohio.

Rep. Ron Magg (to the left of the podium) declared, "There's only *one* Judge I'm interested in pleasing, and He's not on the Supreme Court."

I had an image in my mind of what I wanted the backdrop to be—and these pictures are it. A room filled with red heart balloons—not just for decoration but with purpose. When these balloons were delivered to the offices of the State Reps., there wasn't anyone who didn't know about our bill. Even pro-abort Reps. asked, "Hey, where are my balloons?" To which Lori Viars replied with a smile, *"Oh, they're coming."*

Earlier that morning, we had a room at the Statehouse reserved for the press conference to announce the bill. We brought in big helium tanks through the basement. We were just getting set up when we were told that helium balloons were "not permitted" in the Statehouse. *That would have been nice to know.*

They could be still delivered to the Representatives in their offices (across the street) but, even though the media was showing up in less than 2 hours to our press conference in the Statehouse room, our balloons were not allowed in it. People said, "What's the big deal? Just have the press conference without the balloons." No. That wasn't the vision I had in my heart.

When you have the kind of days that don't go as planned, there's a test. What are you going to do in a crisis? On this particular day, I passed the test. It's not what I planned, it wasn't what I wanted, but I was going to thank God in the midst of it and watch Him turn it for good.

I rushed to meet with the director of the Capitol Advisory Board, the one in charge of the Statehouse grounds. We had less than 10 minutes to figure out what to do. Instead of complaining about a rule I couldn't change, I kicked into high gear. I remember having meetings in a hotel across the street and asked a guy at the desk if he would look up the number for me. I called my Communication Director, Ross Conley, to ask him to get another press advisory with notice of the room change ready to send.

The clock was ticking. I turned to the director and asked if he had some kind of sign we could put outside the Statehouse room to direct the press to our new location. I got the number of the hotel, reserved the room, sent the new press advisory, while the director held the sign for me to write on it. We moved the whole operation—tanks, volunteers, and cases of balloons to the hotel across the street. The "balloon trauma" was a test I had passed, and felt I earned the director's respect that day. The guy in charge of the Statehouse grounds just became an ally. It was a good thing, too. Because we were going to need him.

We had every helium tank flowing—in assembly line fashion, handing balloons off to a second team to tie as they filled. Meanwhile, we stationed volunteers outside the room to man the table where we required the press to sign in, so we would know who was there. One of the volunteers came to me asking, "Planned Parenthood wants to attend our press conference, what should we do?"

That was easy one. "No. Let me clarify—*no way*." We can be friendly to the opposition, but we don't have to be stupid. I had no interest in briefing the baby killers so they could mobilize against us.

It was at that moment that I realized why we had to change locations. If we had announced the bill in the Statehouse hearing room as we had planned, it would have been unlikely we could have kept the pro-aborts out. God worked the balloon trauma for our good.

At that press conference Representative Ron Magg, seated to the left of the podium, answered a hostile question from a reporter about whether he had considered what "the Judges on the Supreme Court" would do. Rep. Magg didn't miss a beat, "There's only *one* Judge I'm interested in pleasing, and He's not on the Supreme Court." Representative Magg not only cosponsored the bill, he also had multiple fundraisers for the Heartbeat Bill in his home.

The balloons were delivered, and the world now knew about our bill. But before there were balloons, the votes had already been counted and a majority—50 of the 99 House members—were already cosponsors with their names displayed on top of the bill.

While we were lining up those cosponsors, there was one day that stood out from the rest. I was walking the halls alone that day, exhausted and depleted, much like our bank account, still a long way from our 50 names. That was when I got a call from American Family Association founder Dr. Don Wildmon, whom I respect like few others. He simply said, "Could you use some help?" I had tears in my eyes as he told me he was sending us a check to help keep hearts beating. After the call, I was no longer dragging from office to office; I felt refreshed, encouraged, and energized knowing we were not alone. As I told the team that day, I want to be like Don Wildmon when I grow up.

The "Youngest to Ever Testify"

The youngest to ever testify in the Ohio House committee—9-week-old unborn baby Halley.

The most powerful testimony I have ever heard was from a child who was not yet born. In the Ohio House hearing in March 2011, we brought in "the youngest to ever 'testify'"—a 9-week-old unborn baby girl whose mother had already named her Halley. We rolled in a mobile ultrasound and revealed little Halley and her beating heart—zooming in on it—so the entire committee could see it in bright red.

The ultrasound image was displayed on a big screen for all to see. It was the image that the media used for the next several years whenever the Heartbeat Bill was in the news. It was like plastering a billboard and free TV ads across the state declaring, "Abortion stops a beating heart." Of course, with the Heartbeat Bill, a beating heart will stop abortion.

I asked Lori Viars to send me a memory from the battle. I'm going to include what she sent because she is Lori Viars, the Heartbeat General who never flinched in battle and never left the field. It gives you a picture of what it's like in the middle of the fight—rarely do things go as planned. Almost always you have to find a way to bypass obstacles and to improvise.

> We were in an important hearing and Janet was sitting about eight or nine chairs down from me. Like the whisper game, a message traveled from Janet, down the row, person to person, until the woman beside me whispered in my ear, "Janet needs some hand sanitizer."
>
> I was thinking, "What!? The hearing is starting! Can't Janet wait to de-germ her hands?"
>
> "No," I was told, "It cannot wait. Janet really needs some hand sanitizer gel."
>
> I rolled my eyes, but gave in and rummaged in my purse, handing a little bottle of Purell down the row, person to person, to Janet. Turns out the pregnancy center folks, whom Janet had arranged to do a live ultrasound during the hearing, had forgotten the conducer gel they put on the pregnant mom's abdomen!

There are two lessons in this. First, check your texts on your cellphone, even during hearings, and second, if I'm asking for something there's usually a good reason. That reminds me of another time Lori begrudgingly did what I asked. She didn't want to drive all the way to Columbus, but I told her I *really* think we should be in the Senate on Tuesday, December 6, 2016 even though there was nothing on the schedule.

We had been blocked in the Ohio Senate for 5 long years. We had run candidates against them in primaries. Pastor Corey Shankleton had run against his senator and I had run against mine, the *President of the Senate*. They hated us. We weren't particularly fond of most of them. But we weren't giving up.

They weren't about to tell us what they were doing, but on that day I had a strong feeling that we needed to be there in the Senate chambers to pray.

So on Tuesday, December 6, 2016, my mom, Pastor Shankleton along with his team, and Lori Viars joined me in the Senate chamber. Lori didn't want to, but came only because I told her it was important. We couldn't have known, but after blocking our bill since 2011, that was the day the Ohio Senate voted to pass the Heartbeat Bill for the first time!

News stories used our ultrasound as constant "B-roll" showing viewers the baby's heart beating strong.

One article announced, "Ohio Senate Unexpectedly Passes Heartbeat Bill," calling it a "surprise vote."[3] It wasn't a surprise to God, and He wanted to make sure we didn't miss it.

Back to our previous story—it's March 2011 and Baby Halley and other unborn babies' hearts were beating strong in the House Health Committee on the big screen for all to see—including the television cameras. The pro-aborts were having a fit, ranting and raving about "Janet's antics, stunts, gimmicks"—*pick a disparaging adjective*—anything rather than face the scientific fact of a live baby's beating heart.

When the cameras were pointed to me, my response was simple, "Isn't it sad that to defend your position you have to deny science and run from technology? That's a *sad* place to be." And it Is.

When dealing with the flat-earth science deniers, the more effective you are, the more names you'll get called.

That little baby's beating heart was so powerful that it actually saved a life before there was ever a vote in committee. A legislative staffer pulled me aside and confided in me that her friend asked her for a ride to get an abortion.

But then she told me, "Once I found out about the baby's beating heart, I couldn't take her." She was still distraught, because her friend hadn't canceled the abortion appointment and was still planning to have her child killed.

About 2 weeks later that same staffer was all smiles when she ran up to me and hugged me, exclaiming, "She canceled the appointment!" The baby was going to live. Several months later I ran into the same woman who told me her friend had a little baby boy named Aiden. All because this staffer heard about the baby's beating heart before a vote was ever cast. That is why even liberal states like New York, California, Oregon, and Massachusetts need to introduce Heartbeat Bills. Whether they pass or not, just the publicity about the bill gets the truth out to the public and saves lives.

I wish I could show you what I saw next. A picture of the most adorable little boy you ever saw—baby Aiden. Posted online by a proud

Baby Halley, who wasn't yet born when she "testified" in the House, made a live appearance in the Senate committee, her little heart still beating strong.

The House heard her heart but the Senate saw her face.

mama. What was once the biggest problem in her life was now her biggest blessing and greatest joy. That is what happens when Heartbeat Bills are introduced, even before they become law.

About 9 months later, our Ohio Heartbeat Bill was being heard in the Senate Committee. Ashland Care Center Director Ducia Hamm called, rather distraught, to inform me that the Senate wouldn't allow us to use the mobile ultrasound.

"That's OK," I responded. "They still allow *video* testimony don't they?"

They did.

So we played the video testimony of little Baby Halley from the House Committee, when she was 9 weeks in the womb. When the Senate Committee had seen it, Ducia said these words:

"The House heard her *heart*. You get a chance to see her face and look into her eyes."[4]

At that moment, one of the Ohio Senators walked in, holding—now born—baby Halley. The same child whose heartbeat was heard from the womb was now seen by all. It was the picture in the newspapers: Baby Halley—the youngest to ever testify—became the face of the Heartbeat Bill.

Federal Heartbeat Bill

But it wasn't until the introduction of the federal Heartbeat Bill in Washington, D.C. that I realized just how powerful a baby's beating heart really was. This ultrasound image is from the U.S. Judiciary Subcommittee hearing where Baby Lincoln (then 18 weeks in utero) "testified" before Congress.[5]

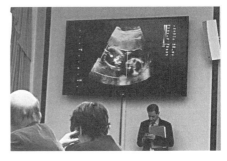

Baby Lincoln "testifies" in the U.S. Judiciary Subcommittee.

When his heartbeat was seen and heard in the committee—the room fell *silent*. Even the most disruptive protestors became still as all eyes were on Baby Lincoln and his beating heart. That was the moment one of the formerly disruptive protestors was seen wiping tears from her eyes. And that was when I realized a baby's heartbeat could reach even the *hardest* of hearts. If it could reach the hardest of hearts, it would reach America.

Baby Lincoln—whose beating heart testified in the U.S. Congress while he was still in the womb.

Baby Lincoln is now born and will be known not only as the youngest to ever testify in the U.S. Congress, Lincoln will be known for his role in emancipating the next generation.

Back in Ohio

Abortion survivor Melissa Ohden and her daughter Olivia.

Meanwhile, back in Ohio, in an Ohio House committee hearing we brought abortion victim Melissa Ohden to testify. Her biological mother had a saline abortion to take Melissa's life at 31 weeks gestation.

Tiny Melissa survived the scalding poison and was born alive.[6] Before Melissa testified, I asked the pro-abortion leaders, "What about Melissa's rights? She's a woman, don't her rights matter?" They looked at Melissa with distain, as if they were sorry the attempt on her life had failed.

Melissa is the founder of the Abortion Survivor's Network[7] and is 1 of only 250 abortion survivors of which she is aware.[8]

While Melissa testified, I held her little daughter on my lap. Melissa was standing at the podium talking about how abortion kills not just the baby, but generations to follow. That's when I looked into the face of her little daughter and said, "Would you like to go see your mommy?" She looked at me as if to say, "It's OK?" I nodded and Melissa's little girl ran to the front of the room just after Melissa urged the members to think about lives like her daughter's, "who would have never had life if that abortion would have succeeded in ending mine. I urge you to think about the ripple effect of abortion in our world, in our community."[9]

At that moment, Melissa picked up her little girl and the point was made visually. It was one of "those moments" where the atmosphere in the room changed. How do you continue to push the agenda of death when you're looking into the eyes of two females who wouldn't be here if abortion had been "successful"?

We had billboards, bumper stickers, baby clothes, buttons, pins, press conferences (from every group imaginable), prayer rallies, heart-shaped chocolates and heart-shaped cookies, multiple rallies inside and outside the Statehouse, yard signs, 2,200 red roses, 4,000 red heart balloons, a

Paula Westwood of Cincinnati Right to Life was one who put up Heartbeat billboards throughout Southwest Ohio.

three-story heart balloon that said "Pass the Heartbeat Bill Now!" and an airplane that circled the Statehouse towing a Heartbeat Bill banner. We left no stone unturned. *No* stone.

Kids for the Heartbeat Bill

The Ohio Heartbeat Bill would save more children every day than all the children at the "Kids for the Heartbeat Bill" press conference.

When I said we had press conferences from every group imaginable, I meant it. We had pastors for the Heartbeat Bill, post-abortive women for the Heartbeat Bill, African Americans for the Heartbeat Bill, and pro-life leaders for the Heartbeat Bill. Jim Bob and Michelle Duggar, with seventeen of their nineteen children, spoke at one of our press conferences. You get the idea. We even had a press conference with all children.

Before the press arrived, I asked if anyone knew the state of Ohio motto. One young boy did, and I made him "chairman" of the committee. We had some children who were speaking at the podium while others sat at in the seats of the legislators.

We lined up the teddy bears to deliver to the Ohio Senators, thanks to Marie Adamo, inside each bear was a recording of an Ohio baby's actual

Seven-year old Christian Harrington speaks at the "Kids for the Heartbeat Bill" press conference in a committee room filled with children. He told the Senators to pass the Heartbeat bill now. "When I say right now, I mean *right* now."

Promise Busby and Christian Harrington in a television interview on their way to deliver the Heartbeat Bears to the Ohio Senators.

Mark Harrington, Christian Harrington, and Janet Porter—at the beginning of the battle and at the end. By the time we finally passed the Ohio Heartbeat Bill, little Christian was taller than me.

heartbeat—which could be heard when you pressed the bear's tummy. The press took their seats and listened to children including 9-year-old Promise, daughter of Julie Busby (small girl to the right of the podium) and 8-year-old Christian, son of Mark Harrington (at the podium). He was standing on a box in order to be seen.

Little Christian Harrington looked straight into the camera and said to the Senators, "I want to tell the senators to pass the Heartbeat Bill right now—and when I say right now—I mean *right now*."[10] A kid after my own heart. In 2019, Christian testified again, in the House Health Committee, but because so much time had passed, he was now taller than me.

The children spoke and then we heard from "the committee" of children sitting in the legislator's seats. Each child introduced themself and cast a vote to protect babies with beating hearts. The kids stated their names and added, "I vote for the Heartbeat Bill." "I vote yes for the Heartbeat Bill," one after the other. Then the 12-year-old "chairman," slammed down the gavel and said, "It's unanimous. The kids of Ohio vote yes for the Heartbeat Bill—the hearts shall beat." And he slammed down the gavel again.[11] Cameras were clicking; reporters were writing.

Television cameras followed as the children took the teddy bears to the Senate offices to deliver them. Even the hardcore obstructionists who had blocked the Heartbeat Bill, along with others who tried to gut it, smiled for the cameras and took the beating heart teddy bears from these amazing children. The children asked the Senators if they would vote to keep hearts beating; after all, it was easy—they had just done it.

One of the members of the press told us that it was the most creative press conference she had ever seen. But we were just getting started.

Appeal to Heaven

At our "Appeal to Heaven" prayer rally with legislators, pastors, leaders, and prayer warriors, we put on display just how many babies the Heartbeat Bill would save each day with seventy baby onesies hung on a clothesline in front of the Ohio Statehouse.

Seventy baby outfits display the number of children the Heartbeat Bill will save each day.

We are not talking about statistics, we are talking about *real* babies who, when born, could wear these outfits. There were three sets of seventy onesies—one for the Governor, the Speaker, and the Senate President.

Janet Porter holding one of seventy baby outfits displayed in front of the Ohio Statehouse—the number of babies the Heartbeat Bill would save each day. Also speaking were pastors J. C. Church and Rodney Lord, along with Reps. John Adams, Matt Lynch, and Ron Hood.

Each onesie had an attached note. The note to the Governor read, "Governor Kasich: Every day in Ohio, 70 babies with beating hearts are brutally killed by abortion—something you pledged to *end* (not just regulate). These are not statistics. They are real babies who will fill these clothes if only you will call upon the legislature to pass the Heartbeat Bill for you to sign into law. Please make protecting these babies a top priority before the election. The price of inaction is far too high."

The back of note said: "After passing the Heartbeat Bill, please consider donating these baby clothes to the Ashland Care Center, so they can be worn by the babies who will be saved." Prayer warrior Terry Conant arranged for the clothesline display—a first at the Ohio Statehouse.

In front of the Statehouse is the state seal with my favorite motto, "With God all things are possible." I pointed out to those attending that we are *literally* standing on the word of God.

At another prayer rally, these prayer warriors spontaneously knelt at the seal to pray for the impossible. Like a persistent widow in the Bible (another campaign of ours), we kept knocking until the door opened to the protection of the babies.

The Ohio motto in front of the Statehouse.

We worshiped God publicly, even though some people (who claimed to be with us) didn't like it. I remember a call from a member of our team who was delivering the message that "Janet shouldn't be so radical," and should only be attending our "private" prayer meetings.

Another prayer rally at the Ohio Statehouse.

"Praying for our leaders in the battle."

I responded, "*Really?* Where are their 'private prayer meetings'? I would like to attend them. Oh, there *aren't any*? That's what I thought." They just wanted to stop us from praying at the Statehouse. I wasn't going to stop. After all, these naysayers hadn't delivered the votes, God was the only one who could.

Every seat in the statehouse was rented and filled with an overflow crowd outside for our Heartbeat Bill rally in the Statehouse Atrium on a Tuesday afternoon in September, 2011.

I haven't always been this bold. During the first year of the Heartbeat Bill battle, I remember one of many prayer meetings in the Statehouse Atrium between the House and Senate chambers. I made a call to Pastor Corey Shankleton, who at that time was just "some guy" who called and offered to help. I took a chance and put him in charge of the prayer rally we had scheduled later that week. We've been friends ever since.

Pastor Corey brought his worship team and banner-toting Christians. I watched the Senators roll their eyes as they walked past our all-day worship and prayer meeting. I pulled Pastor Shankleton aside and said, "We

Janet Porter holding the five-foot list of leaders and groups who supported the first Heartbeat Bill in the Statehouse Atrium adjacent to the Ohio Senate.

CWA of Ohio's Bobbi Radeck, Lori Viars, Janet Porter, Dr. Jack Willke, and Linda Theis at the Heartbeat Bill rally. Dr. Willke is holding his Hero for Life Award we presented to him.

may want to keep the *banner-waving* to a minimum," knowing we were the object of ridicule.

They didn't stop, and I was glad. But by the end of the day, the presence of God so filled the place that, for a moment, I forgot we were in the Statehouse. My eyes were on God, and I no longer cared what people thought. I even picked up a banner and waved it myself. Not bad for a girl raised Lutheran. If you want to see victory, please God, not men.

We had the hearts of the grassroots, and we had the support of the pro-family leaders. By September 2011, the bill had already passed the House (the first time), so we decided to show our support to the Senate. We rented every chair they had in the Statehouse and still didn't have enough for the overflow crowd that came out

"Non-helium" heart balloons from constituents to be delivered to the Ohio Senators following the 2011 Heartbeat Rally.

on a Tuesday afternoon to hear from speakers like Dr. Jack Willke, Joe Scheidler, Troy Newman, Pastors Lou Engle, Dutch Sheets, Jim Garlow, Rick Scarborough, former Congressman Bob McEwen, elected officials and leaders from around the state and nation. People came by the busload from all over the state. That five-foot board I'm holding over my head is a list of groups and well-known leaders who endorsed the Heartbeat Bill. The bunting above us (and all around the atrium) was left over from our Values Voter Presidential Debate.

We fed everyone a huge heart-shaped sugar cookie before they set out to deliver bouquets of (non-helium) heart balloons in glass vases, each with a message from their constituents.

Pastor Tim Sheets from Oasis (far left) prayed for the Heartbeat Bill for years in his statewide prayer network. Pastor Ernie Sanders, of Doers of the Word Baptist Church, is at the podium for the Pastors for the Heartbeat Bill Press Conference.

At this rally a Senator, pretending to be with us, was asked to speak. She then used our microphone to speak *against* the bill. When you're in the battle you have to expect the unexpected and roll with the punches— even the ones that hit you square in the gut. Thankfully, there were bold speakers who followed this public betrayal like Dr. Jim Garlow, who was

Pastor of Skyline Church near San Diego, California at the time. Here's a clip of what he said:

> Any Senator who would dare get on this platform and lecture us about the inappropriateness of a bill that will block 95 percent of abortions must go! This is not going to be tolerated! It is wrong! It is morally, biblically wrong! My wife struggles with stage four cancer—it's been an intense battle. There's an axiom among cancer patients: "If your doctor takes away your hope of life, get a new doctor." If your Senator takes away the issue of life—get a new senator!

His words were met with a standing ovation and more chants from the crowd to "*pass the bill*" which echoed throughout the Senate.

The Senate was still stalling, and we were still hosting press conference after press conference. Exasperated, I took to the air. Television air, radio air, and—*the air*. We rented a plane to fly over the Statehouse when the Senate obstructionists were in town and most likely to see it. The banner said, "OH SENATE: PASS THE HEARTBEAT BILL!"

We took our message to the air: "OH SENATE: PASS THE HEARTBEAT BILL!"

I was with a Senator when the plane flew by. He said, "Oh, they're gonna *hate* this." I remember the reaction of Senate President Tom Niehaus, who had blocked the Heartbeat Bill for years despite his promise to pass it. He talked to the press about "what a stupid idea" it was to fly a plane over the Statehouse since he claimed he "didn't see it." Yet there they all were—talking about it. *Maybe not so stupid.* Lori Viars still marvels at the fact that I had the numbers to multiple airplane banner towing companies in my cellphone from different cities and states. You just never know when you might need them!

Here's one of our early television ads which ran in selected TV markets within targeted Senate districts and online.

In the background we hear children singing "The Wheels on the Bus Go Round and Round."

The Heartbeat Bill, which protects unborn babies with beating hearts, will save the equivalent of a school bus full of children every single day.

That's right, every single day the senate delays a vote on the Heartbeat Bill, a school bus full of children's lives are lost.

> Ask your state senators to persuade senate president Tom
> Niehaus to bring the Heartbeat Bill to a committee and a vote
> today. We can't wait another day. The cost is just too high.[12]

In the original ad, we had video of a school bus going off a cliff, but not surprisingly the television stations rejected it. It seems people are more bothered by a *message* about children dying than children *actually* dying. At least that was the case in the Ohio Senate.

Our big rally inside the Statehouse would be hard to beat. How could we keep the pressure on? You've seen the enormous balloons at the Macy's Thanksgiving Day Parade? I told my husband, "I have an idea! Let's get a huge heart balloon and put it in front of the Statehouse!" My husband didn't flinch—he was used to me by now. He found one we could order online and smiled as he said, *"How is it even possible that we don't own one of these already?"* Just one of the many reasons I love that man.

As I would often remind my long-suffering husband, this whole thing started with his idea to "outlaw abortion while you're here." Here is our Heartbeat Bill balloon outside the Ohio Statehouse at one of our many rallies.

You get a little better picture of just how enormous this thing is when you see it next to people. It actually is three stories high. Thanks to Francis Boysko, who patched it, stored it, and kept it in working order. The Ohio Senate obstructionists were starting to get the idea that  there was nothing we wouldn't do to pass this bill. They were also getting the picture that we weren't going away until it was done.

Katelyn Evans was a girl who shadowed me back when she was in the eighth grade at the insistence of her grandfather Paul Imhoff, a pro-life champion and friend. When she heard about our effort, she weighed in to help blow up balloons, make countless copies, and testify for the bill as an EMS worker. She asked me to be in her wedding and planned to take some of the wedding pictures at the Ohio Statehouse. If you think I was going to let an opportunity like that slip by, you haven't been paying attention. While dressed in our gowns, we stopped by some Senate offices for the word to spread that people were even lobbying for the Heartbeat Bill on their wedding day! They may have thought we were crazy, but they knew we weren't going to quit.

Pointing to our Heartbeat Bill buttons, we lobbied the Ohio Senate in our gowns.

When another Valentine's Day rolled around, we needed something to break through the Senate blockade. We had already done balloons, heart-shaped candy, cookies, and Teddy bears with beating hearts.

We decided to send them the symbol of the pro-life movement—the red rose. Make that *a room full* of red roses. They were ordered online by constituents who wanted to deliver a message that couldn't easily be overlooked.

The Heartbeat Bill would save 2,200 babies each month—the amount of red roses which filled this room.

We tied them in groups of three, the number of babies the Heartbeat Bill would save each hour. The attached message read,

"Bring this bill to a vote before the roses and babies die."[13]

The room had 2,200 roses, the number of babies the Heartbeat Bill would save in a month.

We got all the roses set up about 20 minutes before the press conference was scheduled to begin. People were coming by just to see and smell the beautiful room and have their pictures taken. That was about the time when one of the House staffers came in and blew a gasket. Literally screeching, she screamed, "You can't have these in here! You need to move them—right now! *Right now!* RIGHT NOW!"

I calmly explained that we had permission to use the room and that our state representative sponsor was on his way, "Here, I'll get him on the phone for you." She didn't even take a breath.

She screamed, "*No!* You need to get these things out of here *now— RIGHT NOW!*" I'm pretty sure her head spun all the way around, but I couldn't get confirmation from the others. She kept screaming, threatening to call the Highway Patrol—most of whom were extremely nice and seemingly on our side. It makes sense, after all—their jobs are to serve and *protect*. So I walked over to the homeschool volunteers who had helped us and whispered in their ears:

"Load the roses on the cart as slowly as you possibly can. I'll be right back." They gave the nod and started moving to shut the lady up. I rushed to my director friend down at the Capitol Advisory Board who first helped me manage the illegal balloon incident. Within minutes, he found me another room in the Statehouse that the screaming lady didn't control. We took the signs to alert the press that, in about 15 minutes, the press conference was going to begin down the hall and around the corner. We were still setting up as the press arrived.

That day I got a call from another screaming woman. A Democrat Senator who, apparently, didn't like roses. She screamed that she didn't want any more phone calls and that I had better "Put a stop to them!"

I calmly explained, "I can't tell your constituents not to call an elected official who works for them." She didn't seem to realize that taking calls from constituents is *part of her job*. I had never been in her office since we don't focus our efforts on hard-hearted abortion operatives. We never even targeted her office for phone calls—she was just experiencing the crumbs of what everyone else was getting. After her tirade, I was tempted to put her on the target list to greatly increase her call volume, but decided not to. Not because of any threats, but because that wasn't where the calls would do the most good.

Her pro-abortion tirade didn't really bother me. I don't even remember her name. You see, it's not about what's being said, it's *why* someone is saying it. For example, flattery from obstructionists is meaningless and nauseating. They think saying nice things will get you to back off. If they think it will work, they are mistaken. In the same way, mean calls from people who want to kill babies are encouraging, not just from this pro-abortion Democrat Senator, but from RINOS spewing threats. Expect the RINOs who don't want to end abortion to tell you things like, "You're doing more damage to the cause," and their personal favorite, "You need to stop these phone calls or we won't pass your bill!" Here's the legislative code-talk everyone needs to understand to be effective.

STATEMENT: "You need to stop these phone calls or we won't pass your bill!"

Here's what you need to ask yourself, why haven't they passed the bill yet? Most likely the answer to that question is because they have no intention of ever passing your bill. You see, if a legislator plans to pass your bill, calls aren't a problem—they are an opportunity to tell voters that they intend to do the very thing they're being asked to do. It's a public relations dream. If they want to pass the bill, here's how easy the calls are answered:

Caller: "Vote for the Heartbeat Bill!"

Legislator: "We plan to do that on Tuesday."

Caller: "Thanks so much!"

Easy peasy. It's when you *don't* want to do what callers are asking that the calls are despised.

ACTION TO TAKE: DOUBLE DOWN—Call more and *more often.* You are having an impact, don't stop!

When the Speaker of the Ohio House was complaining about the calls he was getting for blocking a floor vote, a legislator in leadership pulled me aside and whispered, *"It's starting to get to him—keep it up!"*

They don't see the light until they feel the heat.

By the way, that Speaker of the House was someone I once considered a friend. I had known him for decades. He signed my discharge petition when we passed the nation's first partial-birth abortion ban in 1995. He came to my wedding. But when he wouldn't bring the Heartbeat Bill to a floor vote, we called him for 6 weeks nonstop until he did. Calls matter because they work. To everyone who made them, thank you from the bottom of my heart.

There was a fence-sitting legislator we targeted for calls, and we knew he was getting hammered. I saw his aide in the hallway and could barely keep the smirk off of my face.

I glibly asked him, "Are you getting *any calls?*"

He assured me that he wasn't, yet a few minutes into our conversation he slipped up and blurted, "With all your people calling, *I can't get anything done!*"

After reiterating the remedy for the problem—get your boss to *commit to vote for the bill*—I walked away smiling. It was working, and in the end, we got his vote.

There are thousands of babies whose hearts are beating right now who, by tonight, will be legally killed in the United States and beyond. The question is, what are you going to do about it? Are you willing to be a

Ten-year-old Hawke high-fives Senate Sponsor Tina Roegner after he wows them in committee. Proud mom Julie Busby pictured second from the left.

Pastor Rodney Lord, Lori Viars, Jeremy Salupo, Janet Porter, Joshua Hlavaty, and Julie Busby: Part of the unstoppable team who refused to quit.

voice for them even when it makes people upset? Even when they say mean things to you and about you?

Ten-year-old Hawke Busby isn't afraid to speak the truth. Even in legislative committees that tower over him. He stood before the Senators and said what many grown men have been too fearful to say:

"These babies deserve a chance to live their lives and we shouldn't treat them like a piece of trash because God made all these kids special and He has a plan for their lives. We shouldn't abort these babies because God doesn't like that. That's what the devil wants you to do."

Hawke's mom, Julie Busby, is faith filled and fearless and is raising her children to be the same way. We prayed for countless hours together, and she was there at the finish line to see those prayers answered.

Outside the Ohio Senate Chambers in December 2018—just 4 months from victory, this heroic group near the finish line—also ran the race.

Michigan Heartbeat

I spoke at the Michigan Statehouse Heartbeat Bill rally just after the Ohio bill passed. The people in Michigan wanted to keep hearts beating as much as the people of Ohio. Afterward the crowd moved to the rotunda for prayer and worship. Spontaneously from two levels of balconies above came an unmistakable sound.

People began to pound the railings and stomp on the floor to the sound of a heartbeat. Everyone joined. It reverberated throughout the entire Statehouse into the offices of legislators who came to see what was happening. The heartbeat of Michigan had begun to beat, and there is no stopping it.

Pastor Corey Shankleton, who helped us pass the Ohio Heartbeat Bill, moved to Michigan to lead their Heartbeat effort. Pastor Shankleton, Mark Gurley, and I met with dozens of House and Senate members including Michigan house Heartbeat Bill sponsor Rep. Steve Johnson. After lobbying for nearly a week, we were still without a sponsor in the Michigan Senate. That's when we had a divine appointment with Senator Ed McBroom (R-Vulcan). Senator McBroom kept saying there was something familiar about me until he figured out what it was. Turned out

HEARTBEAT
PETITIONS HERE

"A Heartbeat Detected
Is A Life Protected"

Pastor Corey
Shankleton leading
the charge for the
Michigan Heartbeat
Bill.

he listened to my daily radio program for years while farming in Michigan's Upper Peninsula.

Senator McBroom didn't know my married name, but knew every campaign I discussed on the air including the time we mailed 8 million pink slips to Congress, warning what would happen if they voted against our values.[14] We sent so many pink slips that if they were stacked on top of each other, the stack would measure more than four times the height of the Washington Monument.[15] Senator McBroom became our Heartbeat senate sponsor, and we couldn't have asked for anyone better.

I spent another week traveling with Pastor Shankleton and his 9-year-old daughter Moriah, "my assistant," speaking to churches, pro-life groups, and houses of prayer.

They have a pro-abortion governor in Michigan. *No worries*. Michigan has what is called a Citizen Petition Initiative that lets the citizens bypass the governor entirely. Unlike most petition drives, which put a measure on the ballot—where typically the one with the most money wins—in Michigan, just under 400,000 signatures sends the Heartbeat Bill to the legislature. With a simple majority vote in the House and Senate, their Heartbeat Bill will become *law!*

The leadership in the Senate and the Speaker of the House have already pledged to pass it when it comes to them. But Michigan's pro-abortion Attorney General has pledged to not do her job to enforce *any* pro-life laws on the books. That's why I'm so glad Walter Weber, of the ACLJ, thought to put a provision in the Ohio and Michigan Heartbeat Bill (as well as the model bill) that says if the Attorney General won't enforce the law, then a County Prosecutor is authorized to do so. *We don't have to keep being bullied by the lawless left!*

In order to make sure we have enough valid signatures, the Michigan Heartbeat Coalition set the goal at 500,000 signatures by the end of 2020. When I first got there, the Michigan team was asking people to fill out a petition a week for 10 weeks. That's fine, but I told him we can do better than that!

Pastor Shankleton and I told the crowd how easy it was to gather petitions at churches, county fairs, concerts, and outside the Secretary of State's office, where people are waiting in line for their car titles and license plates. We described the romantic date nights husbands could share with their wives—hand in hand, with arms full of clipboards, saying those three special words everyone longs to hear: "*Sign my petition?*"

I let them know that just 500 people in the state of Michigan can end abortion. All that is needed is to gather 1,000 names each, and it will go to the state legislature for a simple majority vote. I brought with me "Heartbeat Hero" pins from the Ohio Victory Party and asked those who wanted to become a "Heartbeat Hero" to come forward. Would people come forward to make such a pledge? Did I set the bar too high?

They came forward in droves! People were crying, saying, "I have prayed for this day to come." Pastor Shankleton also handed out "smooth stones" for these heroes who would slay the giant of abortion. He was in Ohio when the giant fell, and no one can tell Pastor Shankleton it can't be done!

Pastor Corey Shankleton, Beth Folger, Rep. Ron Hood, Janet Porter, Rep. Christina Hagan, Lori Viars, and Rep. Candice Keller just before a floor vote.

The opportunity to end abortion for which we have prayed is *here*. Everything we're believing for is on the other side of not giving up. Sometimes it takes more than a single stone, but once you've seen Goliath fall, giants no longer intimidate you.

CHAPTER 6

The Enemy Within

"If the choice is between unity and life, we choose life."
—Julie Doehner, former president of
Geauga County Right to Life,
former affiliate of Ohio Right to Life

G uess which group has worked the hardest against the Heart-beat Bills? If you guessed Planned Parenthood, NARAL, or the pro-abortion Democrats you'd be wrong.

You wouldn't expect it. Most wouldn't believe it, but the biggest obstacle to passing Heartbeat Bills across the nation is National Right to Life and many of their state affiliates including Ohio, Tennessee, Michigan, Texas, Indiana, Kansas, and West Virginia, which each actively fight against their own mission statements to end abortion.

Don't believe it? Keep reading.

I wouldn't have believed it if I hadn't experienced it—over and over again—for 8 long years. While we lobbied to keep hearts beating in Ohio, we passed Ohio Right to Life in the hallways of the Statehouse actively lobbying *against* the Heartbeat Bill. I was in the committee hearings when Ohio Right to Life testified *against* the Heartbeat Bill, standing alongside Planned Parenthood and the abortion lobby. Then Ohio Right to Life actually called for a veto of the Heartbeat Bill and celebrated, alongside the abortionists, when it came. Not once but *twice*.

One day, while waiting for an appointment with a legislator, I struck up a conversation with the representative from the abortion lobby. I said, "You guys have it pretty easy with Ohio Right to Life doing all the work of fighting the Heartbeat Bill, don't you?"

He agreed, saying, "Yeah, it frees us up for a lot of other things."

There are thousands of news articles to document what took place, many with headlines like this: "Ohio Right to Life and NARAL Team Up Against OH Heartbeat Bill."[1]

For any Right to Life group leaders who may be reading this, unsure whether to support or oppose Heartbeat Bills, here's a friendly reminder:

Live baby (with a detectable heartbeat)—*good*.

Dead babies—*bad*.

If you're still not sure, here a few more hints:

- When your pro-life group is featured on the National Abortion Rights Action League's website as an ally, that's a clue that you may be on the wrong side of the issue.[2]

- When you find yourself celebrating next to Planned Parenthood, NARAL, and the abortionists when a bill is vetoed, you might be on the wrong side of the issue.

- When the number of dead babies could fill stadiums because of your opposition to a bill, there can be no doubt—you are on the wrong side of the issue.

The fiercest opposition to ending abortion came from the group formed to end abortion

I just got *another* call from a frantic pro-lifer saying, "You're not going to believe this, but our state Right to Life group is fighting us!"

Oh, I believe it.

If your state National Right to Life affiliate is not opposing you, thank the Lord. That was the case with Iowa Right to Life, Louisiana Right to Life,[3] and South Carolina Citizens for Life, which actively supported the effort to keep hearts beating. Other Right to Life affiliates claim "neutrality" on the bill that would end most abortions. Almost always, "neutral" means "opposed behind your back." Forget what they say; watch what they do. By the way, if an organization calls itself pro-life and can't support a bill to end abortion, then it either doesn't understand the bill (see Chapter 4), or it should tear up its mission statement to "end abortion."

If your state Right to Life or pro-family group is opposed to the Heartbeat Bill, you need to know what you'll be facing. It's not a pleasant truth but one we must face with eyes wide open. The alternative is to be continually blindsided, in a constant state of shock and disbelief. If you find yourself fighting against people who should be on your side, brace yourself, and get a glimpse of the battle in which you're about to engage.

Ohio Representative Lynn Wachtmann, who in 2011 sponsored the first Heartbeat Bill, produced a timeline of verified events that occurred during the first few months of the effort to introduce and pass the Ohio

Heartbeat Bill. It was distributed widely on Wachtmann's official letter-head, outlining events I would have rather forgotten:

- On November 30, 2010, I had the idea to legally protect babies whose heartbeats can be heard. That night, within minutes of when the idea was first conceived, I approached Mike Gonidakis, then the executive director of Ohio Right to Life (ORTL), at the wake of my friend and former boss Mark Lally. I introduced myself and explained I was supportive of their (incremental) bills, but asked if he would also be supportive of mine—a bill to protect babies whose heartbeats could be detected. There, in front of the past president of Ohio Right to Life and a former legislative staffer, Gonidakis said he would "support" such an effort. He confirmed his support on a phone call on December 20, 2010.

- As a result, I included him on group emails and multiple conference calls. In order to keep the group encouraged, I emailed the group messages like: "We just got another cosponsor!" "Rep. Smith just signed on—we're up to eight!" Little did I know that Gonidakis was using that inside information to peel off cosponsors as soon as we would get them. He even used my confidential email list of attorneys and supporters who had participated in the conference calls to try and talk our own people out of supporting the Heartbeat Bill.

- Legislators complained that they were being "strong-armed" by Ohio Right to Life to come off the bill; others claimed they were outright threatened.

- Before the Heartbeat Bill was introduced, we successfully put every legislator back on the bill that Ohio Right to Life had talked off of it.

- On March 9, 2011, I was with a group including Dr. Willke when we ran into Gonidakis lobbying against us in the Senate once again. He knew he had lost his support in the House, so he was spending his time making sure the Senate would block it when it passed the House floor. Dr. Willke—whose book *Abortion Questions and Answers* has been a handbook for pro-lifers around the world—relayed his 40 years of experience in the pro-life movement and plainly told Gonidakis, "Mike, you're wrong on this."

- Gonidakis responded by telling us that we were a "laughing stock" and that "NARAL and Planned Parenthood are laughing at you." I figured he should know since they were on the same side, opposing our pro-life bill. My mother was with us that day and responded by saying, "There are fifty signatures on the bill." Gonidakis then swung his hand within an inch of my mother's face and exclaimed, "That's enough of that!" Some described Gonidakis's behavior as an "unprofessional display of anger," others called it outright "demonic."

- March 2011, Ohio Right to Life sent a letter to the Ohio Senate, declaring their official opposition to H.B. 125, the Heartbeat Bill.

- On March 29, 2011, Dr. Willke, who was well known for playing his recording of a baby's heartbeat at 6 weeks' gestation, wrote to the board of Ohio Right to Life, the group he founded, stating: "I remain supportive of this bill...I sharply question whether a majority of the ORTL board gave him [Gonidakis] the charge to so vigorously lobby against the Heartbeat Bill even after it became evident that to continue such action will create a tragically divided ORTL organization. This has done serious harm to the Ohio pro-life movement.

Willke continued, "A majority of the Ohio Right to Life Board shares some responsibility here. When it became clearly evident that a substantial percentage of pro-lifers were supporting the new bill, the board should have told him to 'cool it' and let the proposed bill proceed on its own merits. I firmly believe that at this stage of this controversy, the Board should let the chapters and members make this decision."

- On March 29, 2011, Ohio Right to Life sent out a mass email claiming that Dr. Willke had withdrawn his support of the Heartbeat Bill (which was not true). It asked for people to call the Speaker's office to vote no on the Heartbeat Bill.

- On March 31, 2011, Gonidakis told the Associated Press that Ohio Right to Life "will continue to share their thoughts with House members in hopes of blocking a vote by the full chamber."[4]

- By May 2, 2011, there were five hundred national, state, and local pro-life groups and leaders signed on to support the Heartbeat Bill, despite ORTL's concentrated effort to discourage them. The list included four presidential candidates; Dr. James Dobson; Governor Mike Huckabee (who told me how he was being barraged by ORTL to remove his support); four past presidents of Ohio Right to Life; and the vast majority of the local Right to Life members.

- By May 2, 2011, quotes reflecting Gonidakis' opposition to the Heartbeat Bill appeared in 2,130 news sources. And they were just getting started.

- August 2011, Dr. Jack Willke resigned from Ohio Right to Life, the organization he founded, and joined the new pro-life group, Ohio Pro-Life Action, as a vice president in order to help our effort to pass the Ohio Heartbeat Bill. Dr. Willke said Ohio Right to Life was "out of touch with the 'unrestrained enthusiasm' the Heartbeat Bill had unleashed."[5]

- Once the Heartbeat Bill passed in the Ohio Senate, Gonidakis lobbied Governor Kasich to veto the bill. Kasich granted his request. Gonidakis celebrated along with the abortionists when the veto came, praising the governor and giving Kasich pro-life cover for his action.

- The bill passed the Ohio House and Senate a second time in December 2018. ORTL lobbied Gov. Kasich for a second veto—and got it. Gonidakis, again, publicly praised the governor giving him cover for vetoing the most protective pro-life bill to ever pass in the state.[6] On December 27, 2018, the *same day* the effort to override Governor Kasich's second veto failed by one vote, Ohio Right to Life issued a statement in support of the Heartbeat Bill: "Ohio Right to Life believes that *it is now time* to embrace the Heartbeat Bill as the next incremental approach to end abortion in Ohio."[7] They claimed their newfound support was because of the nomination of Justice Kavanaugh, but their support for the bill didn't come at the confirmation of Kavanaugh in October, but rather at the loss of the veto-override in December, when it was clear they could do no more damage to the bill prior to the new pro-life Governor replacing Kasich.

- Gonidakis then stood at the bill signing, pretending Ohio Right to Life had something to do with it passing, hoping everyone would forget how they actively and vigorously lobbied and testified against it for 8 long years and called for its veto not once but twice.

- At a Statehouse press conference following passage of the Heartbeat Law Ohio Right to Life Executive Director Stephanie Krider said, "Passage of the Heartbeat Bill is really our greatest accomplishment to date."

Did you catch that? Passage of the bill they fought the hardest *against* is Ohio Right to Life's "greatest accomplishment to date." *Wow.* Gonidakis then told the press that the Heartbeat Bill was "the culmination of eight years of work."[8] Just not *his* work.

If your "Right to Life" group is anything like Ohio Right to Life, expect to experience the same three stages to passage:

1. They mock you.

2. They fight you.

3. They take credit for what you've done.

Ohio Heartbeat Bill sponsor Rep. Candice Keller (R-Middletown) said, "After working against the Heartbeat Bill, pressuring legislators against it, testifying against it, and twice calling for its veto, Ohio Right to Life had the audacity to actually take the credit when it passed! They have no interest in helping to pass our Life at Conception bill but look for Ohio Right to Life to also take the credit when we pass it without them."

In addition to vehemently fighting the Heartbeat Bill for 8 years before claiming credit for its passage, Ohio Right to Life then refused to endorse pro-life champion Heartbeat Bill sponsor Rep. Candice Keller. Of course this fueled her opponent's nasty mailers with "Ohio Right to Life REFUSED to endorse her." You see how this game is played? I'm going to call it what it is—evil.

In addition to sponsoring the most protective pro-life law to ever pass in Ohio, Rep. Keller is also director of the Middletown pro-life Pregnancy Center and sponsor of the Life at Conception Bill. To deny her a pro-life endorsement is reprehensible. There are always a lot of people at the finish line who never ran the race. But in this case, many standing at the finish line spent most of their time throwing rocks at the runners.

Some frustrated pro-life leaders planned to expose Ohio Right to Life's fierce opposition to the Heartbeat Bill with a protest outside the ORTL office. But I talked the leaders out of it saying, "Let's keep our focus on the goal." But when I reflect on the more than 150,000 lives lost because of Ohio Right to Life's 8-year opposition, I now know my advice was wrong. *Dead wrong—times 150,000.*

Before running to the front of the parade to claim credit, Gonidakis told the *Columbus Dispatch*:

> [Janet Porter] might be one of the best public speakers I've ever seen...She has an amazing gift for communication. Unfortunately she has used that gift for more negative than good.[9]

If only I would use my powers for *good*. For something like...*ending abortion.*

As predicted, Ohio Right to Life experienced a mass exodus from their Right to Life chapters, including Right to Life of Greater Cincinnati (the largest), Cleveland Right to Life, Toledo Right to Life, and many of their county chapters. They joined the new organization, Ohio Pro-Life Action, in droves. That group, now called Right to Life Action Coalition of Ohio, has grown and is stronger than ever.

Geauga County Right to Life was one of many state chapters who left Ohio Right to Life and joined the new organization, which backed the Heartbeat Bill. Julie Doehner, former president of the Geauga County chapter of Ohio Right to Life, told the *New York Times,* "We've had 39 years of talk and regulation, it's time to *win* this war and actually *protect* babies with beating hearts." She added, "If the choice is between unity and life, we choose life."[10]

State "Right to Life" Opposition Continues

One of the first national leaders to sign on to the Heartbeat Bill supporter list was Governor Mike Huckabee, who was targeted by incessant lobbying by Ohio Right to Life from the very beginning. He commented that our fight "was not only against the usual suspects of Planned

Parenthood and the far left who have made the killing of a baby a religious ritual," but we were "even opposed by other elements in the pro-life movement that have never made sense to me."[11]

Sadly, fierce opposition to ending abortion from the groups formed to end abortion was not an isolated anomaly. National Right to Life's state affiliates of Michigan, Tennessee, Kansas, Indiana, Missouri, Texas, and West Virginia were among those who actively fought against their own mission statements to end abortion. When I was legislative director of Ohio Right to Life, I used to dream of the day when the bloodbath was over and I could do something else—*anything else*. Yet it seems these "Right to Life" groups would rather keep abortion legal than find something else to do.

Right to Life chapters across the United States are employing similar tactics to stop Heartbeat Bills in their states.

Michigan

Faith2Action's Michigan director, Pastor Corey Shankleton, is also president of the Michigan Heartbeat Coalition. He spent 8 years helping us pass the Ohio Heartbeat Bill before moving to Michigan to lead the charge there. I was invited to attend a meeting with Pastor Shankleton and the president of Right to Life of Michigan along with Marc Gurley and Rick Warzak of the Heartbeat Coalition. I had a relationship with the president, Barbara Listing, who brought me in to speak at many of their fundraising banquets over the years.

We were told they "weren't opposing" the Heartbeat Bill. Yet we had just come from the Statehouse and saw a copy of their Heartbeat Bill opposition memo, which had just been circulated to legislators.

They admitted they were getting calls from pro-lifers asking for a Heartbeat Bill. We explained that when we started, nobody knew about a Heartbeat Bill. Now *everyone* does. I told them, "It is what your members want, and there's no stopping it." We even offered them the chance to "be the ones to lead and we will follow."

Right to Life of Michigan told us their focus was to pass a dismemberment abortion ban, which bans one method but would allow that same baby to be brutally aborted by another method. We explained, "Pro-lifers are not satisfied with a 'dismemberment ban' that educates but protects no one."

I told Listing what happened before Ohio Right to Life ran to the front of the parade. After opposing the Heartbeat Bill for 8 years, they lost their biggest and most influential chapters, including Cincinnati, Cleveland, and Toledo affiliates.

We told them, "We have the opportunity to protect more babies than every bill we've passed in the last 50 years—*combined*. We can get within reach of *ending abortion!* Isn't that your mission statement?"

Right to Life of Michigan asked us if we could wait 2 years. I responded: "The price of waiting—fifty thousand lives—is just too high."

After the meeting, I sent Listing a dozen roses with a message: "You are the leader—lead the way to the end of abortion." She could have done it, but she chose to manage abortion rather than end it. But we're not just talking about "non support." As of this writing, Right to Life of Michigan is actively and vigorously working *against* the Michigan Heartbeat effort. They will also soon understand that their members didn't join their organization to merely regulate abortion; they, too, want to *end* it. And if Michigan Right to Life won't do it, they will join with those who will in the Michigan Heartbeat Coalition.

While the new Michigan Heartbeat Coalition members were in shock, Pastor Shankleton and I were not. Pastor Shankleton said, "After watching Ohio Right to Life fight against the Heartbeat Bill for 8 years, I wasn't surprised to find the same opposition awaiting us from Right to Life of Michigan. Having lived through this very same nightmare, we had a better idea of what was coming and also what to do."

Pastor Shankleton added, "What did surprise me, however, was the extreme fervor with which they went after each and every supporter, both local and national, in an attempt to peel off their support. All after sweetly saying, 'We would never oppose your bill; that's not our style.'"

I lobbied with Pastor Shankleton and Marc Gurley at the Michigan Statehouse and then spent another week speaking throughout the state, where I was told that Right to Life of Michigan "had just been" everywhere we went. They tried to talk each host out of supporting the Heartbeat Bill.

I recently got a call from a well-known national leader who is being lobbied by Right to Life of Michigan to drop his support of the Heartbeat Bill. *What a shock.* By the way, the leader held firm against the pressure and misinformation with his strong support of the bill.

Why are they doing this? Right to Life of Michigan's website says it all. Their first reason to oppose the Heartbeat Bill is:

> The heartbeat petition drive is not organized by Right to Life of Michigan and is separate from the petition drive to bypass Governor Whitmer's veto of the dismemberment abortion ban.[12]

Allow me to translate: "*It wasn't our idea.*"

Here's another doozy from their website: "Michigan law already bans abortions before and after a heartbeat is detected."[13]

This is deceptive *at best*. They make this claim pointing to an unenforced 1846 Michigan law that protects no one. The only way it could possibly be reenacted is if there is a challenge to *Roe*. And the only way to challenge *Roe* is to pass a law outside its current parameters.

Another common excuse is that the Heartbeat Bill would harm other pro-life laws already on the books. *Nope*. Here is the language from the model Heartbeat Bill, which is similar to what's in the Michigan Heartbeat Bill:

> It is furthermore the intent of the general assembly that the provisions of this bill are not to have the effect of repealing or limiting any other laws of this state, except as specified by this bill.[14]

As Pastor Shankleton told the *Wall Street Journal*:

> A lot of these national organizations have been involved in the fight for 46 years with very few victories to show for it.... This is the best opportunity we've had in a generation to send a real challenge to Roe.[15]

When Michigan and Tennessee pass Heartbeat Laws, every state in the Sixth Circuit will have done so. When they join Ohio and Kentucky, they will send a unanimous message to the court. And it's becoming a very good court. The Sixth Circuit has eleven Republicans and five Democrats along with three Trump appointees—the most of all twelve circuits.[16]

David Fowler, founder of the Family Action Council of Tennessee, went from being an opponent of the Tennessee Heartbeat Bill to a staunch supporter, testifying in support of it in the Senate Committee.[17] Fowler pointed to the recent Sixth Circuit decision to uphold Kentucky's ultrasound law as very hopeful. The Court used the words "unborn child" or "unborn life" thirty times in its opinion, a recognition of the living child in the womb.[18]

Fowler said that "more importantly," in its decision, the Sixth Circuit Court of Appeals "cited approvingly another circuit court decision affirming that abortion 'terminate[s] the life of a whole, separate, unique, living human being.'"[19]

This is our time, and the Sixth Circuit may be our court! Of course, whatever the ruling, it will be appealed, and the final destination will be the U.S. Supreme Court.

Tennessee

Tennessee Right to Life President Brian Harris is also against the Heartbeat Bill that has been introduced in his state. He testified against it in 2017 and continues to actively oppose it.[20]

Harris told the *Memphis Daily News* that introducing Heartbeat Bills can become "demoralizing to pro-life citizens who want to be on a winning team."[21] Anyone who thinks killing a million innocent children each year is "winning" is either delusional or—a terrorist. "Winning" with a bill that protects virtually no one also is not winning. Tennessee Right to Life, like so many, don't want to appear a failure, so they never even attempt to win—to follow their own mission statements to end abortion rather than merely regulate it.

But Tennessee Right to Life took it a step further. Like Ohio Right to Life, they chose to punish pro-life legislators who want to keep hearts beating. Tennessee Right to Life Political Action Committee withheld their endorsement from the Heartbeat Bill's sponsors, Republican Representative Micah Van Huss and Republican Senator Mark Pody, despite their 100% pro-life voting record![22] *The Tennessee Star* reported that Tennessee's Right to Life "cheered when a State Senate Committee sent it off to 'summer study' instead of passing it."[23] That's the same thing the abortion activists did when the Ohio Heartbeat Bill was delayed. There is no other way to describe it, unmistakably—evil.

Andy Schlafly said, "It's terrible to see such a misuse of the Right to Life name."[24] Senator Pody told *The Tennessee Star,* "It's very disappointing that [Tennessee Right to Life] would be the ones standing in the way."[25] I couldn't agree more.

If your desire is to end abortion and there's a bill with that objective that you can't support, why not connect with the sponsors to help make it something you can support? That's not what Tennessee Right to Life chose to do. *The Tennessee Star* reported, "Neither Sen. Pody nor Rep. Van Huss were approached by [Tennessee Right to Life] during this legislative session with regard to making the bill one that they could support."[26]

Joining Tennessee Right to Life in opposing the Heartbeat Bill were the Catholic bishops, while Catholic bishops in Florida and Georgia supported their Heartbeat Bills.[27]

You may have heard that faith is spelled with four letters: R-I-S-K. That means you might fail. Pastor Mark Batterson said, faith is the "willingness to look foolish."[28] But National Right to Life Attorney Jim Bopp, who testified against the Ohio and Tennessee Heartbeat Bills, advocates continuing with the failed incrementalism because to do otherwise might "look foolish." Bopp testified before the Tennessee Senate Committee on August 12, 2019 stating, "I do not want to look foolish."[29] He should worry more about doing what's right.

I was looking forward to responding in person at the committee since Tennessee Senator Pody's office asked if I would testify at their Heartbeat Bill hearing that day. I bought the airline ticket and planned to be there, but on the previous Friday I was informed that the chairman of the committee, a Republican, wouldn't allow it. He wouldn't even allow a substitution to be made for Heartbeat proponents who were on the list but unable to attend. That gives you an idea of the battle being waged behind the scenes. But Tennessee Gov. Bill Lee is bypassing the games and calling for passage of the Heartbeat Bill. I predict he will get it.[30]

In a letter to the editor in *The Tennessee Star*, Frances Arthur, the church outreach associate for Tennessee Right to Life, said, "The smartest, most prudent move for the pro-life leader, activist, and legislator regarding the 'Heartbeat Bill' is to wait."[30]

The idea of waiting is not new. Martin Luther King, Jr. encountered it. And here's what he had to say:

> For years now I have heard the word "Wait!" It rings in the ear of every Negro with piercing familiarity. This "Wait" has almost always meant "Never." We must come to see, with one of our distinguished jurists, that "justice too long delayed is justice denied."[31]

I heard the word "wait" for nearly a decade. It meant "never" when they first said it, and it means never now. Martin Luther King, Jr. didn't wait in the battle for civil rights. Neither will we.

Jim Bopp doesn't have any problem waiting. *It's not like babies are dying or anything.* He told the *Washington Post*, "The Supreme Court will likely consider cases that could eventually limit or overturn *Roe v. Wade*, but it won't happen overnight."[32]

Overnight? It's been nearly 50 years! We need to wait longer because it "won't happen *overnight*"?

The results of waiting: more than 60 million dead.

Tennessee Right to Life flew in attorney Paul Linton to represent them in their opposition to the Tennessee Heartbeat Bill. Linton said he opposed the Heartbeat Bill because "there is no evidence the court is ready, willing and able to reconsider *Roe* at this point."[33]

Let me translate for you: "We better not try because we might fail."

Meanwhile, Linton's former group, Americans United for Life (AUL), has also stepped in. Steven Aden, AUL's chief legal officer and general counsel, encouraged lawmakers to forgo the Heartbeat Bill and instead work to pass "an informed consent provision that would allow women the opportunity to hear a heartbeat that is detected and judge for themselves whether they want an abortion."[34]

Translation: Don't actually *protect* children with beating hearts, just let the mom know about it. The AUL position is to let the woman choose whether or not to kill her baby. That sounds a lot like Planned Parenthood and NARAL to me.

Here's a much better approach. Introduce the model Heartbeat Bill—which has informed consent as part of it along with a severability clause. That means if any portion is found (temporarily) unconstitutional, the remainder becomes law. That's what happened with the Arkansas heartbeat law. During the court challenge to the protective part of the bill, the informed consent portion was allowed to go into effect. Earlier I mentioned the little boy named Duncan whom Arkansas Heartbeat Sponsor Jason Rapert met. Duncan was saved through the informed consent law that was a part of the Arkansas Heartbeat Bill. Informed consent *and* legal protection: Why can't we love them both?

Here's the severability language from the model bill:

> (4) If any provision of this bill is held invalid, or if the application of such provision to any person or circumstance is held invalid, the invalidity of that provision does not affect any other provisions or applications of this section ____ and sections ____, ____, and ___to ____of the Code that can be given effect without the invalid provision or application, and to this end the provisions of those sections are severable. In particular, it is the intent of the general assembly that any invalidity or potential invalidity of a provision of section or sections ___-___of the Code is not to impair the immediate and continuing enforceability of the remaining provisions.[35]

Another objection came from Clarke Forsythe, Senior Counsel for Americans United for Life, who said, "The chance of enforcement for any of these laws is not very good.... The obstacles are substantial."[36]

Imagine a coach at halftime telling his team: "Your chances of winning are 'not very good...the obstacles are *substantial*.'" Not a speech which would lead to victory. It's what we might get if we hired our opponents to lead the cheerleading squad: "Gimme a L-O-S-E! Better not try because you're gonna lose!"

It's a lot like the excuse used by pro-abortion Governor John Kasich, who vetoed the Heartbeat Bill twice, claiming it would be "struck down as unconstitutional."[37] Translation: "The court *may* kill the bill, so I'll beat them to it."

I don't remember Kasich running for judge. A governor is the executive, not the judicial, branch. Kasich's job was to *sign* the laws to protect human life—not anticipate what the courts might do with them.

He said the Heartbeat Bill was "clearly contrary to the Supreme Court of the United States' current rulings on abortion."[38]

These guys need to remember that they swore to uphold the Constitution, not *Roe v. Wade*—which is contrary to the Constitution.

National Right to Life Attorney Jim Bopp, who testified against the Tennessee Heartbeat Bill, is someone I knew from my days at Ohio Right to Life. Bopp, based in Indiana, first testified in 2012 to kill our Ohio Heartbeat Bill.

Speaking against a challenge to *Roe*, Bopp told the *Wall Street Journal*, "The last thing we want to trigger is reaffirming *Roe v. Wade*...That would be a disaster of epic proportions."[39]

Let me try to translate the Bopp doublespeak: We can't challenge *Roe* by protecting children (and try to *change* things) because the Court might say no and keep things as they are. And that would be a "disaster of epic proportions." For a million children this year what's happening *right now* is a "disaster of epic proportions." National Right to Life founder Dr. Jack Willke said it best:

> Whether *Roe* is affirmed or not, the results are the same: Unborn babies are killed for any reason virtually any time

until their birth. We must not wait any longer to protect babies in our state.[40]

Representative Steve King, sponsor of the federal Heartbeat Bill, addressed this issue from the floor of the U.S. Congress:

> If one is not willing to challenge the Supreme Court on abortion, "then you also need to be willing to accept the burden of guilt that comes along with accepting a million abortions a year, in perpetuity, in the United States of America."[41]

The strategy of doing next to nothing because to do more "might lose" has been a colossal failure. If we are unwilling to change and to challenge, we will bear the guilt of a million lives a year lost, in perpetuity, as Congressman King declared. Pro-life leader, film producer, and author Jason Jones said of National Right to Life:

> That was your grandma's pro-life movement, run centrally and ineffectively by a bunch of mediocre white lawyers from Indiana. All its force seemed at the command of the Republican National Committee, whom its leaders would never dare cross. The movement is much more decentralized, diverse, and powerful today. That's precisely because its "central planners" failed to silence dissenting voices and bold, competing visions.[42]

Kansas

Mark Gietzen, Chairman of Kansas Coalition for Life, experienced the same thing from the Kansas Right to Life affiliate, Kansans for Life. Gietzen said they were "discouraging Kansas Senators and Representatives from sponsoring, cosponsoring, or in any way supporting our Heartbeat Bill." He added, "At first, they were going to just remain neutral, but that did not last too long, and when we had some great success, they directly opposed it."

Bill drafters Professor David Forte, Walter Weber, and I testified for the Kansas Heartbeat Bill in 2013 and helped Gietzen lobby for it.[43] I was addressing a large group of legislators when an objection from one of them was raised, "We don't want to get out front on this—only *one* state [Arkansas] has passed the Heartbeat Bill." That was the moment I received a text that the governor of North Dakota had just signed the *second* Heartbeat Bill into law.

Despite the victory in North Dakota, the Kansas legislators still decided not to "get out front." By definition, a leader *must* get "out front." That's what being a leader means.

Gietzen called the Kansas Heartbeat Bill "the most exciting thing that has happened in the pro-life movement since *Roe v. Wade*."[44] Yet the attack from Kansans for Life kept the bill from moving, giving cover to the RINOs who were only willing to regulate abortion.

Indiana

Amy Schlichter, Founder and Executive Director of Hoosiers for Life, worked to introduce a Heartbeat Bill in Indiana. But, once again, the biggest opponent she faced was Indiana Right to Life. Schlichter said, "It's a tough fight to save innocent children from the murderous act of abortion when you have to first fight those that should be your friends in this cause."

Missouri

Lisa Pannett, who led the Heartbeat Bill charge in Missouri said, "Right to Life actively worked against the [heartbeat] efforts that were made by the pro-life citizens of Missouri."

She said, "They lobbied legislators against it for 3 years. They testified in committee hearings that they were in support, and behind our backs were telling them not to pass it. They even published an information piece about its 'unconstitutional nature' and distributed it to legislators."

Even *The Wall Street Journal* took note of Missouri Right to Life's opposition:

> In Missouri, antiabortion activists skirmished with the state's Right to Life affiliate over a Heartbeat Bill.
>
> At the "Pro-Life Action Day" rally at the Capitol in March, traditional members circulated pamphlets that dampened enthusiasm for the activists' proposal: "The courts have ruled that every one of these bills as written and passed in other states, are unconstitutional," the pamphlets read.[45]

What their pamphlet *should* have said is that *Roe v. Wade* is "unconstitutional." That is why it must be challenged. And that is what the Heartbeat Bill is designed to do.

Texas

Texas Heartbeat Bill sponsor Rep. Briscoe Cain (R-Deer Park) with the help of pro-life champion former Majority Leader Tom DeLay made sure the Heartbeat Bill was a priority in the Texas Republican Platform.[46] The bill was introduced with 60 co authors (out of 150 members). But that wasn't enough to counter the strong opposition from the "pro-life" establishment groups.

As the *Dallas Observer* reported, "Texas Alliance for Life, one of the state's biggest anti-abortion advocacy groups, came out against the bill."[47]

Joe Pojman, Executive Director of Texas Alliance for Life, said, "At this time we are not recommending the Texas Legislature support the Heartbeat Bill and other bills that have little chance of surviving a federal court challenge."[48] Also opposing the Heartbeat Bill was Texans for Life Coalition and the National Right to Life affiliate, Texas Right to Life.[49]

Rep. Cain confirmed Texas Right to Life refused to support the Texas Heartbeat Bill stating, "They told House members not to coauthor the bill."

The Associated Press reported, "Texas Right to Life has instead endorsed bills that would curtail late-term abortions and ban abortions based on a fetus' race, gender or disability."[50]

They instead opted to protect a few late-term babies and with the race, gender, and disability ban, protect *no* babies, since all someone has to do is give another reason (or no reason) to abort the child.

Rep. Dustin Burrows (R-Lubbock) said, "As an early co author of the Texas Heartbeat Bill, I was particularly frustrated to learn that the very groups we believed we were allied with were working against us and the bill to protect almost every child facing abortion."

Texas Rep. Steve Toth (R-The Woodlands) said, "It was absolutely surreal. All of these pro-life groups were lining up against the Heartbeat Bill. This bill, took Texas and the cause from the 50-yard line to the goal line and evidently, they didn't want someone else to carry it over the goal line. The Speaker of the Texas House even used their cowardice for cover 'I'm not moving the bill.' The Speaker told all of the Pro Life House Members 'I can't support the Heartbeat Bill when none of the pro-life groups support it.'"

The "pro-life" establishment may fight the bill to keep hearts beating, but as Zach Maxwell, Chief of Staff to Texas Freedom Caucus Chairman Rep. Mike Lang, witnessed, they are out of step with the grassroots. Maxwell confirmed, "There was no doubt a mandate from the grassroots to push and pass the Heartbeat Bill. They could not understand why other states were leading on this issue!"

Maxwell said, "We were so excited that finally we were going to get a Heartbeat Bill until Texas Right to Life single-handedly took it out."

Maxwell explained, "Texas Right to Life approached us several times to urge us—to pressure us—not to support the Heartbeat Bill," adding "They lobbied us very very hard to kill the Heartbeat Bill."

Maxwell explained, "Texas Right to Life knew they had to lock down the Texas Freedom Caucus before the Heartbeat Bill got anymore traction."[51]

Maxwell clarified, "They [Texas Right to Life] were actually out messaging to the grassroots as though they were *supporting* the Heartbeat Bill" while " they were coming to us [in the legislature] and internally saying 'Don't support the Heartbeat Bill.'"

After working to kill the Texas Heartbeat Bill, Texas Right to Life publicly criticized the Texas legislature for not ending abortion. They said:

> The Texas House passed ceremonial, feel-good, and optics-only bills in regard to Life. These bills serve re-election campaigns more than they serve the Pro-Life movement. Such bills fail to directly save lives, fail to focus the cultural conversation on the humanity of the preborn child, and fail to dismantle *Roe v. Wade*.[52]

If they want to know who really backed the "feel-good" "optics-only" pro-life bills, Texas Right to Life needs to look in the mirror.[53] As Texas Right to Life was quoted criticizing Texas legislators in the *Houston Chronicle*, "While other states and the Texas Senate besieged abortion and euthanasia this year with life-saving legislation, the Texas House stopped zero abortions."[54] That's because Texas Right to Life fought the bill to end almost all abortions: the Heartbeat Bill. Their hypocrisy doesn't remove their blame.

As in other states, groups that really want to end abortion (and put themselves out of business) are springing up. One such new group, Texans for Life, is being formed by Zach Maxwell in Granbury Texas. If you want to know who to support financially, the Heartbeat Bill serves as an excellent litmus test. Just remember it's *actions*, not words, that matter.

West Virginia

In West Virginia, there were three Heartbeat Bills introduced during the 2019 legislative session—by Democrat Delegate Ralph Rodighiero

(D-Logan), Republican Delegate Evan Worrell (R-Cabell), and Senator Randy Smith (R, Tucker).[55] There was bi partisan support in the legislature but, once again, the affiliate of National Right to Life fought against them and the babies those bills would protect.[56]

Delegate Evan Worrell stated, "We had a caucus with all GOP leadership and was told that West Virginians for Life did have a meeting with some of our leadership and told them they did not want that [Heartbeat] bill to run again...They said they do not want that [Heartbeat] bill to run in the 2020 session."[57] You cannot be a legitimate pro-life organization and fight the bill that will protect nearly every child facing abortion.

Del. Worrell added, "I believe abortion is murder and I want to outlaw it as much as I can...We campaign on this. It's time to put up or shut up."[58] Well said. It would be nice if West Virginians for Life would do the same.

Idaho

Idaho Heartbeat Bill sponsor Representative Tammy Nichols (R-Middleton) experienced the same thing in Idaho. Once National Right to Life weighed in, all support of the Heartbeat Bill from the Idaho affiliate vanished.

Rep. Nichols addressed the issue head-on. "I've heard that is an issue with the national group" she said, "I don't understand it personally, because I thought all of us were working to end abortion."[59] Rep. Nichols explained her Heartbeat Bill "is actually something that has teeth in it"—something that will make much more of an impact than "running little bits of legislation."[60]

I just received a call from Rep. Nichols to inform me that Right to Life of Idaho, after hearing from their members, has said they will now "support" the Heartbeat Bill and even testify for it. Hopefully, they won't be like the Missouri Right to Life affiliate who publicly testified for the bill while working against it, as reported by *The Wall Street Journal*.[61]

Whether you live in Missouri, Idaho, or anywhere else, we would be wise to heed the words of Texas Rep. Steve Toth: "If you judge a person by their actions, their words will never disappoint you."[62]

We have been accused of dividing the pro-life movement. But if people got a glimpse into what lengths we have gone to try and keep the pro-life movement united, they would never say that. In the end, as Julie Doehner of Geauga County Right to Life said, "If the choice is between unity and life, we choose *life*."[63]

A Meeting with the National Right to Life Committee

Former Majority Leader Tom DeLay, Rachelle Heidlebaugh, Attorney Larry Cirignano, Rebekah Gantner, of Phyllis Schlafly's Eagles, and I met with the co directors of the National Right to Life Committee, David O'Steen and Darla St. Martin, in 2017. I had known both of them for decades.

In late 2002, I approached O'Steen with an idea for a campaign in conjunction with the thirtieth anniversary of *Roe v. Wade*. I envisioned an ultrasound image of a baby with the words "I am an American." The idea started on a napkin while sharing pizza at Union Station with my friend Deirdre O'Sullivan. I told her, "It'll be on billboards and bumper stickers." She politely smiled. I called her while on the road in Michigan

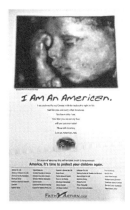

The campaign I shared with National Right to Life, which became newspaper ads around the nation, billboards, and bumper stickers. Faith2Action ran this ad in the *Washington Times* on the thirtieth anniversary of *Roe v. Wade*.

and said, "Do you remember when I told you the 'I am an American' baby would be on billboards and bumper stickers?"

She remembered.

I asked, "Did you ever think it would happen?"

That was an easy one. "No."

I told her, "Well, I'm looking at an 'I am an American' billboard right now!" It was also made into bumper stickers.

Faith2Action ran it as an ad in the *Washington Times* with thirty-five organizations listed on the bottom. It also ran as newspaper ads by pro-life groups and National Right to Life affiliates around the country and was the sign printed and distributed at the March for Life that year.

All of that is to say I had a working relationship with National Right to Life. In fact, one of the first calls I made before introducing the first Heartbeat Bill in Ohio was to O'Steen to give him a heads up and get him to commit to not oppose it. On that call he agreed to be "neutral." I got a better idea of what "neutral" meant when National Right to Life's attorney, Jim Bopp, came to our Ohio hearing to testify *against* the Heartbeat

Bill—standing right beside Planned Parenthood, NARAL, and the abortionists. In the 2-hour meeting with O'Steen and St. Martin, we laid out
the case. Tom DeLay told them about his greatest regret—leaving Congress without ending abortion. Rachelle told the heart-wrenching story
of the abortions she'd had, pleading, with tears, for them to help protect
babies. This was their moment to lead.

In a patronizing tone, they commended me for my "enthusiasm." They
didn't itemize the "Jim Bopp talking points" from their attorney on a
rampage to kill any Heartbeat Bill that surfaced. National Right to Life
had been distributing "Abortion Stops a Beating Heart" bumper stickers
for decades, but they had no interest in the bill to ensure that a beating
heart would stop abortion.

I reminded them of National Right to Life's mission statement:

> The mission of National Right to Life is to protect and
> defend the most fundamental right of humankind, the right
> to life of every innocent human being from the beginning of
> life to natural death.[64]

I commended them for their work in electing pro-life legislators and
presidents, and I reminded them of the *reason* they did it. The reason for
which we've all been working to elect all those pro-life people and pro-
life presidents to nominate pro-life justices is to...*end* abortion. At least
that's what their mission statements led us all to believe.

We delivered some other news they seemed to have missed. President
Trump won the election! A pro-life justice had just been ushered onto the
Supreme Court, and there would be more to come with Trump as president.

Because of this, DeLay explained that the window to pass the Heartbeat Bill was now open. "We have a pro-life Republican House, Senate, president, and Supreme Court—and by the time the Heartbeat Bill makes it to the Supreme Court, there will likely be more justices ready to embrace it."

National Right to Life said *no* to supporting the Heartbeat Bill. And during the 2018 midterms, the window closed on the Republican-led U.S. House of Representatives as Democrats took the majority in the November 2018 election.

When a pro-life group, with the mission to end abortion, chooses not to, there is a problem. As I said earlier, almost always, "neutral" means "opposed behind your back." This is no exception. It can also mean "let someone else (who works for you) oppose it for you."

If National Right to Life's Attorney Jim Bopp is acting on his own, why does National Right to Life continue to let him use their name when testifying against Heartbeat Bills?[65] That doesn't sound "neutral" to me. If someone worked for me and was misrepresenting my organization they would be fired and an official public correction would be issued. There has been no such action from National Right to Life. No, they just let Jim Bopp go around the country touting their name to kill Heartbeat Bills and the babies they would protect.

By the way, it's not just Heartbeat Bills that National Right to Life's General Counsel Jim Bopp is against—he's also against Personhood efforts to protect babies from conception.[66] He is actually quoted on NARAL's "pro-choice" America's website to help them in their effort to kill babies.[67]

Whose payroll is Bopp on again? NARAL's? Planned Parenthood? Oh yeah, National Right to Life. Troy Newman, President of Operation Rescue, was right when he said, "If you do not support the bill, you oppose it."[68]

Rachelle Heidlebaugh said, "National Right to Life is the perfect example of insanity—doing the same thing over and over again and expecting different results."[69]

Liberty Counsel founder Mat Staver, former dean of Liberty University School of Law, told the *New York Times* that National Right to Life has "lost its legitimacy" and is "on the wrong side of advancing human life protections."[70]

In a January 17, 2018, editorial in the *Washington Times* Tom DeLay explained:

> Today, National Right to Life, the only national group that doesn't support the Heartbeat Bill's substantial protection for unborn children, thinks "success" is to kill only a million children a year. We reject the establishment's approach.
>
> We also reject those who have the thoughtlessness to continue it. We have more than enough blood on our hands and Congress has the means to stop this loss in nearly every case.[71]

When few others would stand up to the establishment giant that grants political endorsements, federal Heartbeat Bill sponsor Rep. Steve King courageously did. Taking the floor of the U.S. Congress, Rep. King said:

> It is a curious thing, indeed, that National Right to Life is the only one of 131 major pro-life leaders and organizations that has failed to express support for HR 490, and it is tragic that babies continue to die from abortions as this

one organization exerts a unilateral veto over House consideration of the [Heartbeat Bill].[72]

How could a group claiming to be "neutral" block the Heartbeat Bill in the U.S. Congress? Rep. King explained that after meeting with former House Speaker Paul Ryan and other members of House leadership, he discovered an "informal rule" that "no pro-life legislation" could be brought to the House floor unless it had the support of National Right to Life. National Right to Life's "non support" gives RINO (Republican in name only) leadership the excuse to do nothing. This must change. President Trump is right, it's time to drain the swamp.

Congressman Steve King (R-Iowa) courageously exposing the truth on the floor of the U.S. House of Representatives.

King said from the floor of the U.S. House:

Is there no one on the National Right to Life Board of Directors that supports making a simple, supportive phone call to Speaker Ryan that would save unborn lives? Is there no one within National Right to Life that wishes to publicly support the efforts of the Heartbeat Protection Act's 170 House cosponsors? Is there no one within National Right to Life that finds it odd that they are on the wrong side of 130 dedicated pro-life leaders and organizations? If not, then there is something seriously wrong within National Right to Life.[73]

As Dietrich Bonhoeffer is credited with saying, "Silence in the face of evil is itself evil: God will not hold us guiltless. Not to speak is to speak. Not to act is to act."[74] King continued in his floor speech broadcast on C-Span, "I've saved a spot up here in red for [NRLC President] Carol Tobias and David O'Steen, and if National Right to Life just gives us a call, sends an email or text, picks up the phone and calls the Speaker, we'll move this bill."[75]

The question on everyone's mind is, *Why?* Why would a group with a mission statement to end abortion fight against a bill that would protect more babies than every bill they've passed in the last 50 years—*combined?*

My first theory was that it had to do with a defeatist mindset. Maybe because they had fought so long and lost, they couldn't really picture actually winning. Maybe they were like a barracuda in a fish tank.

You see, barracudas are natural predators to Spanish mackerels. They eat them for lunch. But researchers in Southern California did a study where barracudas were placed in a fish tank on one side of an invisible glass barrier. On the other side of the glass barrier were the Spanish mackerels—their food. Every time the barracuda tried to eat a mackerel, it would bounce off the glass between them. It failed over and over until it finally quit trying to get the fish on the other side of the glass.

Then the scientists removed the glass barrier. Finally, the predator could eat the mackerel. But it didn't. Even though the mackerel swam right in front of the predator's mouth, bumping into it repeatedly, the barracuda would not eat it. It had failed so much, it would no longer try.[76]

Has the pro-life movement become a barracuda in the fish tank—so used to failing that they refuse to try anything new? I believe this is true for some.

But we need to look at another possibility. Not just that Right to Life groups are well-meaning defeatists. You've heard of fake news. Well, there is such a thing as a fake pro-life group. You cannot be a legitimate pro-life organization and call for a veto of a bill that protects nearly every child.

Some say they simply have an honest strategic disagreement over the bills—the time is not right due to the makeup of the Supreme Court. This excuse is completely invalid. Donald Trump won. The court has shifted. The time is now.

Given what we have seen in state after state, I believe we are seeing the maturing of the wheat and tares, as stated previously. The seeds that have been growing together are coming to maturity—making it a lot easier to tell them apart—especially the pro-life pretenders who claim to want to end abortion but frantically oppose the efforts to do so. A Heartbeat Bill litmus test clearly divides the wheat and the tares.

What appeared to be "pro-life wheat" are really tares working against their very mission to end abortion. And it's not just the Heartbeat Bills they don't like; it's also the bills that protect babies from conception and most every other pro-life bill that wasn't their idea. There were a lot of surprises at who failed the Heartbeat litmus test. Not just National Right to Life and several of their affiliates, but many "pro-life Republicans" and people whose pro-life rhetoric was all for show.

Not Pure Enough

While the Right to Life groups oppose the Heartbeat Bill because they claim it goes "too far," the Personhood groups *criticize* it for not going far enough. Personhood groups want to protect babies from conception, as we all do, but oppose any effort that falls short of perfection. After being blasted from the platform by the Personhood leader at a pro-life event because our Heartbeat Bill wasn't perfect, I walked over and signed their Personhood petition. That's because I support every effort to protect life. Sadly, not everyone does.

Here's the analogy. Imagine a day care center is on fire. We are standing on the corner, watching it burn. What *should* we do?

A. Go in and rescue as many children as we can, then go back for more.

B. Stand there with arms folded and watch it burn because we can't possibly rescue every child at once (the Personhood position).

C. Only rescue the few children on the playground, since we are 100% sure we can rescue them without risk (the incremental, "Right to Life" position).

I choose A. The "purists" opposed the Heartbeat Bill because it doesn't save every child, or in the case of Georgia Right to Life (which is not affiliated with National Right to Life) because the Georgia bill had exceptions for rape and incest. Instead of supporting the effort to rescue as many children as possible, they stood on principle, folding their arms while the building burns because every child wasn't rescued at once. That is also the position of Abolish Abortion Texas, who opposed the Texas Heartbeat Bill on "principle."[77] Personhood groups like Personhood Florida oppose Heartbeat Bills even after admitting "if the Heartbeat Bill were really enacted, it would end practically all surgical abortion."[78]

To be clear, I agree with the position of protecting children from conception. I agree with no exceptions for rape and incest, and I fought with everything I had to make sure such attempts to weaken our Ohio Heartbeat Bill were blocked. In fact, no Ohio pro-life law on the books has a rape or incest exception—none. And that didn't happen without fierce battles. I agree with Rebecca Kiessling, who was conceived as a result of rape; we should punish rapists, not babies.

Kiessling had a different *fireman* analogy. She said, "Now imagine you are on the fire department and you are hiring potential firemen. One candidate wants to rescue every human being from a fire while another candidate is racist. He's really strong and very capable, but tells you up front that he refuses to rescue black people or Jewish people. Not someone you would want to hire, right?" You want the fireman who will try to rescue everyone. However, if because of the threatening blaze the fireman can't get everyone out at once, does that mean we forget about trying to save the rest? That's what purists like Georgia Right to Life (GRTL) and Abolish Abortion Texas think.

All or Nothing?

Georgia Heartbeat Bill sponsor Ginny Enhart said GRTL threw "the proverbial unborn baby out with the bathwater," rejecting the bill in it's entirely because it wasn't perfect. In a letter to the editor she stated:

> Let's be very clear. Like it or not, the chance of HB 481 passing out of committee without the exceptions was zero. It did not have the votes. There were only two options: Pass it with

> exceptions or let the bill die, along with thousands of unborn
> babies.[79]

She stated the similarity Solomon faced with the two women who both claimed to be the mother of a single baby. When Solomon suggested the baby be cut in half, the real mother objected—caring more that her child was saved than who would raise him. The pretender's position was fine with the killing—either she would be his mother or there would be no child at all. Enhart stated:

> That's exactly what happened to the Heartbeat Bill. GRTL, spurred by its own pompous hypocrisy, told the Georgia Legislature to cut the baby in half. To kill HB 481. All or nothing. Given the chance to save some or none, they chose none.[80]

The *Atlanta Journal-Constitution* reported that the Georgia Life Alliance, which is affiliated with National Right to Life, said though their state's Heartbeat Bill isn't perfect, "it's the only pending bill this year that 'can save lives in the womb.'"[81] *It's not what I would call enthusiastic support, but at least the National Right to Life affiliate of Georgia didn't oppose it.*

When I look back to my early days in the Right to Life movement, there was forceful, unified, and overpowering resistance at the slightest suggestion that we do more than regulate abortion. When I proposed the idea to protect babies from the point of heartbeat in the early 1990s, it was like being surrounded by "pro-life" piranhas—determined to kill the suggestion at all costs. I saw it in the many years that followed. Every time I suggested we do more than regulate around the edges of abortion, I was berated and beaten down. This isn't natural. You would expect this from the pro-abortion side, but not from pro-lifers whose very mission statements are to *end* abortion. When something doesn't make any sense, you have to look behind the people and their positions. Could it be that this is spiritual? It's the only explanation that makes sense to me.

The same resistance I encountered then is the very same resistance we are experiencing now. The difference is now we have the courage to stand up to it and call it what it is—evil. Bowing to the "pro-life" bullies has cost more than 60 million children their lives. They didn't perform the abortions, but it was their failed incremental strategy which allowed it. We let them beat us down before, but there's not a chance we're going to let it happen again!

Heartbeat Bills are going to pass. My message to the Right to Life groups—lead, follow, or get out of the way. If you fight the effort to keep hearts beating, your pro-life followers will leave you in droves. Because it's not about you; it has always been about the babies.

As Dr. Willke told *The New York Times*, "I was Mr. Incremental...But after nearly 40 years of abortion on demand, it's time to take a bold step forward."[82] The founder of the pro-life movement is right. We're moving forward. And there's no turning *back*.

CHAPTER 7

Whatever It Takes

"Sometimes our best is simply not enough...We have to do what is required." —Winston Churchill

W hat would you do to end abortion? What happens in your state or nation will depend upon your answer to that question. Of course, I'm not suggesting anything immoral or illegal, but if we really want to end abortion, we're going to have to get out of our comfort zone—sometimes *way* outside.

As mentioned, we introduced the nation's first Heartbeat Bill in February, 2011. The House passed it by June of that year, but the Senate wouldn't budge no matter how many balloons, roses, or heart-shaped chocolates we sent them. By the second year, we had to call them out and expose their obstruction. By the fifth year, I was running in a primary against the Senate President.

If you really want to end abortion, expect to see "comfort" in the rear-view mirror.

It all began with our answer to this question:

Q: What would you do to end abortion?

A: Whatever it takes.

If you want to end abortion, you're going to have to do "whatever it takes." But if we're really honest, that's not the answer most pro-life people give. They may say it, but I found very few who were willing to pay the price and actually *do* it. As I said earlier, "Actions are what you believe." Winston Churchill put it this way, "I no longer listen to what people say, I just watch what they do. Behavior never lies."

The same holds true for those in political office.

There will likely come a time in your battle to keep hearts beating when it becomes evident that those who hold office have no intention to keep their pro-life promises. That is when you have a decision to make. Do you really want to end abortion, or do you want everyone to like you?

But don't confuse the real answer with the answer you most want to hear: "If I'm nice and everyone likes me, they will vote to protect babies *later.*" Of course, the problem with later is that later never comes. No one does what they don't want to do when there are no consequences. Everyone knows that actions have consequences, but legislators we hire must also learn that *inactions* have consequences.

Arkansas State Senator Jason Rapert, sponsor of his state's Heartbeat Bill, said, "Be prepared. There are going to be people that you *knew* would be with you, and they absolutely will not be there for you." What do you do about it? The two basic methods of persuasion are the carrot and the stick—reward and punishment. In Ohio we gave those senators so many carrots they spit them out in our face. Our lobbying efforts included multiple meetings, rallies, billboards, bumper stickers, yard signs, television, radio and full-page print ads, 4,000 red heart balloons, heart chocolates, heart cookies, heartbeat teddy bears, 2,200 red roses, an airplane that flew over the Statehouse, and tens of thousands of calls. It was time for a *vote*.

It was also time for another *more direct* approach, one that would not let them get away with further delay and more excuses. Heart-shaped cookies and candy were a thing of the past. As Morton Blackwell of the Leadership Institute said, "In politics, nothing moves unless pushed."[1]

Confronting the RINOs

We started off mild. We weren't calling anyone names; we just asked them to take the "RINO Test." In 2012 we distributed neon-pink postcards to all the Republican members of the Ohio Senate that asked a very simple question: Are you a Republican or a Republican in Name Only (RINO)? Then we gave them two possible responses:

_____ A. I stand by the Republican Platform and call for the protection of unborn children with an immediate floor vote on the Heartbeat Bill (H.B. 125). *Roe v. Wade* must be challenged and overturned and there is no better time than now.

_____ B. I am Republican in Name Only and am content with merely regulating abortion. I will continue to stall and make excuses rather than call for a vote to protect unborn children with the Heartbeat Bill (H.B. 125). I accept and conform to *Roe v. Wade* and have no desire to challenge it.

We then urged them to stand by the Republican platform and bring the real Heartbeat Bill (not a weakened informed consent only bill) to an immediate floor vote. We reminded them that inaction cost nearly 26,000 Ohio babies their lives that year alone because those babies could have been saved if the Ohio bill had become law.

We made it clear: Either they would stand by the pro-life Republican platform and bring the protective Heartbeat Bill to a vote, or they were RINOs, plain and simple. We handed out pink RINO postcards at our rallies by the stack and had people sign them for all twenty-three Republican senators while they were there. We also recorded video messages from Heartbeat Bill supporters, which we posted on line and emailed to the senators. Others at the rally recorded messages from their phones. We made use of every public event we could including concerts, conferences, and festivals.

As I was searching the Internet for the rhino graphic we ran in full-page ads in newspapers across the state, I found a forgotten article I wrote which featured an electronic "RINO button" used to enlist people across the nation to join us. Clicking the button would  send all twenty-three Republican senators a RINO postcard, which we hired a vender to both electronically sign and physically mail.

Here's an excerpt from that article, which ran in *WorldNetDaily*: "I'm not asking you to fly here and walk door to door. You don't have to work the phone banks. I'm asking you to click one button to bombard the Senate with more pink postcards than they have ever seen, calling them to make the choice that will label them for the rest of their political career: Republican or RINO? Let them know the nation is watching...Please help us break through the wall of resistance, because when the Senate votes, the killing stops."[2]

If you're fighting to keep hearts beating with a Heartbeat Bill in your state, feel free to use any of our ideas and graphics—it's the reason I'm writing this book! If you are working against Heartbeat Bills and the babies they will protect, everything herein is copyrighted and completely and legally off limits.

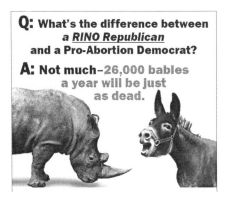

When a Republican state senator failed the RINO test, we let the world know about it. This phase of our campaign began with full-page newspaper ads across the state and postcards mailed to the senators' districts. The postcards and ads said, "What's the difference between a RINO Republican and a pro-abortion Democrat? Answer: Not much— 26,000 babies a year in Ohio will be just as dead."

The ads read: "DON'T BUY THE SENATE'S FLIMSY EXCUSE that they should kill the Heartbeat Bill because the court 'might' find it 'unconstitutional.' Nearly every pro-life law on our books was first challenged in court and later *upheld*—including Ohio's ban on partial-birth abortion!"

You can be effective even if you don't have a lot of money to spend. Here's the secret: don't send postcards to everyone. Mail them to only the key people on a highly targeted list. Lori Viars is amazing at constructing mailing lists.

She found the senators' friends on Facebook, key members of their county and state Republican central committees, along with elected officials in their district, and sent postcards to them. We even mailed their relatives and Republican neighbors in hopes they would be "neighborly" and mention they had received the negative mailing. By doing this, the senators thought *everyone* in their district got a postcard that exposed them as a RINO and pro-life fraud, when we actually only mailed a few hundred cards for each senator.

On the back of the card and in the full-page ads were the words: "If you want us to trust you in the *next* election, do what you promised in the *last* one!" Mark Crutcher of Life Dynamics is the guy who gets the credit for that gem. I can hear his voice as I write those words. He told me many times that I should forget about people ever liking me, because "this is about ending abortion, not making friends at the Statehouse." He was right. We made the senators' lives miserable—but they weren't nearly as miserable as the babies they refused to protect.

It isn't just the people at the Statehouse who will hate you; it's also your faint-hearted friends whose decisions are driven by the "fear of man." The hand-wringers are worried about offending their so-called "friends" who hold office. As I mentioned before, if your "friends" in the Statehouse won't protect babies with beating hearts, they are not your friends—they are abortion enablers. They have the power to stop the killing but won't. Babies are dying because of their inaction and, well, those aren't the kind of friends I want to have.

If you aren't comfortable causing discomfort to the abortion enablers, the alternative is to become comfortable with what they enable—abortion itself. For those who want to end abortion, this is "a time for choosing,"[3] to borrow a phrase from Ronald Reagan. If you're not sure what do, ask yourself, "Which course of action will save the most lives?" And then, "Am I willing to do it?"

The antidote to obstruction is bold, unrestrained truth. Arkansas State Senator Jason Rapert put it this way, "Speak the truth even if the ground shakes."[4] Brace yourself, because it will.

I was astounded by the people who choose to remain friends with the obstructionists rather than expose them. Instead, they distanced themselves from *us*—the ones willing to stand and fight for the babies the Ohio Senate refused to protect. I wouldn't have believed it if I hadn't seen it with my own eyes, but I actually watched people who had been part of our heartbeat effort cozy up to a politician who had just publicly spoken against our bill. *Unbelievable.* We all watched as several of our *former* Heartbeat team members followed this senator around like he didn't just stab us in the back.

Sadly these hand-wringers choose access over influence, mistaking proximity for results. It happens all the time. But getting people to take your calls and meetings is very different from getting them to do what you ask. The options we face are clear and simple:

A. Remaining friends with the abortion enablers = dead babies.

B. Exposing them = live babies.

If you chose "A," keep regulating. If you chose "B," keep reading. When Mississippi Senator Michael Watson was confronted about cost to defend a heartbeat law in court, his answer was simple, "What is a life worth?"[5] To end abortion, we have to forget about the approval of men and be ready for their criticism. You'll be maligned and ridiculed—but saving human lives is worth it. Whether it's good or bad, you can't let what men say matter more than your mission. As Pastor Bill Johnson of Bethel Church said, "If you don't live by the praises of men you won't die by their criticisms."[6]

This stage of your effort also serves as an excellent litmus test to see who is willing to pay the price to end abortion and who is not. At this stage, you may be able to count your friends on one hand, but at least you will know who they are.

Rep. John McCravy, sponsor of the South Carolina Heartbeat Bill, put it this way: "The number one key thing is: You need one person to be a tenacious bulldog and then you need a group of people that are willing to sacrifice to get it done."[7] He couldn't be more right.

But all the things we had to do to pass the Ohio Heartbeat Bill would have been unnecessary if only we had leadership in the state senate like Senator Rapert and his allies in Arkansas. When the House public health committee chairman refused to move the Senate-passed Arkansas Heartbeat Bill, Senator Rapert and Senate leadership had a meeting with the chairman.

This group of Senate champions banded together to form a blockade. They told the chairman that if he didn't bring the Heartbeat Bill to a vote, all legislation was coming to a screeching halt. Senator Rapert clarified, "In general terms, there would be no more House bills voted or moving forward in the Senate until they allowed the Heartbeat Bill to move forward."[8]

Because of the stalwart senators who stood with Senator Rapert as a united front, the Heartbeat Bill passed the House committee and then passed the Arkansas House. It was vetoed by Governor Mike Beebe, but that veto was overridden with a simple majority vote. That is why Rapert not only introduced the Heartbeat Bill, but also was the one who ultimately signed it into law.

Senator Rapert donated a framed copy of the signed Arkansas heartbeat law to our Faith2Action silent auction and banquet, where he came to speak. Knowing that I *really* wanted it, Pastor Corey and Hannah Shankleton along with Heartbeat Bill volunteers Jay and Jodi Horn entered into a bidding war so they could give it to me! The nation's first heartbeat law was on our mantle the next several years as a reminder that our efforts were not in vain.

Senator Rapert and his family paid a high price to lead the way to keep hearts beating. There were credible death threats against them, and he had to move his wife and children out of state for a time to protect them. All the while, Senator Rapert's wife stood strongly with him, texting him Bible verses of encouragement and support.

Senator Rapert has launched the National Association of Christian Lawmakers (NACL), which offers issue and policy research, training, and support for lawmakers and those running for office. When Christians share ideas and strategies, we multiply our effectiveness. If ever there was a man qualified to lead this charge, it is Senator Rapert, and I am honored he asked me to serve on his NACL board. Of course, we will help every state leader who asks, but once the NACL is up and running, we'll have a way to provide the model Heartbeat Bill to representatives from all fifty states at once.

If your Heartbeat Bill is being blocked, don't be discouraged. I recently told Texas legislators facing obstruction the South Carolina story. In South Carolina, twenty-eight House members of the Family Caucus "dedicated to preserving and protecting families in South Carolina"[9] stood together to make it a priority to pass a Heartbeat Bill in their state. The first thing you see on their website are the words from Joshua 24:15, "But as for me and my house, we will serve the Lord."[10]

Even though the South Carolina lawmakers had the support of their Statehouse speaker and Republican majority leader, their fight was to get the bill out of committee. That committee vote likely would not have happened if the Family Caucus hadn't stood united, using their political capital for all it was worth. South Carolina State Rep. John McCravy explained, "If the leadership won't go along with you, then you have to find something that they care about."

McCravy said, "You have to get the leadership on board however you have to do it. Until you get that commitment, you've just got a bunch of weak, wishy-washy politicians—you're not going to get it done."[11]

On April 24, 2019, the South Carolina Heartbeat Bill passed in the House by a 70–31 vote.[12] South Carolina Governor Henry McMaster has pledged to sign it once it clears the Senate and reaches his desk.[13]

"In our family caucus we prayed for this bill to pass, over and over again," McCravy said. "I think the Lord honors that, I really do." McCravy also credited a unified pro-life movement in South Carolina with "getting them all in the same room and praying about it...and including them in the process...giving them a voice, letting them be heard."[14] A unified pro-life movement shouldn't be the exception.

When Senator Rapert first met with leaders from Arkansas Right to Life, they asked him, "Do you think maybe you're going just a bit too far?"

Rapert replied, "At what point do you say that enough is enough? Is 50 million enough? 60, 70, 80 million?" Senator Rapert discovered, "You're going to see a separation of the wheat from the chaff."

If your state lawmakers won't unite to block all legislation until the Heartbeat Bill is passed, as they did in Arkansas, find out what your opposition most wants—like a budget or some other high-priority bill that they absolutely need votes from Heartbeat Bill supporters to push through. This is the next best way for your leaders to join together as a united front.

Bold Truth

If your legislative leaders aren't willing to play hardball from the inside, you will have to expose the obstruction and generate the consequences from the outside—which is a *much* harder task. The antidote to obstruction is bold truth, and the good news is there are lots of ways to express it. One of my favorites is a cartoon. Everyone likes cartoons—well, not *everyone*. When the Ohio legislators refused to pass the second Heartbeat Bill, we ran this cartoon as a television ad and blasted it across social media.

Thanks to my media-buying buddy Chad Scalf from my days at Coral Ridge Ministries, we selectively aired this ad in the district of Senate President Keith Faber, beginning with the broadcast of the Macy's Thanksgiving Day Parade. Even if he didn't see it, his pro-life mother and her friends were about to find out what Faber, who told everyone how pro-life he was back home, was really doing in Columbus. Once he became senate president, Faber blocked the bill to protect babies with beating hearts, and our cartoon exposed it. It also ran during the Ohio State University football game, so, as an alumnus, he could see it directly and hear from his former Ohio State classmates who were also likely watching.

The cartoon featured a "school bus a day" (that the Heartbeat Bill would save) going over a cliff while the senate delayed and delayed bringing the bill to a vote. Here's what the ad said:

Announcer: "If you hired someone to do a job and they didn't do it, would you hire them again? Four years ago, we hired John Kasich to be our governor."

Governor John Kasich: "I'm pro-life!"

House Speaker William Batchelder: "We regulate how and where we kill babies."

Senate President Keith Faber: "Yes, now we only kill a stadium full of Ohio children each year."

[On screen]: "According to the Ohio Department of Health, there were 23,226 abortions in 2013, more than a capacity crowd at Canton's Fawcett Stadium."[15]

Kasich: "Isn't that great?"

Announcer: "What?"

Batchelder: "Oh, come on. There's no hurry. We'll protect children later."

[On screen]: School buses roll by and off a cliff.

Announcer: "Every day of delay we lose a school bus full of children the Heartbeat Bill would protect."

Batchelder waves to the school bus as it goes off the cliff.

Faber: "It's not a priority."

Kasich: "What's another 4 years?"

Football stadiums fall from the sky, and Faber kicks the fourth stadium off the cliff.

[On screen]: The busses and stadiums are on the ground, burning.

Announcer: "We need you to fight for the lives of our children right now! Because the price of delay is just too high."

The cartoon displayed the governor's phone number and the words: "Brought to you by the people who hired you," along with a list of eighteen pro-life, pro-family, and tea party groups.[16]

How times have changed since I served as Kasich's campaign spokesperson, debating his opponent for him because I believed his pro-life campaign promises. Kasich has since become a political commentator on

CNN. It's a perfect fit, really. That way they can all bash President Trump and report fake news together.

In a private meeting, a subsequent speaker of the House admitted he was bringing the Heartbeat Bill to a floor vote because he "didn't want to be featured in a cartoon." That's reason enough to run ads like this in your state. Both Batchelder and Faber eventually voted for the bill, when the consequences of inaction became too great.

A Movie Scene That Led to a Vote

(Left to Right) Rep. Ron Hood, Congressman Steve King, Gov. Mike Huckabee, Janet Porter, and Beth Folger get ready to shoot a movie scene at the Ohio Statehouse.

I had been trying to make a movie for years about how we passed the nation's first ban on partial-birth abortion. The twist in the story: I dated the son of the woman who killed it in committee—think Ann Coulter dating the son of Nancy Pelosi. Yes, it *really* happened. How is that movie relevant? I had an idea if we could film one scene of that movie at the Ohio Statehouse before the clock ran out for a vote, we could use it to let the senate know they were going to be exposed nationally and finally held accountable for their obstruction. One more thing, it was November

2016, and the clock ran out in December, after which we would have had to reintroduce the bill yet again, and pass it in the House *again* before pushing for a vote in the senate—*again*.

I made the case to an investor that we could get our long-awaited senate floor vote if we filmed just *one scene* of the movie now. "I think we can get the Ohio Senate to break their 5 year blockade of the Heartbeat Bill by filming a scene from my movie at the Statehouse."[17] A long shot? The very *definition* of a long shot.

I knew how ridiculous my idea sounded when I said it. Yet that is exactly what happened.

With the incredible help of my friend Alfons Carroll, we filmed the last scene, which shows us coming up with the idea for the Heartbeat

Congressman Steve King and Governor Mike Huckabee on the steps of the Ohio Statehouse to film the final scene of *What's a Girl to Do?* which led to the first passage of the Ohio Heartbeat Bill in 2016.

Governor Huckabee shakes Janet Porter's hand while Rep. Ron Hood, Beth Folger, and Art Ally (playing the part of Jim Folger, Janet's dad) celebrate the passage of the nation's first ban on partial-birth abortion.

Bill, at the Ohio Statehouse. We enlisted Governor Mike Huckabee to play the part of a former Ohio governor, Congressman Steve King to play himself, and Heartbeat Bill sponsor Representative Ron Hood to play himself, the "future" sponsor of the nation's first Heartbeat Bill to let the state Senate know they were about to be exposed nationally.

Here's the scene. My parents are with me at the Statehouse when we passed the nations' first ban on partial-birth abortion. I had just connected with Congressman Steve King and had the idea to protect babies from the point of detectable heartbeat. That's when we run into Governor Huckabee (playing the part of former Gov. George Voinovich, Ohio's governor at the time the partial-birth abortion bill passed) and pitched him our new idea to introduce a Heartbeat Bill.

> **Dad**: "But could you get a bill like that through the Senate?"
>
> **Rep. Ron Hood**: "They'll regulate abortion, but I'm not sure the Senate is willing to actually *end* abortion."
>
> **Gov. Huckabee**: (playing the part of former Ohio Gov. George Voinovich): "But that's what elections are for."

Governor Huckabee: "That's what elections are for."

That's what elections are for. That was the line I wanted the Senate to hear—keep obstructing the Heartbeat Bill, and the world will know about it and vote you out. I emailed the trailer to the state senators' personal and Statehouse offices, as well as to tens of thousands of people on our email list. Less than a month after we released the trailer, the Heartbeat Bill passed the Ohio Senate for the first time. It sounded like a ridiculous idea, but we got our vote—and it *passed*. Sadly, our victory was followed by the first veto from RINO Governor John Kasich, now on record as a pro-life pretender, one of many things that hurt him in his bid for President.

When you set out to do whatever it takes, rest assured there will be disappointments. In December 2012, Senate President Tom Niehaus whispered the order to "kill the bill" into the committee chairman's ear in the middle of my testimony—it was a devastating blow.

That was when Mark Harrington of Created Equal sent me a movie about Alice Paul and said, "This is you." Paul (1885–1977) was a brave woman who went against the establishment to fight for women's right to vote. As I watched the film about her life, I could see in their battle the *very same* characters we were fighting, and those you will likely face. There were the establishment "women's suffrage" groups who fought Paul's efforts, just like the Right to Life groups fought us. And fighting against the establishment for the right to vote were people who looked a lot like us. It was uncanny.

Alice Paul faced the *very same* battles from those who should have been her allies. The similarities were remarkable, as if I had dropped all the characters of our struggle into theirs. I wondered if maybe *everyone* blazing a trail to a breakthrough faces this kind of opposition from groups who are more establishment than authentic.

In 1923, when Alice Paul proposed an amendment to the U.S. Constitution, the conventional women's organizations claimed such a move would set them back and hurt their legislative efforts.[18] I lost count of the times I heard this excuse. Over and over those fighting our efforts proclaimed, "Heartbeat Bills threaten the pro-life laws on the books!" Nothing could be further from the truth. The provision not to touch any other pro-life law is spelled out in every Heartbeat Bill. But that didn't stop our opponents from using it in Ohio and virtually every state. As we go to press, this remains the primary fraudulent argument against the Michigan Heartbeat Bill.

Here's another recycled objection. They didn't like Alice Paul's "tactics." She led pickets at the White House and Congress, refusing to abandon such "extreme" tactics despite America's entry into World War I.[19] While I did not orchestrate it, some of our supporters picketed the governor and obstructionist senators at their homes. One such champion was a man named David Law. While picketing Senator Keith Faber's home, he went to the door and politely introduced himself, explaining why he was there. He noticed the senator had an injury and asked if he could pray for him. He did. Then he respectfully went out to the sidewalk and prayed for the senator to have a change of heart as he became the voice for the voiceless—a voice the senator's neighbors could now hear.[20]

There were *a lot* of people who were angry that we wouldn't stop speaking the truth. A reporter from a pro-life news site kept sending me nasty emails about his "problem" with our tactics. I responded, "When we end abortion, you can write about it." Exactly what happened. Without the determination to do whatever it takes there would never have been a Heartbeat *law*.

Pulitzer Prize winner Laurel Thatcher Ulrich wrote a book titled *Well-Behaved Women Seldom Make History*.[21] She was right about that.

I once thought Jesus was rather harsh against the Pharisees, but I no longer think that. The very people who should have recognized Him as the one Scripture foretold were the ones who sought to kill Him. Martin Luther King, Jr. experienced the very same thing:

> I must confess that over the past few years I have been gravely disappointed with the white moderate. I have almost reached the regrettable conclusion that the Negro's great stumbling block in his stride toward freedom is not the...the Ku Klux Klan but the white moderate, who is more devoted to "order" than to justice; who prefers a negative peace which is the absence of tension to a positive peace which is the presence of justice who constantly says: "I agree with you in the goal you seek, but I can't agree with your methods of direct action"; who paternalistically feels that he can set the time-table for another man's freedom; who lives by a myth of time and who constantly advises the Negro to wait until a "more convenient season." Shallow understanding from people of goodwill is more frustrating than absolute misunderstanding from people of ill will. Lukewarm acceptance is much more bewildering than outright rejection.[22]

Maybe this opposition from establishment moderates *is* something everyone must first overcome to see a significant victory. But how do you keep going when even your "allies" are working against you? One thing that kept me going was a note that hung on the wall by my desk from Dr. Jack Willke.

Dr. Jack Willke's note was a daily encouragement to me to keep going. Next to it was his nametag from one of our Heartbeat Bill events in Cincinnati, which I kept and treasured.

In the midst of the battle, when even those around him were advising him to distance himself from our effort, Dr. Willke sent me a note to "keep making trouble." The founder of the Right to Life movement was with us. That was good enough for me. You never know what a note of encouragement can mean to someone on the front lines. For me, it was invaluable.

Challenging What They Care About Most—Their Jobs

There will always be those who say it can't be done or that the time is not right. But they don't have to work for you or represent you in office. One of my favorite things about living in America is that we don't have to accept the status quo or bow to those who hold office. We can challenge the pro-life pretenders publicly and when they still won't keep their pro-life promises, we can challenge them in a primary. *I love America.*

Sometimes you have to challenge what they care about most—*their jobs.* When our representatives don't do what we hired them to do, it is our *duty* to fire them.

To pass the Ohio heartbeat law, we ran candidates in senate primaries across the state against almost every Republican in the senate...in *three* election cycles. But when the senator from my own district, the senate president pro tempore, was up for election in 2016, I wasn't able to recruit anyone. *Oh, I tried.* My husband and I invited a pastor and his wife over for dinner to make the case for him to run for office. I gave it my best shot, telling him he was perfectly positioned to run for the senate and lead the way to the end of abortion "for such a time as this," hoping the Esther reference would help. I assured him we would support him, pleading, "We can use this election to expose their obstruction and get the Heartbeat Bill passed!" He turned me down flat, along with *every* other person I asked. The filing deadline for the primary was upon us, and no one was willing to challenge the next senate president. That was when I got a call from Lori Viars on my cell phone.

Lori: "Did you find anyone?"

Janet: "No."

Lori: "We have a lot of other candidates filed, but it sure would have been nice to have someone run against the next senate president."

Janet: "Yeah, I know."

Election Clerk: "Just sign here."

Lori: "Where are you?"

Janet: "At the Board of Elections."

Lori: "What are you doing?"

Janet: "Filing to run against the next senate president."

Somebody had to put their faith to action. After all, *actions* are what you believe. We spoke the truth, and the ground began to shake. I was told that two polls showed me dead even with the current senate president, causing the opposition to spend a reported $1.3 million of their war chest against me. Then they started launching attacks, claiming I was the one who supported abortion. They did this on every television and radio station and in scores of large, glossy, false, and nasty postcards.

They hired a guy to stalk me at every event, filming and recording me even after we asked him to stop. He came to our banquet and left with my books so he could try to find something against me. After hearing the incessant barrage of attacks, even on Christian radio, my niece said, "They really don't know Aunt Janet." The one thing they did know is that I was not going to give up until the Heartbeat Bill was law.

In my campaign literature, I explained why I was running: because my state senator was blocking the Heartbeat Bill. In *his* campaign literature, he called me a liar. But watch what he did. He didn't outright deny my claim; he just changed what my claim really was.

This is what they do. My opponent's fliers never said my claim that he refused to pass the Heartbeat Bill was false—because it wasn't. Instead they said, "claims Larry isn't pro-life enough" with the word "false," because he was endorsed by the staunchest opponent to the Heartbeat Bill—Ohio Right to Life. You see how this works? If you have a state

If you challenge the establishment, expect to see mailers like these calling you a liar for telling the truth.

Right to Life or pro-family group that opposes your Heartbeat Bill, they provide cover for all the RINOs who block the bill in the legislature.

I had to register as a lobbyist to work on the Ohio Heartbeat Bill, and the vast majority of my work was unpaid. Yet that didn't stop my opponent from making the false claim (lie) that I was a "high-paid government lobbyist!"

The opposition also made the claim that I filed my "corporation" in Florida to "avoid Ohio tax law"—which is also a lie since Faith2Action Ministries is a 501(c)3 and therefore tax exempt! There are no Ohio taxes to avoid! But this lie was repeated on every television and radio station, where ads ran nonstop. They ignored the fact that I filed Faith2Action Ministries in Florida in 2003 because I lived in Florida at the time—7 years before I ever thought of the Heartbeat Bill!

There were other lies, but the most ridiculous were the ads and mailers that told the world that *I* was the pro-abortion candidate and the senator blocking the Heartbeat Bill was the pro-life champion. The opposition knew we couldn't match their budget to counter the barrage of bold-faced lies.

Sandy Rissler, Violet, Campaign Manager Shari Bascom, Janet Porter, Secretary Susan Gardicic, and Beth Folger at a campaign event for Janet's primary run for Ohio Senate.

Then came the attack from my former employer, Ohio Right to Life. While I was legislative director of Ohio Right to Life, there were more than a few election cycles when I also served as political director, overseeing the endorsement process. We were always careful to be nonpartisan and completely factual, a policy of the *past*. In my primary race for the Ohio Senate, Ohio Right to Life ran newspaper ads and mailings that claimed I "refused to support personhood status for unborn crime victims." Not only was this not true, I was the one who lobbied to pass one of the nation's strongest laws against fetal homicide on the books—protecting unborn victims of crime *from conception*. I also signed the personhood petition for Ohio and supported it nationally, but their ad made it look like I opposed it.

If your state Right to Life affiliate is fighting your Heartbeat Bill, expect them to not just provide cover to obstructionist RINOs; expect them to *actively campaign* against Heartbeat Bill candidates like they did me. They even used Obama Logo's in place of the "o's" in my name— *sound impartial to you?*

Expect to be maligned for speaking the truth and having the audacity to challenge those in office. The problem is that when people hear the lies on every TV and radio station and read it in ads and postcards over and over (and over), they start to believe it. I spoke at one church where a woman came up to me and said, "If you hadn't come today, I would have believed the lies against you." The problem is you can't get to every church or speak to every person.

While many churches are afraid to let candidates speak to their congregations, there are still courageous pastors like John Bouquet of Bethel Baptist Church in Ashland, Ohio. He invited all the candidates to speak at his church and said he couldn't tell people who he was voting for unless he was asked. After a moment of silence, he asked, "Well, isn't anyone going to ask who I'm voting for?" A member of the congregation shouted out, "Who are you voting for?" to which he replied, "Janet Folger Porter." We need more courageous pastors like John Bouquet. And more friends like Dr. James Dobson and Larry Pratt of Gun Owners of America, who endorsed me and Phyllis Schlafly, Governor Mike Huckabee, Operation Rescue founder Troy Newman, and General Jerry Boykin, who all made videos of endorsement.

Truth in Elections

Pastor Corey Shankleton, who ran against his state senator said, "The first thing I realized is when people aren't interested in doing what is right,

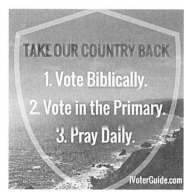

Make the iVoterGuide pledge and then tell others.

My campaign literature made use of the iVoterGuide rating of "Very Conservative" (in red) next to my opponent's "Somewhat Liberal" (in blue).

Janet's parents, Jim and Beth Folger, then U.S. Senator Mike DeWine, and Janet Folger Porter. Note now Governor Mike DeWine is wearing a Janet Folger Porter campaign button.

truth is irrelevant. They will do almost anything to protect their seat of power... However, one thing must lead us in this fight; we must never let go of truth and righteousness, nor let those who disregard it sideline us."

What can we do? Let me introduce you to the best friend of the truth in elections: iVoterGuide.com. It's the way you can get past all the false advertising that happens in every election at both state and federal levels.

It will help you when you vote, and it will help you if you run. I recommend pro-life candidates use iVoterGuide's assessments in their campaign literature like I did, pictured with the red "very conservative" graph next to my name and a blue "somewhat liberal" describing my opponent. Our biggest challenge is lack of funds to get this information out to voters compared to the enormous war chests we face. iVoterGuide may be our most untapped political weapon providing the truth about every major state and federal race, thoroughly researched, in every state!

When you're merely regulating abortion, the establishment runs to endorse you and has no problem taking pictures with you. State office holders lined up to help me unseat the secretary of the Republican Party for the state central committee back then. But when we introduced a bill to end most abortions and exposed those blocking it, it was a different story.

Like Gideon, sometimes you can glean encouragement from what the enemy has to say about you. When the leftist group Right Wing Watch ran an article about me running for the Ohio Senate, I did something I never do—*I read it.* And I found out that they had written more than 500 articles about the things I had been doing. In fact, I found out that I was the second most "watched" woman in America, right after former Congresswoman Michele Bachmann. Great company if you ask me. It doesn't feel good to be attacked, but the Bible says, "Woe to you when all men speak well of you" (Luke 6:26). We can't let what others think of us dictate our actions—at least not if we want to get anything done.

There were county Republican groups that tried to prevent me from speaking at their meetings, but at the insistence of some of their pro-life members finally allowed it. When I shared how I was the left's second "most watched" woman in America, the very people who had tried to block me were now giving me a standing ovation. Learning how much the enemy hated me cut through the clutter of disinformation. I should thank them.

I didn't win, but ultimately the babies did. Opposing us was costing them. When we ran against them, we made them spend a lot of money, and we made them work to keep their jobs. We had passed the Heartbeat Bill many times in the house, but that year we got our first vote in the Ohio Senate.

If you want to end abortion, you have to do "whatever it takes" even when you have absolutely no chance of success. As Morton Blackwell said, "Don't fully trust anyone until he has stuck with a good cause which he saw was losing."[23]

"Let's Get Our Vote"

It was 2018. The Ohio Heartbeat Bill had been introduced for the fourth of five times. It had passed in the House and Senate 2 years earlier, but Governor Kasich had vetoed the bill, and we didn't have the votes to override it. Now, it was November and the bill had not passed in either the house or senate and the clock was about to run out (for the fourth time) in just over a month. Our champion, Ohio Rep. Ron Hood, called me suggesting we wait until January 2019 to try again because Mike DeWine would be sworn in as governor, and he had already promised to sign the Heartbeat Bill.

I told him emphatically, "No."

I believe you need to take *every* chance you can get in this battle, so I argued against waiting. Of course, I almost always argue against waiting.

"The speaker promised us a vote after the elections," I said. "Hold him to his word. Let's get our vote."

Less than 2 weeks before Thanksgiving 2018, we were told we would get our House vote on Thursday, November 15. On Wednesday, November 14, I made the long drive to Columbus once again.

I know I said that a true leader leads even when success is not guaranteed. But this was ridiculous. We were fifteen votes short of the sixty-vote supermajority needed to override Governor Kasich's promised second veto. And we had a day and a half to get them. I'm not saying it's easy, but sometimes you have to fight even when winning is impossible.

We had lost several of our cosponsors because those representatives had resigned or moved to another office. So a day before the vote, we had to find fifteen votes that were never there before.

No one else could make it to lobby that day and, as I told supporters on the phone on the drive down, it was going take an "act of God." I wasn't exaggerating. But isn't that what we'd been counting on all along?

I spent the day handing out my whip lists to our cosponsors as my friend Tom DeLay had taught me. I'd ask one person, "Can you get these two?" Then another, "You're in committee with this guy, can you get him?" By the end of the day I was so exasperated, I was asking people, "Can you try to get these five, these ten?"

By Thursday, November 15, the day of the vote, we were still two or three votes short. The vote was at 1:00 p.m. At noon, I met with our pro-life hero, Rep. Bill Patmon, an African-American statesman from Cleveland who was the only Democrat with the courage to vote for life.

But if we were to succeed, we would need to get at least one more Democrat—something we had never done in this battle. Representative

Janet Porter between Democrat hero Rep. Bill Patmon and Republican hero Rep. Ron Hood.

Patmon and I tried to win over a Democrat House member, but we couldn't persuade him. I told Bill there was one other Democrat we had a chance to get, Rep. Glenn Holmes. We had less than 20 minutes to try. I gave Bill the copy of the heartbeat legislation with the representative's concerns addressed in yellow highlight and said, "Text me if you get him."

Minutes before the session began the pro-abortion witches and satanists made a gauntlet, wearing their "PRO ABORT WITCH" T-shirts accessorized with huge pentagram earrings, all aiming their video phones at me. *Lovely.*

I handed out "Keep Hearts Beating" gift bags filled with chocolate hearts and talking points printed in color. We were still short of the votes we needed, and I wanted to use every moment before the vote to try and get them. I took my reserved seat in the gallery as the session began.

Ohio Rep. Nino Vitale voting "Yes" to keep hearts beating.

Rep. Christina Hagan began her floor speech carrying her newborn twins—perfect visual aids. That was when I got the text from Rep. Patmon. It said one word: "Done."

My heart leapt. We might actually have a chance. At that moment, the Democrats on the floor called for a recess. No one really knew what was going on, but I was about to find out. I stood on my tiptoes looking in the chamber doors in hopes of gaining another critical vote or two. That's when Representative Patmon walked up and told me I might strain myself standing on my tiptoes so long. I thanked him for his critical help in getting our Democrat vote. Speaking of the Democrat caucus, he then said, "You know what they're doing, don't you? They are beating him up, threatening him to try and flip him."

I asked, "Is he going to hold firm?"

Patmon responded, "I don't know."

We held hands and prayed outside the chamber. The Republicans recessed as I followed them to the room where they caucused, still trying to secure the last few votes.

They reconvened and debated for hours. I had been told not to take any more pictures in the balcony, but my intern Joshua Hlavaty had not. So I instructed him to get a picture of the display board when the votes were cast. In his usual fashion he replied, "Got it."

We needed sixty votes to have a shot at avoiding or overriding a veto. The vote was cast and it came in 58–35.

Something wasn't right. I thought we had more votes than that. We left the balcony and went outside the chambers

Joshua Hlavaty with Janet Porter in the Senate Committee.

downstairs. Ten minutes later, Rep. Glenn Holmes, the Democrat who was threatened by his caucus, went forward and voted yes.

We were then at 59–35—one vote short of being veto-proof. As we looked intently at Josh's phone picture of the votes, the yes votes were green, no votes red, and the ones in orange hadn't voted. We noticed that Rep. Marilyn Slaby's name was in orange.

"Hey! Why is Marilyn Slaby's name orange?" I asked.

"Maybe she's not here," someone suggested.

"I saw her! I gave her a gift bag as she went in!"

"Maybe they flipped her," another said.

"Not her. She is a cosponsor, and her husband was a cosponsor of the first Heartbeat Bill when he held the seat before her!" We had three bills on the roster and less than an hour to get her back.

Rep. Nino Vitale, a pro-life leader, came up to us and volunteered to "self-identify as a female" to look for Marilyn in the ladies' room. We declined his offer, but our team set out to look for her while I started texting to find Marilyn's cell number. Rep. Kristina Roegner texted me Marilyn's husband's number. I called, and fortunately he picked up. "Lynn, it's Janet Porter. Marilyn is the swing vote on Heartbeat, and we have less than an hour to get her back."

Lynn responded, "We are 2 hours away for a mandatory meeting that I just can't miss." He pointed out that to get her back would be a 4-hour round trip.

It was impossible. There was absolutely no way to stall for 4 hours. But I believe in the God of the impossible, as our state motto proclaims. We did not come this far to lose, and without even thinking about it, I found myself asking, "Can you pull off the highway? Because I'm on my way to get her right now!"

He said, "Yes."

Josh handed me my coat while I told one group to pray and another, "Tell them to stall until we get back!"

The snow was coming down heavy, and I was parked more than two blocks away. I crossed the street and ran as fast as I could to my car. When I got there, I realized I didn't have my keys.

As I started to search my purse, still out of breath, I looked up to see a very calm man who walked up to me holding my keys. He said, "Here, you dropped these in the crosswalk." As my husband said, he was either a marathon runner or an angel.

I thanked him profusely and got on the highway. I remembered that Josh's mother, Raylene Hlavaty, who was an intern back when I was at Ohio Right to Life, served on the board of Wayne/Holmes County Right to Life. That's where our swing vote was waiting for us. I called Josh and asked him to see if his mom could pick up Marilyn.

Raylene did, driving south as I drove north, while the snow was getting heavier. My husband called and asked me what I was doing.

"I'm driving through a blizzard to go get our swing vote. Pray we make it."

He laughed, and then prayed. I pulled off at our agreed upon exit in Mansfield and got gas as Raylene pulled in with Marilyn.

I was apologizing to Marilyn for my somewhat less than pro-life driving, when the answer to our prayer came in. Our champion sponsor, Ron Hood called. "Jan, I talked to the speaker and got him to recess the session instead of adjourning it."

He explained, "If two members are present, we can reconvene after everyone leaves, readjourn session, and let her cast the sixtieth vote."

When Marilyn and I arrived at the Statehouse, we met Ron and the team in the parking garage and all walked to the chamber. It was like a dream.

Our champion Ron Hood took hold of the gavel and called for the session to reconvene. "I call House Bill 258 for third consideration..."

Marilyn Slaby, still in her coat, signed yes on the official form.

As Ron slammed the gavel down and called for session to be adjourned, I fell to my knees and cried, "Thank You, Jesus." He truly is the God of the impossible.

I introduced myself to the clerk, thanking him for staying late. He replied, "I know who you are. I've known you since the 1980s and 1990s when you were Janet Folger."

I then made a rather unusual request. When we first passed the Heartbeat Bill through both the Statehouse and Senate in December 2016, we all stood in the Statehouse atrium, where we held many rallies and prayer

Heartbeat Sponsor Rep. Ron Hood, Janet Porter, and Rep. Marilyn Slaby after she cast the 60th veto-proof vote.

meetings. That night, around midnight, we all joined together at the plaque designating where Abraham Lincoln spoke in front of the Statehouse Christmas tree. We worshiped God, singing "Oh Come Let Us Adore Him," like never before.

I didn't know how Rep. Marilyn Slaby and the others would feel about it, but I asked anyway. Could we all sing that song again? We had just seen an impossible victory; it was only fitting that we take a minute and praise the one who gave it to us.

We sang it. And then Marilyn Slaby led everyone in the *second* verse. Every time I hear that song, I am taken back to those moments, when the God of the impossible came through for us.

We had the votes to be veto-proof in the Senate, but on December 12, 2018, following the veto and the House vote to override it, Senate President Obhof refused to bring the Heartbeat Bill to an override vote. That is when Rep. Christina Hagan and I stood directly in front of Obhof on the Senate floor staring him down. I had every influential person I knew text him that day, including former House Majority Leader Tom DeLay, members of Congress, and other influential leaders. I watched as Senate President Obhof stood at the podium looking down to the texts on his phone I knew he was getting. Rep. Ron Hood had a key Statehouse leader text him a warning that if he blocked the vote, he would "own" the loss. Obhof knew that was true. I had cost him a boatload of money in the primary by running against him, but Rep. Christina Hagan, who lived in his senate district, was about to cost him even more. She was leaving office at the end of the month but told him that day, "I thought I was done with politics, but I guess not."

We were two women standing side by side in the Senate chamber, willing to "do whatever it takes." What was the result? A 180-degree turn:

Senator Obhof brought our Heartbeat Bill to a vote. I learned: When you challenge what people care about most—their jobs—they are more, *not less*, likely to listen.

We had the votes to override Kasich's second veto—that is until Senator Bill Beagle flipped his "yes" vote from the previous week and voted against overriding the veto.

Instead of protecting babies with detectable heartbeats, he voted to kill them.

His reason: Gov. John Kasich. Flip-flop Beagle said, "This is as much about Gov. Kasich...and Gov. Kasich has been supportive of me, and I think we have a good working relationship and that weighs into the question as well."[24] After betraying babies neither John Kasich nor Bill Beagle can ever get away with pretending to be pro-life again.

Our victory came 4 months later, but the lesson is clear. To get to the finish line, you have to keep going. Even when it's impossible. Even when the finish line is nowhere in sight.

This battle isn't about how many stand with you. It is about the remnant willing to stand and do whatever it takes. Feel outgunned and outnumbered? Doesn't matter. Even our American history proves God is famous for working through remnants.

In my documentary film *Light Wins*, historian David Barton of Wall-Builders said:

> We look at the American Revolution. We look at the freedom from Great Britain that we had—throwing off the tyranny—and say, "Oh that's a cool story—all those patriots back then." ...No they weren't all patriots back then. As a

matter of fact, you will find only about 25 percent of Americans supported the American Revolution. You'll find that only about 7–8 percent actually participated in the American Revolution. The guys who fought and won were a tiny minority! But they changed the direction of the nation. They brought them all to their position because they wouldn't quit fighting. They wouldn't back up. They wouldn't stand for tyranny. You don't have to have 51 percent to win something—just look at American history—it's never been that.[25]

Our founders didn't need a majority and neither do we. But we do need persistence. Remember, we are talking about *ending* abortion—not merely regulating it. So don't expect the battle over life and death to be easy. But, as my father used to tell me, "If it was easy anybody could do it." Anybody *can* end abortion—if they are willing to do *whatever it takes*.

Whether it's challenging the status quo or the job of a RINO, we must stand up to those who stand in the way of ending abortion. No matter the cost. At the end of the assault against you, your name, your reputation, your family, and your finances, lives will be saved. And they are worth it. You also get to find out who your real friends are.

Though the truth causes the ground to shake, tell it. Though it cost you everything, shout it. Because, in the end, it is the truth that sets us free and paves the way to victory. What must we do to bring the killing to an end? The answer remains, "whatever it takes." As Winston Churchill, the man who saved Western civilization, declared, "Sometimes our best is simply not enough...We have to do what is required."

CHAPTER 8

The Federal Heartbeat Bill

"No dream is too big. No challenge is too great.
Nothing we want for our future is beyond our reach."
—President Donald Trump

I told you what happens at the state level when you blaze the trail to keep hearts beating. But if you're going to be an effective leader on the side of righteousness at the *national* level, dial up the threat to DEFCON 1. Those who take a strong stand to advance the kingdom of God at the federal level can expect to be falsely accused, maligned, and attacked through every means possible, especially if they're effective like President Donald Trump, Congressman Steve King, and former House Majority Leader Tom DeLay.

It begins with character assassination and old-fashioned name-calling seen on playgrounds for centuries. Yeah, you remember. It's what they say when they can't argue a case on its merits. And when challenged, they just say it over and over and louder and louder beginning with their favorite word:

January 2017, the launch of the federal Heartbeat Bill with Sponsor Rep. Steve King, co-sponsors and group leaders. "President Donald Trump said 'we are going to make America safe again.' The Heartbeat Bill is the first step to make America safe again for every child whose heartbeat can be heard."

> **Ra-cist**: 1. adj. what to scream when you are losing an argument with a conservative—especially if they are effective, talented, or successful; Syn. white privilege, white supremacist, white nationalist, Nazi, and assorted profanity.

To the left, everything is racist. *Everyone* is racist. Don't believe me? That's because you're a racist! Unless you are nominated to the U.S. Supreme Court or a swing vote in the U.S. Senate, in which case you are also a rapist and a pedophile.

It's a tried and true strategy of Democrats and RINOs. It even has an official name. In a briefing on June 22, 2016, Nancy Pelosi explained something her party has perfected: a political tactic she called the "Wrap-Up Smear."

It's a self-fulfilling prophecy, you demonize and then...we call it the "Wrap-up Smear." ...You smear somebody with falsehoods and all the rest, and then you merchandise it. And then you [speaking to the press] write it and they'll say see, it's reported in the press that this, this, this, and this, so they have that validation that the press reported the smear. And then it's called the "wrap up smear." And now I'm going to merchandise the press's report on the smear that we made. It's a tactic. And it's self-evident.[1]

Here's the playbook:

1. Demonize/slander a candidate with false accusations.
2. Then, get the smear printed in the press for credibility
3. Merchandise it to the public.

The character assassins simply load their manufactured accusations into media machine guns to besiege the blameless. After rapid-fire rounds of "Russia, Russia, Russia," failed, they just reload with new rounds of rhetoric: "Ukraine, Ukraine, Ukraine," and "Impeach! Impeach! Impeach!" When none of that worked, they just hit restart and shouted "Russia, Russia, Russia" again.[2]

I know of no American in our lifetime who has been as targeted, maligned, or mistreated as President Trump. As President Trump said at the 2020 March for Life, "They are coming after me because I am fighting for you and we are fighting for those who have no voice."[3] When my husband and I were at his inauguration, I saw what I have not seen at any other inauguration. In the crowd were covens of witches cursing our president. So nasty I almost mistook them for CNN. Every time you see the assault against our president—which is every time you turn on the news—let that serve as a reminder our prayers need to be that constant.

Our prayers are what break those curses. God heard our cry for mercy and our prayer to end abortion. If President Trump had not won, we would be mourning the death of the Constitution right now, with no hope of stopping the slaughter of babies in our lifetime. Keep that in mind next time you're tempted to criticize him for being imperfect. Turn those words into a prayer *for* him and for our nation.

Because Congressman Steve King, the sponsor of the federal Heartbeat Bill, was so effective he was next in the crosshairs. King made a mistake of consenting to an interview with *The New York Times* without recording it. That meant they could make up whatever they wanted, and there was nothing he could do about it. In the interview, like in hundreds of previous interviews, King defended Western civilization.[4] The foundational principle of our Western civilization begins with the self-evident truth that "all men are created equal." But *The New York Times* claimed King was defending racism, instead.

It's funny that when an Ohio legislator introduces an amendment, in committee and on the House Floor, to exclude legal protection from just the black babies with detectable heartbeats no one is calling for the resignation of the Democrat author of that lethally racist amendment that equates to prenatal lynching. But when Congressman Steve King defends Western civilization but is misquoted by *The New York Times*, everyone calls for his head. He must be a "racist" because *The New York Times* said so!

Congressman King was railroaded over a false quote. While Democrats will fervently protect even their guilty, Republicans are famous for sacrificing their innocent. When the mud starts flying, Republicans don't want any of it splashing onto their tailor-made suits.

Republican leadership, desperate to appear pious to the press, chose to believe *The New York Times*, famous for their left-wing bias, over a sitting Congressman with no history or connection to the allegations made against him. They stripped King of all of his committees—denying King's voice in the powerful Judiciary Committee.[5] As journalist Brit Hume said, it's "completely bogus."

I hand delivered a letter signed by 200 pro-family leaders including Rev. William Owens, Founder and President of the Coalition of African-American Pastors; Pastor Stephen E. Broden, President of the Black Pro-life Coalition; and Dr. James Dobson to Leader Kevin McCarthy urging him to not to "make the fatal mistake of turning the reigns of the U.S. Congress over to the liberal media, allowing them to target, misquote, and falsely brand any member of Congress they wish to remove."

If we don't stand with these good men and women against the media-manufactured assault today, none of us will be safe from it tomorrow. I knew Congressman Steve King was a good man; that's why when I saw him on the floor of the Republican National Convention on July 20, 2016, I pitched him the idea for a federal Heartbeat Bill. Our Ohio Senate was still holding our bill hostage—for the fifth year. It was time to go over their heads with a federal Heartbeat Bill—that could override the obstruction and protect beating hearts across the country.

How do ordinary people get a Congressional bill heard in Congress? One with more cosponsors than any pro-life bill backed by the multi-million dollar establishment groups? It's unheard of. But God is famous for working through remnants. The people to whom I will introduce you are a team of volunteers sold out to God and the belief that He is everything

He claims to be and empowers His people to do the impossible. This rag-tag team literally met with hundreds of Congressmen, getting 174 as cosponsors of the 218 votes needed to pass it.

If we can do it, so can you, on this and any other issue for which we are willing to step out and try.

The conversation that began at the Republican National Convention ended at a funeral. Rebekah Gantner, a former intern at Faith2Action and executive director of Phyllis Schlafly's Eagles, called to relay Phyllis's invitation to come and speak at their 2016 fall conference. If Phyllis was asking, my answer was yes.

Sadly, Phyllis didn't make it to her fall conference. On September 10, 2016, I attended her funeral at the Cathedral Basilica of St. Louis where then-candidate Donald J. Trump gave the eulogy. He attended along with his wife, Melania; Kellyanne Conway, now a counselor to President Trump; and Stephen Bannon, who became White House chief strategist after Trump's election. I was in the row behind them and asked Morton Blackwell, founder of the Leadership institute, Congresswoman Michele Bachmann, and Congressman Steve King to join me there. I told Congressman King, who sat next to me, how highly Phyllis had often spoken to me about him, and we briefly talked about a federal Heartbeat Bill.

Then in the eulogy, Father Brian Harrison spoke about Phyllis's "ceaseless combat against the scourge of abortion." That's when Congressman King leaned over and said, "We have our charge, don't we?" I let Congressman King know that another memorial service for Phyllis was being held at the Eagle Forum conference the following week in St. Louis and suggested that he come and speak there. He did.

I had the honor to emcee the memorial service for my friend Phyllis Schlafly and presented Representatives Louie Gohmert of Texas and

Rachelle Heidlebaugh and Janet Porter with our fearless leader Fmr. Majority Leader Tom DeLay.

Heartbeat co-sponsor Congressman Jody Horn (R-GA) with Janet Porter and Larry Cirignano in St. Louis.

Steve King with packets containing information about the Heartbeat Bill. I know Phyllis would be honored that her favorite congressman, Steve King, agreed to sponsor the Heartbeat Bill that day, and another favorite, Congressman Gohmert, became a key cosponsor.

Our federal Heartbeat Bill team began with Rachelle Heidlebaugh, whom I met during the Ohio heartbeat battle in 2011, although it seems like we have been friends for life. She prayed that if she was supposed to be a part of the national effort, I would call her while we were in Washington for President Trump's inauguration. I called, and she spoke at our first national Heartbeat Bill press conference days later.[6]

Rachelle volunteered to become the scheduler, and I have never met anyone better at it. She scheduled meetings with congressional offices on the same floor of the same building when possible—starting at the top floor, working our way down. She was organized and efficient beyond words, briefing us as we walked toward offices on whom we were meeting and their staffer's names.

Another member of the team is Larry Cirignano. I've known Larry so long, I can't even remember where we met. He represents the choose-life license plates in Washington, D.C. and can be found on the front lines of most pro-life battles. He's an attorney, but he has the heart of an activist. As long as I've been involved in the pro-life and pro-family movement in Washington, D.C., Larry has always been there doing the heavy lifting without fanfare or spotlights. Unlike Rachelle and myself, Larry is laid back. One day when Rachelle stayed back in the cafeteria to line up appointments, Larry and I went to a congressional meeting without her. On the way there, I asked Larry, "Who are we meeting with?" His nonchalant reply, "Oh, some guy in some office from some state."

Larry is not only a lawyer but the kind of guy who has been around Washington since he served as an advance man for President Ronald Reagan. He traveled ahead of the president to arrange the details of his schedule, security, and the like. To this day, as some student pro-life activists noted while holding signs at one of Washington's metro stations, "Everyone in a suit knows Larry."

Larry is the guy who helps us find our way around the congressional offices, especially when we have to go underground to avoid the snow. He points out all the fun facts, like the pictures on the wall in Congressman Claude Pepper's former office. Hanging next to a picture of Congressman Pepper with one of the Wright brothers is a picture of him standing next to Neil Armstrong—spanning the first flight all the way to the moon. Here's another fun fact: the Wright brothers and Neil Armstrong were all from *Ohio*.

Rachelle Heidlebaugh, Janet Porter, Congressman Jim Jordan (R-OH), Rebekah Gantner, Joshua Hlavaty, and Larry Cirignano talk strategy.

Marty Angell, Fmr. Majority Leader Tom DeLay, Larry Cirignano, Rebekah Gantner, Janet Porter, David Porter, and Rachelle Heidlebaugh working on the Hill to keep hearts beating.

Janet Porter, Fmr. Majority Leader Tom DeLay, and Congressman Steve King strategize in Congressman King's office.

The only time I saw Larry get angry was a day we faced yet another insurmountable obstacle, and I got discouraged. It was one of the few times I voiced discouragement to the team, but Larry wasn't about to hear it. It's just one of the many reasons everybody loves Larry. His favorite memory was watching the congressmen "light up" with hope when we told them "We're going to end abortion!"

Also key to our team is Rebekah Gantner. When she was in high school in Wisconsin, Rebekah listened daily to my Faith2Action radio program. She wrote me to ask if she could become my intern. I said yes—one of my *better* decisions.

We had a handful of cosponsors for the federal Heartbeat Bill and I explained on the phone to Larry and Rachelle, "We need help." I suggested we pray. They were used to that suggestion, but none of us were used to how immediate the answer came. I prayed, "God, who do we know that we're forgetting about who could help us?" Immediately, it was like someone whispered the thought in my mind, "Tom DeLay."

Like President Trump and Congressman King, former Majority Leader DeLay was also falsely accused and maligned in an effort to remove his legendary effectiveness. After losing his reputation, millions in legal fees, and his powerful position, he was finally fully exonerated.

Leadership Institute's Morton Blackwell stated, "The only fire under all that smoke generated by the leftist attacks is their burning hatred of a good man."[7] Rush Limbaugh agreed, "Tom DeLay was despised because he was good."[8]

Was it even possible a good man who had been treated so badly in politics would be willing to go back to Capitol Hill? Our desperate prayer for help was answered by one of the most powerful men to ever serve in Washington. The former Majority Leader said "yes!" That was the moment the federal Heartbeat Bill came to life.

Tom was nicknamed "the Hammer" by the *Washington Post* because of his effectiveness. I can vouch for it. When Tom DeLay joined the Heartbeat Bill team everything changed. Instead of marching uphill, meeting mostly with staffers, when Tom DeLay led the charge, doors swung open—literally. We had our own parking place at the Capitol Hill Club, across from the Congressional offices. Instead of waiting in long lines, we were waved through security by police officers who all knew and adored Tom.

Congressmen ran across the street to hug him and tell him how much he was missed. Several said things like, "We were just talking about how much we need you to come back here and run things!" He was revered and respected on Capitol Hill like few others I have ever seen. And when the members and staff weren't asking for photo ops with him, teenage girls and middle-aged women were begging the former "Dancing with the Stars" contestant for a picture.

Tom showed us how to develop a "whip team" and turn congressmen into an active lobbying force. We printed "whip cards" listing members who had not yet cosponsored the Heartbeat Bill on a vertical half-sheet of card stock, which fit neatly inside a man's suit jacket. They could easily pull it out while they were on the House floor and cross off members as they signed on the bill. I utilized this at the state level, and those whip cards got us within one vote of a veto-override on our Ohio Heartbeat Bill.

One of my favorite moments with Tom was walking down the hall one day between congressional appointments. He had stressed the importance of getting 218 votes in the House—the majority vote needed to get a bill passed.

Heartbeat Bill Hero Dr. Ames Curtright joined the battle and helped finance it. Pictured: Ames Curtright and Tom DeLay leading the charge with Janet Porter and Jeremy Salupo close behind in route to another meeting.

Rebekah Gantner, Fmr. Majority Leader Tom DeLay, and Janet Porter on the way to 218 Congressional votes for the federal Heartbeat Bill.

Fmr. Majority Leader Tom DeLay, Rachelle Heidlebaugh, then Rep., now U.S. Senator Marsha Blackburn (R-TN), Janet Porter, Anna Little, Larry Cirignano, and Rebekah Gantner.

I told him, "Tom, I think we're going to get our 218."

He looked at me like I was crazy—but not the kind of crazy I had become accustomed to, you know, the "you'll never be able to pass this bill" kind of crazy. His reply was, *"Of course we will! Why do you think I'm here?"*

My heart leapt. Finally, someone who knows what they're doing who *actually believed* this can be done!

Tom has said repeatedly that his biggest regret upon "leaving Congress is that we didn't end abortion."[9] He, like so many in the pro-life movement, believed the lie that "all we could do" is regulate abortion and move a millimeter down the field each year. He implored members and leadership to not make the same mistakes he made: "Don't leave this place with the same regret."

The Congressional Wives Whip Team

I met Nancy Schulze, wife of former Congressman Dick Schulze, while speaking on the "Liberty Bus Tour" in Florida with our mutual friend Art Ally. She is the founder of *Republican Congressional Wives Speakers*. I asked for an opportunity to speak to the Congressional wives—the *real* movers and shakers on the Hill. Nancy agreed to fit me in her packed schedule and the wives became energized to keep hearts beating. I handed out whip lists, and before lunch was served, they were already on the phones with their husbands.

After my talk, they crowded around bursting with enthusiasm, pointing to the whip list, saying, "I'll call his wife tonight." "My husband and I are *very* good friends with this one. He'll be on!" "We live next door to them; I'll get him." When I pointed out to one of the

Congressional Wives Whip Team Cindy Ross, wife of Congressman Dennis Ross (R-FL).

Nancy Schultz, Christine DeLay, and Fmr. Majority Leader Tom DeLay at a meeting of conservative leaders in Washington, D.C.

Janet Porter with Christine DeLay, who spoke on the Congressional wives' conference calls, encouraging them to use their influence to save lives. Christine sacrificed many weeks and months while Tom lobbied with us on the Hill.

David and Janet Porter with Kellyanne Conway discuss the Heartbeat Bill. Kellyanne is wearing our Heartbeat Bill pin before giving a speech.

Heartbeat Bill Congressional Cosponsor lapel pin.

Larry Cirignano, Janet Porter, Congressman Doug Lamborn (R-CO), Rachelle Heidlebaugh, and Fmr. Majority Leader Tom DeLay presenting the Heartbeat Bill Cosponsor lapel pin.

wives that her husband was not yet a cosponsor, she replied, "Oh, he *will* be!" We'd just come across the real power brokers!

At that event, I had the opportunity to make an elevator pitch to Kellyanne Conway—*literally*. I had met her at a few other events and gave her our "sponsor" pin. At one dinner of Conservative leaders in Washington, she gave the Heartbeat Bill a shout out from the podium, saying, "We need to do away with 'heartbeat abortions!'"[10] I was the first one to my feet, applauding and cheering.

Janet Porter, Larry Cirignano, Josh Hlavaty, Rachelle Heidlebaugh, and Rebekah Gantner. "Who do we still need?"

We were picking up steam meeting with hundreds of members of Congress. Each member who cosponsored the bill was given the custom-made official "sponsor" pin of "precious feet"—the actual size of a baby's feet at 10 weeks—inside a red heart. We had an official "pinning ceremony" and photo op with each one in their offices. Many tweeted the photos to their followers.

Everyone on the team was used to hearing me say, "We're gonna end abortion." But one of my favorite moments with Rebekah Gantner was sitting in the House cafeteria in Washington, D.C. when Rebekah asked me how many cosponsors we had. I told her "seventy-three." She looked at me with surprise and delight and exclaimed, "We're gonna end abortion!" It finally hit her! It wasn't long after that we had 174 cosponsors—more cosponsors than any pro-life bill in Congress. Sometimes you have to keep proclaiming the vision and moving toward your goal until others can see what you know in your heart.

The Scenic Route to a Divine Appointment

I asked Tom DeLay if he could get a meeting with Vice President Mike Pence. He called to inform me that "all he could get" that week was a meeting with the vice president's policy director—did I still want it? *Of course.*

A "Divine Appointment" with Vice President Mike Pence. Also pictured Janet Porter, Fmr. Majority Leader Tom DeLay, and Rachelle Heidlebaugh.

After the very positive meeting, the policy director asked, "How would you like to leave the White House?" I suggested, "How about the scenic route?"

That scenic route ran us smack dab into none other than Vice President Mike Pence, who called the meeting a "divine appointment." Tom DeLay was Majority Leader when the vice president was a member of Congress. Like so many others have done, when the vice president saw Tom DeLay, he stopped in his tracks exclaiming, "Tommy!" and briskly walked over to hug him. We told Vice President Pence about the Heartbeat Bill, which the vice president said he "loved," and he spent 20 minutes with us talking about it. After instructing his staff to take pictures of us together, the vice president promised to personally deliver to the president's desk our letter signed by more than 120 national leaders asking for support of the federal Heartbeat Bill.

Rachelle Heidlebaugh, Rebekah Gantner, Congressman Mike Kelly (R-PA), Janet Porter, Larry Cirignano, and Fmr. Majority Leader Tom DeLay. Congressman Kelly took charge to reach out to the entire Pennsylvania delegation for the Heartbeat Bill.

Anna Little, Beth Folger, Rachelle Heidlebaugh, Larry Cirignano, Janet Porter, Jeremy Salupo, and Josh Hlavaty after another Heartbeat Bill press conference on the Hill.

Dated September 13, 2017, the letter reads as follows:

September 13, 2017

Dear President Trump, Vice President Pence, Speaker Ryan, and Leader McCarthy,

On Nov 8th of last year, 81% of Evangelicals voted to put President Donald Trump into the White House and Republicans in control of the House and Senate. They are now watching closely, wondering if Republicans in Washington will keep their campaign promises. One of the most important campaign promises was the protection of unborn life.

We, the undersigned, have united to protect human lives with HR 490, the Heartbeat Protection Act, which is co-sponsored by two-thirds of the Republicans in Congress—more than any other pro-life bill. It also has more public support than any other pro-life bill. Simply put, the Heartbeat Bill ensures that "if a heartbeat is detected, the baby is protected." To deny the child's beating heart is to deny science. To ignore it is heartless.

According to the father of the pro-life movement, the late Dr. John Willke, the Heartbeat Bill will protect 95% of the babies who would otherwise be aborted. Simply recognizing this universal indicator of life—a heartbeat—is the most effective way to "Make America Safe Again."

While we support pro-life bills that protect preborn children, the Pain Capable Bill (HR 36) would only protect babies after five months—that's only 1.3% of the babies facing abortion, according to CDC statistics.

As Dr. Willke stated, "When I founded the pro-life movement, it wasn't to regulate how abortions would be done, it was to bring the abortion killing to an END. We have waited too long and that wait has cost us too much."

After 44 years, an "incremental approach" has left us with a body count of nearly 60 million. We are a far cry from success when nearly a million abortions are still being committed each year. But in order to achieve a different result, we must do something different. The Heartbeat Bill is different.

According to a 2017 George Barna poll, 69% of Americans support the Heartbeat Bill—most of them strongly. The bill

Josh Hlavaty, Larry Cirignano, Rebekah Gantner, Janet Porter, Rachelle Heidlebaugh, and Congressman Steve Chabot (R-OH), who insisted I sit in his chair.

Congressman Louie Gohmert (R-TX) has always been my favorite. I am honored he would tweet about the Ohio motto plaque I gave him.

Heartbeat co-sponsor Congressman Ken Buck (R-CO) shares his appreciation for the 2nd Amendment. Following Biden's announcement to put Beto O'Rourke in charge of gun control if elected, Buck tweeted, "I have just one message for Joe Biden and Beto O'Rourke, if you want to take everyone's AR-15s, why don't you swing by my office in Washington, D.C. and start with this one? Come and take it. #2A"

has support from the vast majority of Republicans (86%) and Independents (61%). Even 55% of Democrats believe "If a doctor is able to detect a heartbeat of an unborn baby, that baby should be legally protected." The Eighth Circuit Court of Appeals declared that the heartbeat is a more "consistent and certain" indicator of life than "viability," the arbitrary standard the U.S. Supreme Court currently uses to allow legal protection of children in the womb.

While respecting all pro-life efforts, after four decades, it's time to achieve the goal for which we have marched, prayed, and voted. With a Republican House, Senate, White House, and new Supreme Court being ushered in, we can do more than protect 1.3% of the babies, we can protect every child whose beating heart can be heard.

We urgently and respectfully request that you lead your legislative agenda this fall with HR 490, the Heartbeat Bill, supported by two-thirds of the Republican members of Congress, seven out of ten Americans, and millions of pro-life voters who will be greatly encouraged by its passage prior to the midterm elections.

Among the 120 leaders who signed our letter were:

♥ Dr. James Dobson,

♥ Governor Mike Huckabee,

♥ Don Wildmon, Founder, American Family Association and AFA Radio,

Heartbeat Bill Hero Challenge Coin given to Congressional Co sponsors of the federal Heartbeat Bill.

♥ Troy Newman, President, Operation Rescue,

♥ Penny Nance, CEO and President Concerned Women for America,

♥ Joe Scheidler, National Director, Pro-life Action League,

♥ Pastor Bill and Deborah Owens, Founder, Coalition of African American Pastors,

♥ Ed Martin, President, Phyllis Schlafly's Eagles,

♥ William G. Boykin, Lt. General, Retired, U.S. Army,

♥ Former Congressman Bob McEwen,

♥ Steven F. Hotze, M.D., President Restore Our Godly Heritage PAC, Founder and CEO, Conservative Republicans of Texas PAC,

♥ Former Congresswoman Michele Bachmann,

♥ Dr. Rick Scarborough, Founder, Vision America,

♥ Abby Johnson, author of *Unplanned*,

♥ Dick Bott, Founder, Bott Radio Network,

♥ Lou Engle, Co-founder, TheCall Azusa Now,

♥ David Barton, Founder, Wallbuilders,

♥ Mat Staver, Esq. B.C.S. Founder and Chairman, Liberty Council,

♥ Rep. Gary Glenn, Associate Speaker Pro Tem, Michigan House of Representatives and American Family Association, Michigan,

♥ Pastor Rick Joyner, Chairman, The Oak Initiative,

♥ Jason Jones, Founder and President, Movie to Movement,

♥ Andy Schlafly, Esq., Phyllis Schlafly's Eagles,

♥ Gary Bauer, Esq. President and Founder American Values,

♥ Alan E. Parker, Jr. President, The Justice Foundation,

♥ Patrick Mahoney, Director, Christian Defense Coalition,

♥ Dr. William Ames Curtright, Founder, Ames's Gathering of the Eagles,

♥ Mark Crutcher, President, Life Dynamics, Inc.,

♥ Joel Brind, Ph.D., Co-founder, Breast Cancer Prevention Institute,

♥ William Murray, Chairman, Religious Freedom Coalition,

♥ Pastor Paul Blair, President, Reclaiming America for Christ,

♥ Dr. Jimmy Draper, President Emeritus, LifeWay, former president, Southern Baptist Convention, and

♥ Thomas Glessner, J.D. President, National Institute of Family and Life Advocates.

Congressman Glenn Thompson (R-PA) already has his Heartbeat Bill Hero Coin displayed in his office.

In January 2018, I was invited to attend a reception at the White House with about 300 people in attendance. I had a "Heartbeat Hero" coin in my hand and declared to our Heartbeat team Jeremy, Rachelle, and Larry that I was going to give it to the vice president. Looking at the crowd, Jeremy quipped, "Of course you are." When the vice president came in, I gave him the coin, and I also was able to speak to him afterward about the Heartbeat Bill once again. At the reception, we also bumped into Kellyanne Conway, who asked for an extra sponsor pin for her son. When she later ran into Congressman King at the Fox television studio, she also asked him for his pin, so she could wear it on her next interview with CNN. *I really like her.*

Another day, while having dinner at the Capitol Hill Club, I spotted former Speaker Paul Ryan across the room. I walked up to his table and gave him a Heartbeat Bill Hero coin. He said, "What's this?"

"It's *you*, if you will just bring the Heartbeat Bill to a floor vote." I mentioned to him that we had 174 cosponsors on the bill and told him we had the forty-four additional votes needed to pass it. If he would call a vote, he could be the "Heartbeat Hero"—the guy who ends abortion for babies with beating hearts.

Sadly, his answer was "no." He and the Republican leadership instead chose to regulate abortion. That was just before they lost the majority of the U.S. House.

Other members of our federal team included David Porter, Jeremy Salupo, Josh Hlavaty, Dr. Ames Curtright, Anna Little, Madeleine Castle, Marty Angell, and Pastor Paul Blair. Jeremy helped wherever needed in both the Ohio and federal Heartbeat battles—often performing thankless duties and whatever needed to be done. Jeremy often led the prayers with members of Congress, who were visibly touched and greatly impacted. I thank God for sending Jeremy to become a key member of the team.

No matter what you ask Josh to do, his response is, "Got it," right before he gets it done. The favorite memory Josh relayed was when we were stuck in traffic and had to run to a meeting with the legal counsel of the U.S. House Judiciary Committee. While Jeremy parked the car, Larry, Josh, and I ran for what seemed like miles—*full sprint*—down the hallways to the meeting, which started the moment we arrived. I was still out of breath when I started our presentation. We ran *a lot*—"dignity" is overrated.

Dr. Ames Curtright was a friend of Tom's who quickly became a friend of ours. To generate support, we hosted a banquet at the Capitol Hill Club attended by more than 100 members of Congress. It was a pricey endeavor, and afterward Ames asked me to send him the bill so he could pay half of it. I will always be grateful to him for his generous help.

Anna Little is now a federal judge, but she wasn't too important to help the effort to keep hearts beating. Her favorite memory was Baby Lincoln—the youngest to ever testify in Congress. As described in Chapter 5, it was a sacred moment in the U.S. House Judiciary Committee when

Janet Porter presents Chairman of the House Freedom Caucus Congressman Andy Biggs the Heartbeat Hero coin with his wife Cindy at a Phyllis Schlafly's Eagle's event in St. Louis.

Fmr. Chicago Bears player Pastor Paul Blair gets a Heartbeat pin as he joins the team in D.C. to lobby for the Heartbeat Bill.

18-week unborn Baby Lincoln's heart was seen and heard via ultrasound beating strong. It even brought a pro-abortion protestor to tears. Also at that hearing, Heartbeat Bill co drafter Professor David Forte testified, much to the chagrin of every abortion activist who dared question him.

Madeleine Castle was an intern for Rebekah Gantner of Phyllis Schlafly Eagles and made herself indispensable. On the way to the offices, she found pertinent information about the members like "Planned Parenthood hates this guy!" Just the kind of person we couldn't wait to meet and get on the bill!

Marty Angell helped the effort and also provided comic relief. When you visit the representatives' offices in Washington, they often offer you refreshments or something representative of their district. In Georgia's congressional offices, for example, you'll likely be offered peanuts. In

Florida, it's orange juice. By the end of the day, an exhausted Marty was asking, "Which office represents My Pillow?"

Former Chicago Bears player Pastor Paul Blair also joined us on the Hill, lobbying in the U.S. Senate as well as the House. He is also the president of Reclaiming America for Christ and Founder and President of Protect Life and Marriage OK. People on the Hill wanted their picture with Pastor Paul, often asking what it was like to play football during the famous Mike Ditka era of the Bears.

Think about this. We weren't part of the Washington establishment. We didn't have a big budget or any special talents or connections. Just a rag-tag team of ordinary people willing to step out to do what has never been done. It wasn't until we already had the bill, some cosponsors, and our first press conference that God dropped the idea in my heart to call Tom DeLay. I have found that when you step out to obey God, He brings you what you need along the way. Starting with nothing but an idea, we ended up with more cosponsors than any other pro-life bill in congress and a congressional hearing where a baby's beating heart brought witness to his humanity and need for legal protection. Now we just need you—to join the effort to keep hearts beating beginning with a call to your congressman and a vote in the next election for the candidate who'll keep hearts beating. Then, go over their heads and place a call to the Creator. That's what we did.

Prayer was central to all we did in the federal and state battles. We made it a habit to pray before we went into each representative's office, and as former intern Madeleine Castle pointed out, it was amazing to see the way God prepared their hearts before our arrival. Many members of Congress joined us in prayer once we were inside.

God said He is no respecter of persons. He has no limits and He has no boundaries. He can enable you to pass a Heartbeat Bill and advance His

Additional members of the Heartbeat team (left to right): Joe Shrewsbury, Jeremy Salupo, Adam Schindler, Janet Porter, Congressman Clay Higgins, Jonathan Shek, Matt Geppert, and David Porter.

Kingdom in your state, our nation, and nations beyond. Take the model Heartbeat Bill and these principles to keep hearts beating in your nation. Begin with two (or more) coming into agreement in prayer. Then ask God to show you the people to invite on your team. Find your champion to sponsor the bill, then, like Peter, step out of the boat. Forget about the storm and the waves, keep your eyes on God with each meeting and watch how He prepares the hearts before you say a word. If, like with us, you don't see victory right away, that just means the story isn't over. As Winston Churchill said, "Success is not final, failure is not fatal; it is the courage to continue that counts."[11]

Grassroots Effort Plus Technology

One of the great assets in our Congressional and state battles was the use of technology, thanks to our friend Steve Ensley of American Family Online (AFO.net), who is available to help in your Heartbeat battle.

I'm a big believer in turning emails into something tangible—something hard for representatives to ignore. With that in mind, we launched our Congressional battle with Valentine cards. Colorful Valentines like the kind you used to get in grade school on card stock, only with messages about the Heartbeat Bill. With the click of a button, they were ready to be personalized and mailed from you to U.S. House leadership and committee members, to every Republican, or every member of Congress. In just a few weeks, supporters sent tens of thousands of personalized Valentines cards by the box-full to members of Congress. The messages ranged from "Have a Heart, Support the Heartbeat Bill," to "Hear my heart, Save my life." We also printed bar graphs of the George Barna Poll depicting the 86% of Republicans who support the Heartbeat Bill and another majority—55%—of Democrats also supporting it!

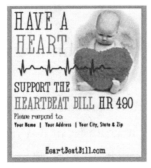

400,000 Faxes

We got word that while written correspondence and emails and are handled by staff, in many cases faxes are delivered directly to a congressman's desk. That news set the stage for our next campaign—faxes.

With the click of a button, people could send seven free faxes to then-House Speaker Ryan and key members or hundreds to every Republican in both their D.C. and local district offices. The result: 400,000 faxes![12]

We shut down Congressional faxes with members and staff complaining their lines were tied up and they could get nothing else done! Message delivered. They knew about our bill, and they knew people wanted it.

More Than 910,000 Emails

We then we turned to emails to thank cosponsors and encourage the others to sign on as a sponsor of the Heartbeat Bill and call for a vote. We sent 910,294 emails to Congress before members begged us to stop. If I had known we were so close to a million, I would have probably kept going. There wasn't a member of Congress or their staff who didn't know about the Heartbeat Bill's overwhelming support.

Between the emails and faxes, our supporters provided well over a million communications to members of Congress. The support for a Heartbeat Bill was demonstrated. Now we just needed a vote.

Dr. James Dobson of Family Talk stood with me from the beginning with a 2011 broadcast about the Heartbeat Bill before anyone outside of Ohio knew what it was. I was on his program again in 2019, when he played a clip of another show I recorded in 2017 from a congressional office in Washington, where I said, "We've waited 44 years. It's time to *do* what we've been marching about. This is the moment where we've got the Republican House, Senate, White House. We've got new Supreme Court justices being ushered in. This is our moment, and we had better seize it, because it may not come again."[13]

Sadly, that window closed when the Democrats took the majority of the House in 2018. The Republicans could have passed the Heartbeat Bill, but instead they chose to continue to regulate abortion, costing nearly a million children their lives each year. While Democrats will fight for death to the death, Republicans in leadership didn't even have the courage to call for a committee or floor vote to keep hearts beating.

Janet Porter presents Dr. James Dobson with a Heartbeat Bill Hero award. Dr. Dobson was there at the beginning of the battle in 2011.

The Republican Senate made the same choice, claiming to be bound by their self-imposed sixty-vote rule—a rule they can change whenever they please with a simple majority vote.[14] Just as the Senate removed the sixty-vote cloture requirement to confirm all executive and judicial nominations in 2013, requiring only 51 votes when Vice President Pence's broke the tie to confirm Betsy DeVos as Secretary of Education in 2017.[15] The vice president was also the tie-breaking vote to overturn a rule blocking states from defunding Planned Parenthood, a tax-related amendment, a banking regulation, and repealing some provisions of Obamacare.[16] If they can break their 60-vote rule for these, they can do it again to keep hearts beating.

Republicans in leadership need to muster the courage to turn away from the "right to regulate" movement that has been whispering in their ears and call for a vote on H.R. 490, the Heartbeat Bill. We already know seven out of ten Americans will stand with them as will nearly nine out of ten Republicans.

How do we get to a heartbeat vote in Congress? First, the Republicans must regain the majority. But to do that they must regain voters' trust. I believe it's time to bring back the Contract with America—with protecting babies with beating hearts first on the list of promises. If America knew that members of Congress were willing to go on record with promises they intend to *keep*, voters would have the confidence to give them another chance in office.

With the upcoming elections, it is grassroots who have the power to bring this to the forefront at both the state and federal level. When politicians come asking for your vote, ask for theirs—to cosponsor and call for passage of the state and federal Heartbeat Bill. While many on the campaign trail give lip service to "protecting life," it's time to get specific. We're not looking for them to support some vague protection or regulation *sometime in the future,* we want to keep hearts beating now! If you're ever going to get a promise from a politician, it is right before an election, so ask! Then we must hold them to those promises.

President Donald Trump has what the Republican Party most lacks—courage. If our anti establishment president called for the Heartbeat Bill to become law, it would pass in the U.S. House *and Senate* and be delivered to his desk for his signature. If ever there was a president who could get it done, it is President Donald Trump. The Left may say he's crazy, but the truth is he is both courageous and smart. Who else could have defunded Planned Parenthood without ever having to go through Congress?

If you want to see babies with beating hearts protected, President Trump is the only choice. He will fight for their lives while his opponent (no matter which announced Democrat it is) will force us to pay for abortion until birth and stack every court with pro-abortion judges. Nothing you can say about President Trump could convince me to vote to dismember innocent children by the millions. *Nothing.* We prayed for mercy and God's answer was authentic anti establishment President Trump, who loves babies and has the courage to do what it takes to protect them. As President Trump said at the 2020 March for Life, "Unborn children have never had a stronger defender in the White House."[17] He is right.

Passing the federal Heartbeat Bill can be done, and it can be done in the *next* election. After all, President Trump is the one who promised to "make America safe again."[18] Ask him to keep hearts beating as he makes his way across the country. Even if you can't be heard, you can make a sign or a banner to hold at the rallies. This is our moment and President Trump is the man. He also said, "No dream is too big. No challenge is too great. Nothing we want for our future is beyond our reach."[19]

I, for one, believe him.

CHAPTER 9

Courageous Truth

"The Party told you to reject the evidence of your eyes
and ears. It was their final, most essential command."
—George Orwell, 1984

We're used to *The New York Times* writing their "news" stories straight from Planned Parenthood's talking points. But now the *Times* is taking their legendary bias to a whole new level—attempting to rewrite *science*. The overwhelming public support for Heartbeat Bills has put the pro-abortion mob in a frenzy, frantic as they witnessed heartbeat laws pass in six states in the first 5 months of 2019. They lose on the issue of "heartbeat," and they don't like it.

That's because everyone knows what a heartbeat is, and everyone knows what it means. They had to do *something!* They can't let the word "heartbeat" kill their plans to kill babies with a heartbeat! Based on the results, I imagine their panicked pro-abortion "crisis meeting" went something like this:

> **Baby Killer 1**: We're losing ground and we're losing business on these wretched Heartbeat Bills! When people hear the word heartbeat they picture the product of conception as... *human*.
>
> **Baby Killer 2**: Let's just change the name of heartbeat to something people don't recognize, like we did by calling the baby a fetus.
>
> **Baby Killer 1**: Brilliant! What's the Latin word for heartbeat?
>
> **Baby Killer 3**: I'm tired of Latin, I was thinking about calling it "electrical pulse" or "cardiac activity..."
>
> **Baby Killer 1**: Perfect! But the name of the bill is "heartbeat," the scientific term we're describing is "heartbeat," will the press go along with denying science and ignoring the name and subject of the bill?
>
> **Baby Killer 2**: Of course, they'll do whatever we say! (followed by evil laughter and hand-wringing).

To avoid using the medical term "heartbeat" when referring to an unborn child, *The New York Times* has replaced "detectable heartbeat" with "embryonic pulsing."[1]

Funny, the pulsation that causes blood to circulate and makes a beating noise isn't called a heartbeat, just like the human being scheduled for abortion isn't called a baby. They simply took a page from their playbook that's worked for decades. The pro-abortion operatives lost the debate when it came to protecting a "child," so they merely slapped on a Latin label and called the baby a "fetus" to make it sound less like a living human being. It worked so well, why not just do it again?

A baby is a choice. A heartbeat is a pulse. Sounds like the talking points from George Orwell's Big Brother: "War is peace. Freedom is slavery. Ignorance is strength."[2]

Ohio Heartbeat Bill sponsor Ron Hood suggested *The New York Times* might follow suit and rename Neil Diamond's "Turn on Your Heartlight" theme to the movie *E.T.*: "Turn on Your Extraterrestrial Embryonic Pulselight." *Catchy*. It's funny, *The New York Times* never questioned the premise of an extraterrestrial having a beating heart, only fellow human beings.

We know the universally recognized indicator of life—*the heartbeat*—is currently detectable at around 6 weeks. Of course, we want to protect life from the moment the unique, distinct, individual life begins—at fertilization. But for the Supreme Court (and anyone else unsure about basic biology), there can no longer be any doubt that the human heartbeat indicates that a human life has, in fact, already begun. That's why those who want to kill babies with beating hearts have to pretend there is no baby and pretend there is no heart.

The Washington Post also got the memo to deny science, referring to the baby's heartbeat as "the electric pulsing of what will become a fetus's heart."[3] Wikipedia calls the heartbeat at 6 weeks' gestation "a group of cells with electrical activity."[4] *Newsweek's* version is "pulsing that becomes the fetus' heartbeat, often simply referred to as the 'fetal heartbeat.'"[5]

Yeah, it's often referred to as a heartbeat because that's what it *is*. National Public Radio (which is supported by our tax dollars) has also forbidden the use of "heartbeat" when describing Heartbeat Bills lest they accidentally humanize the child with a beating heart.[6] The science denying revisionism has even gone international. The UK-based *Guardian* declared, "The *Guardian* will no longer use the term 'Heartbeat Bill' in reference to the restrictive abortion bans that are moving through state legislatures in the US," because the legal killing of babies "is under serious threat for the first time in generations."[7] They claim Heartbeat Bills are "arbitrary bans that don't reflect fetal development." Think about that for a minute. If there wasn't a beating heart that we could detect, the bill wouldn't provide legal protection. It is precisely *because* of "fetal development" that they're running from science and running scared. Not surprisingly, their revisionism has now reached the Statehouse. I just got a call from a legislator in South Carolina asking for help with medical testimony since abortion lobbyists' new tactic is to claim that there is no "heartbeat," it is merely a "pulse."

By the way, here's a medical definition of *pulse*: "The rhythmic dilation of an artery that results from beating of the *heart*."[8]

The Endowment for Human Development states:

> By 7 weeks, the heart has 4 chambers. The pacemaker center is already well-established in the right atrium. The embryonic heart rate peaks at 7 weeks and now beats approximately 167–175 times per minute. This rate gradually declines to about 140 beats per minute at birth.[9]

If it beats like a heart, circulates blood like a heart, and has four chambers like a heart, guess what? It's a heart. And when it beats, we call that a "heartbeat."

When the abortion mill known as Preterm filed suit against our Ohio heartbeat law, bill co drafter Walter Weber, an attorney with the American Center for Law and Justice, pointed out how Judge Michael Barrett followed NARAL/Planned Parenthood's instruction manual to the letter:[10]

> **Don't call it a "heartbeat."** The slogan, "Abortion stops a beating heart," has long been an effective way to highlight the injustice and inhumanity of abortion. The Ohio Heartbeat Protection Act directly incorporates this notion—that abortion stops a beating heart—into law...which the abortion proponents hate. But they can't avoid the centrality of heartbeats to the law and thus to their constitutional challenge. In fact, the pro-abortion challengers admit that a heartbeat can be detected as early as six weeks of pregnancy. So a cardinal rule is to find some way of saying "heartbeat" without using that word. Thus, even though the law itself says "heartbeat," Judge [Barrett] uses only the far more technical jargon, "cardiac activity" (pp. 2–4, 8).
>
> **Don't even admit there is a "heart."** Judge [Barrett] does not even refer to the organ producing the "cardiac activity" as a heart. Instead, he refers (p. 3) to "cells that form the basis for the development of the heart later in gestation." In other words, there's no heart there, just some "cells" that are the "basis" for what will "later" develop into a heart. (Never mind that those cells are pumping blood!)

It appears they were under the misconception that George Orwell's *1984* was an instruction manual, taking literally the novel's words: "The Party told you to reject the evidence of your eyes and ears. It was their final, most essential command."[11]

Abraham Lincoln understood that changing words doesn't change reality. Lincoln asked, "How many legs has a calf?" "Four, of course," answered one of the delegates. ..."But," said Lincoln, "suppose we call a calf's tail a leg, how many legs will that calf have?" ..."Why, in that case, the calf would have five legs." "No, he would not," exclaimed Lincoln... "Our *calling* a calf's tail a leg, would not make it a leg."[12]

Calling a tail a leg doesn't make it a leg. Calling a heartbeat something else doesn't change scientific facts. Winning the debate begins by taking back the language. He who defines the terms wins.

When speaking at a high school in Pennsylvania, I asked a boy near the front of the class if he believed in the "right to choose." He emphatically said, "Yes." Then I started taking his belongings from his backpack and desk. His response was, "What are you doing? That's mine!"

I replied, "Oh, I was just exercising my 'right to choose'...*to take your stuff*."

Abortion really isn't about the "right to choose"; it's about *what's being chosen*. I learned from Dr. and Mrs. Willke, who taught those of us in the pro-life movement to specify what choice we're talking about when it comes to abortion by adding the words "to kill" after they say "right to choose." Don't let the people on your team use the abortion lobby's language whether it's on a conference call, standing at the podium at a press conference, or floor debate. Words matter.

You may have noticed I refuse to use the word "progressive" to describe the government takeover of everything. A more accurate term would be *regressive*—going back to the failed policies of socialism and government control of healthcare, business, the press, and speech. Sen. Bernie Sanders and the parade of socialists' slogan *should* be, "You make it, we take it." Their love of socialism could be cured by a single field trip to Venezuela, where socialism has worked so well people are eating rancid meat out of dumpsters.[13] Newsflash for the millennials who think socialism is a great idea—when the Berlin wall fell, *nobody* ran to the East.

Here's an idea, if Senator Sanders is looking for a catchy name to call his movement, why not the National Socialist Party? Oh, wait, that was already used *by Hitler*, the acronym was NAZI. Maybe he could borrow from the Union of Soviet *Socialist* Republics. Yes, the communists of the USSR called themselves socialists. Even Mayor Bloomberg understands that. In the February 19, 2020 Democrat debate, Bloomberg said, "We're not going to throw out capitalism. We tried that. Other countries tried that. It was called communism, and it just didn't work."

Communism is really just socialism at gunpoint. By the way, no politician who supports gun control (including Joe Biden) should get armed protection paid for by those they are trying to disarm.[14] The only reason why the government would want to disarm you after 244 years is because they intend to do something for which you would shoot them.

It's all about the words we use. If their slogan doesn't work, they just switch—*midstream*—to one that does. Like when too many "global warming" conferences kept getting snowed out—boom! It's now called "climate change"! Unlike "warming," which can be measured and debunked, they can now use each fluctuation in temperature and seasons to incite panic, pointing to their predetermined "cure"—less freedom, more taxes, and more government control. If repeating the slogan doesn't work, just make stuff up to scare people into your point of view like the signs at Glacier National Park, which stated, "The glaciers will all be gone by the year 2020."[15] *Oops.* Or when Rep. Alexandria Ocasio-Cortez (D-NY) said, "The world is going to end in 12 years if we don't address climate change."[16] I'm guessing Chicken Little already had dibs on "The sky is falling!"

Joseph Goebbels, Hitler's propaganda minister in Nazi Germany, summarized the pro-abortion strategy being utilized:

> Tell the masses a lie often enough and for long enough, sooner or later they will all believe it.[17]

It appears he got his idea from his boss, who wrote in *Mein Kampf* (*My Struggle*) the idea of the "*Große Lüge*"—the Big Lie. Adolf Hitler said:

> But the most brilliant propagandist technique will yield no success unless one fundamental principle is borne in mind constantly and with unflagging attention. It must confine itself to a few points and repeat them over and over. Here, as so often in this world, persistence is the first and most important requirement for success.[18]

First you speak a lie, then you repeat the lie, and repeat the lie, and repeat the lie, and eventually people believe it.

Today's lie: Babies aren't babies. Pretend they don't exist and keep screaming "Choice!" and you have abortion on demand. Say it for nearly 5 decades, and you have more than 60 million dead.

Yesterday's (*and today's*) lie: "Jewish people are bad." Say the lie often enough, and you have the Holocaust.

I included a chart from Dr. William Brennan's book *Dehumanizing the Vulnerable: When Word Games Take Lives*, in my book *True to*

Life. Brennan, a professor at the Saint Louis University School of Social Work, outlines how seven categories of people were characterized in the same eight ways in order to oppress them.[19]

Here's a sample of dehumanizing labels used against African Americans, European Jews, and "unwanted" unborn children to legitimize enslaving, gassing, and brutally dismembering fellow members of our human family. Every single victim had a heartbeat and a God-given right to life and liberty. Those rights were stripped from them, and it began with words that described them as a disease, inanimate object, waste product, non person, deficient human, non human, an animal, and a parasite.

1. Disease

- **African Americans:** "Free blacks in our country are... a contagion" (American Colonization Soc., 1815-1830).

- **Jewish People:** "Someday Europe will perish of the Jewish disease" (Joseph Goebbels, Nazi Propaganda Minister, 1939.)

- **"Unwanted" Unborn:** "Pregnancy when not wanted is a disease...in fact a venereal disease" (Professor Joseph Fletcher, 1979).

2. Inanimate Object

- **African Americans:** "A negro of the African race was regarded...as an article of property" (U.S. Supreme Court, 1857).

- **Jewish People:** "Transit material" (Portrayal of Jews dispatched to Nazi death camps, 1942-1944).

- **"Unwanted" Unborn:** "People's body parts (embryos) are their personal property" (Attorney Lori Andrews, 1986).

3. Waste Product

- **African Americans:** "The negro race is...a heritage of organic and psychic debris" (Dr. William English, 1903).

- **Jewish People:** "What shall we do with this garbage (Jews)" (Christian Wirth, extermination expert, 1942)?

- **"Unwanted" Unborn:** "An aborted baby is just garbage... just refuse" (Dr. Marti Kekomaki, 1980).

4. Nonperson

- **African Americans:** "In the eyes of the law...the slave is not a person" (Virginia Supreme Court Decision, 1858).

- **Jewish People:** "The Reichsgericht itself refused to recognize Jews...as persons in the legal sense" (1936 German Supreme Court Decision).

- **"Unwanted" Unborn:** "The word 'person,' as used in the 14th Amendment, does not include the unborn" (U.S. Supreme Court, 1973).

5. Deficient Human

- **African Americans:** "A subordinate and inferior class of beings" (U.S. Supreme Court on the status of Black people, 1857).
- **Jewish People:** "The inferior Jewish race" (Dr. Rudolph Ramm, Nazi medical educator, 1943).
- **"Unwanted" Unborn:** "The fetus, at most, represents only the potentiality of life" (U.S. Supreme Court, 1973).

6. Nonhuman

- **African Americans:** "The negro is not a human being" (Buckner Payne, Publisher, 1867).
- **Jewish People:** "Jews are undoubtedly a race, but not human" (Adolf Hitler, 1923).
- **"Unwanted" Unborn:** "A fetus is not a human being" (Rabbi Wolfe Keiman, 1984).

7. Animal

- **African Americans:** "The negro is one of the lower animals" (Professor Charles Carol, 1900).

- **Jewish People:** "The prisoners here are animals" (Nazi Anatomy Prof. Dr. August Hirt, 1942).

- **"Unwanted" Unborn:** "Like...a primitive animal that's poked with a stick" (Dr. Hart Peterson on fetal movement, 1985).

8. Parasite

- **African Americans:** "They (Negros) are parasites" (Dr. E.T. Brady, 1909).

- **Jewish People:** "The Jew is a parasite" (Nazi propaganda booklet, 1944).

- **Unwanted Unborn:** "The fetus is a parasite" (Prof. Rosalind Pollack Petchesky, 1984).[20]

Dr. Brennan points to historical evidence proving that social engineering always begins with verbal engineering. His research proves false the often-repeated children's adage, "Sticks and stones may break my bones but names will never hurt me." Quite the contrary, Dr. Brennan proves, "disparaging designations may inflict greater damage than physical blows and foster a climate of antagonism leading to the actual breaking of bones and other forms of violence."[21]

Just as the U.S. Supreme Court ruled blacks "non persons," they made the same colossal mistake when it came to the youngest members of the human family who had not yet changed their address to "outside the womb."

How does a nation get to the point where they allow the mass murder of children? We could always ask someone who knows:

> The receptivity of the masses is very limited, their intelligence is small, but their power of forgetting is enormous. In consequence of these facts, all effective propaganda must be limited to a very few points and must harp on these in slogans until the last member of the public understands what you want him to understand by your slogan. —Adolf Hitler[22]

The Left knows Hitler's premise of harping on slogans very well—especially the fake news. How long did we hear "Russia, Russia, Russia!" before it was "Ukraine, Ukraine, Ukraine!" and "Impeach, Impeach, Impeach!" How many decades have we heard "choice, choice, choice!"?

John Diggs, MD, pointed out in my film *Light Wins* that the Left's attempt to take over our language is nothing new.

> Political correctness, as people may not recall, is a term that was born in the Soviet Union, where thousands, if not millions, of people died because they tried to quash religion and because they tried to quash political dissent by sending people to gulags. Don't let this happen in America.[23]

Yet, bringing gulags to America is exactly what Bernie Sanders's paid campaign worker seeks to implement. In January 2020, just before being kicked off Twitter, Project Veritas exposed Sanders's Field Organizer, Kyle Jurek, revealing his plan.[24] "There's a reason Joseph Stalin had gulags, right?...gulags were actually meant for like reeducation...I feel as though there needs to be reeducation for a significant portion of our society."[25] Jurek added, "If people are going to fight back against the revolution," they need to be "eliminated."[26]

Jurek continued, "Greatest way to break a f---ing billionaire of their like, privilege and their idea that they're superior, go out and break rocks for twelve hours a day. You're a working-class person and you're going to learn what that means."[27]

As of this writing, Senator Sanders has refused to fire his pro-gulag communist worker.[28] Remember, actions are what you believe; everything else is political posturing.

All of this matters because truth matters. I began the journey to end abortion as an undergraduate in college. As president of Students for Life, I made sure the issue was front and center in many creative ways (covered in my book *True to Life*). But in today's environment, that freedom of speech and expression would have been choked out before it began.

This matters because our pro-life leaders in training are being beaten down before they can say the word heartbeat, uh, *embryonic pulse.* Conservative radio host Dennis Prager, founder of PragerU, defines *politically incorrect* as "a truth that people on the left find too painful to acknowledge and therefore do not want expressed."[29] Greg Lukianoff, President of the Foundation for Individual Rights in Education, noted that "highly restrictive speech codes are now the norm on campus, not the exception."[30]

Words are beliefs you can see and hear. When words are suppressed, beliefs are crushed, along with the people who have them.

It used to be that college campuses welcomed the free exchange of ideas. That freedom is our nation's lifeblood, as the Supreme Court ruled in *Sweezy v. New Hampshire*:

> Teachers and students must always remain free to inquire... otherwise our civilization will stagnate and die.[31]

Schools and corporations are now dictating to their subjects, er, *students* and *employees,* who is allowed to speak and what they are allowed say. They have constructed committees from which permission must be granted with speech police and Orwellian tribunals to enforce infractions and silence dissent.[32]

College campuses have become a place where everyone is a victim, unless you're a pro-life Christian, Jewish, or a heterosexual white male. It's where incessant "offense" drives people into "safe spaces"—a grown-up version of "the fort" made with a security blanket and a cardboard box—to protect their Leftist opinions from the uncomfortable challenges of logic and facts.

If any of these university leaders ever bothered to read our Constitution, they would find that there is no right in it to be an "unoffended listener." The freedom of speech was specifically put in the Constitution to protect unpopular speech—and prevent the government from shutting down dissent. Shutting down dissent is the very *intention* of speech codes, which makes the Left's agenda mandatory and defines biblical and scientific truth as "hate." Truth is hate for those who hate the truth.

What do you do when those who refuse to march in lock step won't sit down and shut up? Protest, threaten, and disinvite any "unauthorized" speaker with the courage to disagree and face the Left's vocal and violent intolerance. Then, shield people from ever coming into contact with contrary views by ostracizing opponents to small and restricted "free speech zones,"[33] pushing pro-lifers, conservatives, and Christians to no-man's land where they won't be seen or heard.

They then issue what's known as "trigger warnings" to keep people away from these speech ghettos lest students experience an uncomfortable challenge to their state-sanctioned views. These publicly posted warnings are the modern-day equivalent of shouting "Unclean!" outside the leper colony of those who refuse to recite the party line.

Why does this matter? Speech codes not only silence the case for life, they also lead to the criminalization of Christianity. How? For starters, they change "evangelize" to "proselytize," a toxic way to depict the Great Commission in order to prevent it. When I was writing *The Criminalization of Christianity*, my assistant asked me what that word meant. Here's the response I sent her, recorded in my book:

> Proselytize is the negative code word used to prevent us from spreading the Gospel. They use it to silence Christians and penalize anyone with the audacity to tell them how to keep from going to hell. When you see it, know that they are evil.[34]

Think that's an exaggeration? When I lived in Hollywood, Florida the city commission tried to outlaw Christian speech by calling it...*proselytizing*. They, too, designated a no-man's land where Christians would be forced to go in order to speak. After a quick call to Liberty Counsel to ensure they would represent me (for free), I testified before the commission telling them if they dared push Christians to the back of the bus I would be the first one to sue them for violating my constitutionally pro-tected freedom of speech and freedom of religion. My staff and I were the only ones who stood against it, but because we showed up they backed down. The price of freedom really is eternal vigilance.[35]

I thought about that as I watched my sister-in-law's Christian dance company performance about the true meaning of Christmas on Holly-wood Beach's stage—a message the city had tried to outlaw just a few years earlier. The only way to keep our freedom is to use it.

Thankfully, the voice for freedom is being heard. The University of Chicago rightly issued a statement advocating freedom of expression that said, "It is not the proper role of the University to attempt to shield indi-viduals from ideas and opinions they find unwelcome, disagreeable, or even deeply offensive."[36]

The university also issued this statement to incoming freshmen, alert-ing them that free speech was still exercised on campus:

> Our commitment to academic freedom means that we do not support so-called "trigger warnings," we do not cancel invited speakers because their topics might prove controver-sial, and we do not condone the creation of intellectual "safe spaces" where individuals can retreat from ideas and perspec-tives at odds with their own. Fostering the free exchange of ideas reinforces a related University priority—building a campus that welcomes people of all backgrounds.[37]

Thanks to the courage of those who refused to bow to the bullies, free speech is making a comeback. Fifty-five institutions including Princeton,

Purdue, Columbia, Georgetown, and American universities as well as the University of North Carolina at Chapel Hill have adopted the Chicago statement on free speech or a significantly similar one.[38]

This is a good start, but the Orwellian police state has reached its tentacles beyond campuses, corporations, and city government, into our conversations. Even cowardly conservatives have sanitized their speech to comply with the PC mandates of the tyrannical Left. If you celebrate the day when the Savior of the world came to earth in order to die for our sins with a "holiday party," I'm talking to you.

Courage Is the Key

If you faint in the day of adversity, your strength is small (Proverbs 24:10).

The rewriting of science, the agenda-pushing slogans, and the speech codes are really about bullying us into submission. In addition to your lunch money, the baby-killing bullies want you off the playground entirely. And the only way to deal with a bully is to stand up to him and not back down. The key to victory is courage. When Georgia passed their heartbeat law, in a last-ditch effort to stop them, the pro-abortion extremists called in the big guns—the bullies from Hollywood.

In an effort to justify her two abortions, actress Alyssa Milano joined Hollywood celebrities—including Jason Bateman, Ben Stiller, Christina Applegate, and Don Cheadle—in threatening to boycott Georgia because of their heartbeat law (scheduled to go into effect January 1,

2020).[39] Abortion activist Amy Schumer, Hugo Chavez groupie Sean Penn, and actress Mia Farrow signed a letter to Governor Kemp calling the Heartbeat Bill he signed "so evil."[40]

Actor Dean Cain said, "And now we have Hollywood coming in and saying, 'Listen, we want you to have our values. We're going to tell you what you should do and how you should do it in your state.' I don't think they understand civics very well...it ain't gonna happen."[41] Cain added, "Hollywood pretending to be the bastion of moral superiority is an absolute joke."[42] When *Variety* magazine asked me for a quote about the celebrity pushback, here's what I told them:

> We didn't pass Heartbeat Laws to impress Hollywood; we passed them to protect babies with beating hearts. So many states want to keep hearts beating that those who want to boycott them will soon run out of places in which to work. No one is worried about it—there will soon be thousands more actors, producers, and directors because their lives were protected instead of killed.[43]

Governor Kemp didn't back down to the bullies. He gladly signed the Georgia heartbeat law despite their threats. Kemp said: "I understand that some folks don't like this new law. I'm fine with that...We value and protect innocent life—even though that makes C-list celebrities squawk."[44] I really like this guy.

Kemp said in Georgia, "We stand up for those who are unable to speak for themselves."[45] He blamed the hysteria on an "agenda-driven media," "talking heads and the Twitter trolls," adding, "Our best days are ahead in this great state."[46]

Then abortion activist Alyssa Milano and Bette Midler called for a sex strike until Georgia's Heartbeat Bill is overturned.[47] Finally, the pro-abortion activists are embracing abstinence. Abby Johnson thinks we should broaden Milano's sex strike to the schools, renaming abstinence education "sex strike education"—something the liberals, apparently, now embrace.[48] Johnson stated, "It...demonstrates that sex can equal a baby, and confirms what pro-lifers have been saying for years: that humans are not wild animals and we can control our sexual impulses."[49]

Did Georgia suffer for passing their heartbeat law? *Nope.* While there were multiple threats to boycott Georgia's film industry following the passage of the bill, it remains "business as usual."[50] Nearly 40 movies and television shows were scheduled to film in Georgia the same year the Heartbeat Bill was signed—all their threats to boycott fizzled.[51] The "sex-strike" also had no effect. Turns out no one really cares whether Alyssa Milano or Bette Midler have sex.

After Netflix threatened to boycott Georgia, their "shares fell 17 percent following quarterly results...and the U.S. subscriber count fell for the first time in a decade.[52] Netflix "reported a loss of 126,000 domestic paid subscribers compared with analysts' expectations for a 352,000 gain"—the first time they lost paid subscribers in the last 8 years.[53]

Boycott Netflix

Some suggest this huge loss isn't entirely due to pro-life backlash. I agree—people are also leaving Netflix because their programs are terrible. Netflix programming includes a depiction of Jesus as a homosexual, the Virgin Mary as an adulteress, and Lucifer as a cool guy a priest turns to for help.[54,55] That's reason enough to boycott them, but they are also using your movie money to fight Heartbeat laws in court. Following the passage of Georgia's Heartbeat Bill, Ted Sarandos, Netflix's chief content officer, told *Variety*: "We will work with the ACLU and others to fight it in court."[56]

Faith2Action joined the official boycott of Netflix. Unless you want your money used to fund the court battle against babies and horrific, blasphemous programs, I'd encourage you to join it, too. Here's yet another reason: instead of watching movies, let's end abortion!

Not backing down to the bullies isn't just for lawmakers, lobbyists, and pro-life leaders; it's for all of us. If the truth is worth speaking, it is worth fighting for. I took a poll on a conference call recently where I asked, "How many of you have received death threats for your biblical stand?" Everyone on the call answered in the affirmative. That's when I knew I was in the right company. If you take a stand, especially an effective one, you will see pushback.

Now even wearing a red "Make America Great Again" hat sparks hostility from people who, apparently, don't want to make America great again. I wear my Trump 2020 shirt as much as I can—especially when traveling. When a woman at the Cleveland airport announced her disapproval, it gave me the opportunity to announce to hundreds waiting for a plane, "We're gonna make America great again!" I wore my Trump shirt while my husband and I were in Key West recently, and received countless high-fives and very few disapproving looks. It's a great litmus test. When a souvenir shop owner asked, "That's sarcastic, right?" I replied, "No, I use it to determine the stores in which to spend my money. Thanks for your help!"

If hostile Trump-haters approach you, just have the video on your phone ready to document what happens. Why? Reagan answered that question, "Evil is powerless if the good are unafraid."[57]

I've also learned that sometimes the bullies do more than talk.

In 1994, I drove a Porsche. I bought it used and spent my life savings—$8,000—on it. On the back I put a bumper sticker—*yes, I put a bumper sticker on a Porsche*—which read, "Abortion? Pick on Someone Your Own Size." I don't really recommend that one, because some people see that as an invitation.

That was when I was spokesperson for the state Right to Life and had files full of hate mail and death threats. I even had someone with a violent criminal record stalking me. I never paid attention to any of it. I lived alone but had no fear whatsoever. Then one night I heard a noise I thought sounded like someone walking on leaves outside my garage. I got up and turned on the light, but didn't see anything. Thinking it must have been my "DeWine for Senate" sign flapping in the wind, I went back to bed.

As I backed my car out of the garage the next morning, I saw a trail of fire behind me. When I turned around, I saw the fire was coming from under my hood, which was now flaming and billowing smoke. I jumped out as my beloved car burned. I called the fire department but was told they were already on their way.

The *Columbus Dispatch* put the story on page 5-C next to: "Jury Ponders Rights to Glow-in-the-Dark Lingerie"—*you know, just like they would do if there was an attack on an abortion clinic.*

Abortion foe must deal with violent disagreement

Janet L. Folger stands next to her burned-out 1987 Porsche 924S, which erupted in flames at her Columbus home. Fire inspectors suspect tampering by someone opposing her work as lobbyist and spokeswoman for the Ohio Right to Life Society.

But the *Cleveland Plain Dealer* made it a front-page story with the headline, "Right to Life Leader's Car Sabotaged—Odds Are Fire Is Connected to Abortion Issue, Police Say."

I remember feeling fearful for a few weeks until I got back to a place of trusting God who promised to "fulfill the number of [our] days" (Exodus 23:26). In retrospect, I think the attack made me even *more* pro-life—beginning with my *own*. It also made me a stauncher supporter of our Second Amendment.

We have to quit cowering to the threats of the hate-spewing bullies including those wearing pink hats:

> F--- you. F--- you...Yes, I'm angry. Yes, I'm outraged. Yes, I have thought an awful lot about blowing up the White House. —Madonna[58]
>
> I'm a nasty woman, a loud, vulgar, proud woman. —Ashley Judd[59]

Just the kind of woman every little girl longs to be when she grows up. I can't write the other things she said, nor can I describe the profanity-laced and graphic signs. The Women's March was filled with vulgarity, people dressed as body parts, foul language, hate, and threats of violence—exactly like *none* of the pro-life marches.

Here is just one example from feminist activist and screenwriter Krista Suh:

> My dream is that a grandmother will give her granddaughter her p---y hat and say, "I wore this on January 21, 2017."[60]

And who can't picture their grandmother saying those words? What planet are these people from?

Tamika Mallory, co president of the Women's March, appeared on *The View* and defended her friendship with Nation of Islam leader Louis Farrakhan,[61] who praised Hitler as a "very great man"[62] and compared Jewish people to "termites."[63]

Funny, Twitter didn't see fit to censor Farrakhan's horrific anti-Semitic tweet, which remained posted for almost a year.

Farrakhan's anti-Semitic rhetoric is not unlike the weekly anti-Jewish rant of "the Squad" in Congress including Democratic representative Ilhan Omar of Minnesota, who constantly displays her anti-Jewish hatred for all the world to see.[64] A fierce contender for the anti-Semitic bigot award is Rep. Rashida Tlaib of Michigan who actually said, "There's always kind of a calming feeling, I tell folks, when I think of the Holocaust, and the tragedy of the Holocaust."[65]

"More than six million Jews were murdered during the Holocaust; there is nothing 'calming' about that fact," declared House Minority Whip Steve Scalise (R-LA). Adding that the heinous anti-Semitic comments are "now the norm for their caucus" and called on Speaker Pelosi "to take swift action and make it clear that these vile comments have no place in Congress,"[66] None was taken, signaling Democrat approval of the continuous anti-Semitic assault.

It was back in January, 2019[67] that Rep. Tlaib publicly declared her mission to "Impeach the motherf---er."[68] Nasty enough for you? The reason they despise President Trump is because he is pro-life and pro-Israel. My two favorite things about him.

The antidote is truth, but the key is courage. What God told Joshua, He is telling us: "Be strong and very courageous" (Joshua 1:7a). We see the results of not standing up to the bullies every day. They now want submissive subjects who beg permission to speak. They want control of the words we say while they invent new language to alter its meaning, pushing us into speech ghettos where we can't be heard.

In order to see victory, we must first take back the language and the freedom to speak it. We must recognize their tactics and their propaganda's deadly destination. We must rip up the PC-approved lists and never—*I mean never*—submit to them. It is not "polite"; it is evil. A heartbeat is not a "pulse" and a child is not a "choice."

To those reading my book for opposition research—first, thanks for the contribution; you're going to hate what we do with the money you just spent. Here's the message to run back to your baby-killing buddies: We're not backing down to foul-mouthed women in pink hats. We're not concerned with C-list celebrities or campus, corporate, or government speech police. We don't need your permission to speak, and we're not asking for it. We will speak the truth even when your PC list forbids it—and we're not going to stop.

No matter what hats you wear, no matter what language you use, no matter what threats you make, we will use our freedoms to defend their lives. We will speak the truth until it prevails. We will end abortion. Not sometime in the distant future. We're gonna end abortion—*now*. Take a look around. The end of abortion has already begun.

CHAPTER 10

Behind the Mask: Greed and Racism

"More than 20,000,000 Black lives have been lost to abortion—more than the entire Black population in 1960."
—Catherine Davis, President of the Restoration Project[1]

How can you tell the difference between an abortion mill and a pregnancy resource center? That was a question I was asked while debating some lovely ladies peddling an at-home abortion kit on national television. I brought up the fact that for every abortion mill charging to kill her child, there were several pregnancy centers offering women a free choice she and her child could "live with."

The mic was given to an angry member of the audience who accusingly said, "I've seen *60 Minutes*, I've seen *20/20*—you're talking about those *fake clinics* that try to *trick* women into having their child."

I responded, "If you're looking through the yellow pages, and you're not sure whether you're looking at a pregnancy resource center or an abortion facility, here's a good rule of thumb: If you see any reference to VISA or Mastercard, *that's abortion*. Our services are *free*."

That comment was cut from the program when it aired. Color me surprised.

The abortionists are charging hundreds of dollars for every baby they kill while pro-life advocates are saving babies for free—at great cost to *pro-life people*, not pregnant women.[2] If you knew nothing else, you would be able to tell who is really "pro-women" just by knowing that fact.

I just spoke for the Community Pregnancy Center in Middletown, Ohio, run by Ohio Heartbeat Bill sponsor Representative Candice Keller. They offer diapers, infant and toddler clothes, coats, shoes, furniture, and more. And like other pregnancy centers across America, everything they do is *free*. They also offer counseling, training, adoption assistance, and parenting classes where Moms2B and Dads2B earn credits for items like cribs and strollers.

Other centers like Lori's House near Branson, Missouri, founded by Jim and Lori Bakker, provide a beautiful home, giving pregnant mothers and their children a safe and loving place to live. They provide meals, child care, jobs, and education—*all free*.

Does anyone know of a single abortion clinic doing *anything* like that? No, they're too busy killing babies for profit.

Carol Everett was part-owner of several abortion mills near Dallas. In the documentary *Blood Money*, Everett admits her goal was to sell abortions in schools through sex education.[3] According to Ed Szymkowiak, National Director of STOPP International, a division of American Life League, "Planned Parenthood's entire business relies upon sex education, which corrupts young minds and increases youth promiscuity." He said,

"This in turn establishes a customer base of contraception users, and eventually abortion clients."[4]

It's not just leaders in the pro-life movement who've discovered this. Arizona House Speaker Rusty Bowers, a Republican, attacked his state's proposed comprehensive sex-education curricula, saying they are "grooming children to be sexualized" with their "drawings of people engaged in sex acts."[5] Bowers said Planned Parenthood has "created the business plan of hell" by developing programs that lead to high-risk behaviors and pregnancy, which lead students back to their doors for STD treatments and abortions.[6]

Everett confirms that assessment. "So they would turn to us...we would give them a low-dose birth control pill they would get pregnant on or a defective condom," she said, adding that they "bought the *cheapest* condoms" because their "goal was three to five abortions from every girl between the ages of thirteen and eighteen."[7]

Everett explained, "Who does she call when she's pregnant? She calls us. We're the experts. And we were ready. We used a script to overcome every single objection. That's what sales is—overcome the objection, and you get the order—in this case, the abortion."[8] She said the abortion "counselor" is "really a telemarketer" who is "selling abortions over the telephone."[9]

Former sex educator Monica Cline, who worked with Planned Parenthood for 10 years, agrees: "The sex education grooms them for promiscuity. Grooms them for STD treatment, and grooms them for abortion."[10] Cline told how they were instructed to identify with student's fears, "Say, 'you're just a teenager, the last thing you want is a baby.' 'Your parents are probably going to be so mad at you. We can take care of this for you, it's not a problem.'"[11] Cline added that Planned Parenthood employees "always went to the extreme," saying, "If we don't do this for this girl, she will live in poverty. Or her parents will commit acts of violence."[12]

Planned Parenthood operates 45% of all abortion clinics.[13] Their 2017 annual report revealed Planned Parenthood performs more than 320,000 abortions per year,[14] killing thirty-seven babies each hour. That's one baby every 98 seconds around the clock, bringing in annual profits of nearly $100 million.[15] President Trump pulled the plug on $60 million that went to Planned Parenthood through Title X funding.[16] Yet taxpayers are still forced to pay the abortion giant about a half-billion dollars of our hard-earned money every year—something even Republicans in Congress have refused to change.[17] That takes Planned Parenthood to over a billion dollars in annual revenue.[18] Not a bad profit for a "nonprofit."[19]

And do you want a glimpse into how they're spending that blood money? They give it to those who will vote to fuel their abortion frenzy with our tax dollars. Planned Parenthood announced they expect to spend $45 million or more in the 2020 election season in hopes of unseating President Trump and flipping the narrowly controlled Republican Senate.[20] They want more people to enable them and turn a blind eye to even confessions of crimes caught on video.

You see, Planned Parenthood and the abortion industry aren't just making money killing babies; they are making money selling the organs of those babies. In an undercover video released by the Center for Medical Progress, Dr. Mary Gatter, a Planned Parenthood Medical Director, is seen saying she wanted to charge enough for aborted baby organs to afford an expensive sports car. The undercover video captures her telling actors posing as fetal tissue buyers, "I want a Lamborghini."[21]

Gatter haggled over the price she would charge for intact organs from the aborted babies, making sure her compensation was commensurate to that of other Planned Parenthood clinics.[22] As if this weren't horrifying enough, Gatter discussed changing the method of abortion from a vacuum aspirator to what she called a "less crunchy" method to retrieve the aborted baby's organs intact.[23]

In the seventh video the Center for Medical Progress released, Holly O'Donnell, a former technician for a biotech company called StemExpress, described the organ harvesting or "procurement" conducted at Planned Parenthood's clinic in San Jose, California. Her supervisor called her over to take a look at what she described as "the most gestated fetus and the closest thing to a baby I've seen."[24]

> My supervisor said, "I want to show you something"...And she just taps the heart, and it starts beating. And I'm sitting here and I'm looking at this fetus, and its heart is beating, and I don't know what to think.[25]

O'Donnell added, "It had a face...its nose was very pronounced; it had eyelids, and its mouth was pronounced."[26]

Like they were in some kind of ghoulish science-fiction movie, O'Donnell's next task was to help her supervisor procure the baby's brain.[27]

O'Donnell was told what to do next:

> "OK, so what you do is you go through the face"...And she takes the scissors and she makes a small incision right here [pointing to her chin], and goes, I would say, to maybe a little

> bit to the mouth. And she's like, OK, can you go the rest of the way? And I'm like, "Yes." And I didn't want to do this.[28]
>
> And so she gave me the scissors and told me that I have to cut down the middle of the face. And I can't even, like, describe, like, what that feels like. And I remember picking it up and finishing going through the rest of the face, and Jessica picking up the brain and putting it in the container... and I'm just sitting there like "What did I just do?" And that was the moment I knew I couldn't work with the company anymore.[29]

In another Center for Medical Progress video removed by YouTube, Planned Parenthood executives made jokes about eyeballs from aborted babies "rolling down into their laps."[30]

How will history view this? How has history viewed the killing of innocent human beings in the past? The International Military Tribunal at Nuremberg answers the question.

Killing Jews was not only "legal" in World War II Germany; it was ordered. Yet the judges at Nuremberg rejected the "I was just following orders" defense.[31]

Rudolf Höss, the commandant at Auschwitz, testified:

> Don't you see, we SS men were not supposed to think about these things; it never even occurred to us...We were all so trained to obey orders without even thinking that the thought of disobeying an order would simply never have occurred to anybody, and somebody else would have done

> just as well if I hadn't...I really never gave much thought to
> whether it was wrong. It just seemed a necessity.[32]

The Nuremberg judges declared it was impossible for the defendants to "not know that murdering civilians was both illegal and immoral."[33] Twenty Nazi leaders were found guilty by the court, four of whom were executed.[34]

If it's ever unclear about which side of history to be on, choose God's side. God's side will always be the right side of history.

But the abortion lobby would rather forget about history, forget about what's impossible not to know—because there's money to be made! A StemExpress flyer distributed to Planned Parenthood clinics promised "financial profits" and fiscal rewards for clinics that supplied aborted fetal tissue.[35] After all, Gatter needs to be able to afford her Lamborghini.[36] StemExpress' annual revenue is a reported $4.5 million.[37] Where do those profits go? It's not just for sports cars; they are padding the pockets of pro-abortion politicians who enable all they do. As mentioned, Planned Parenthood plans to spend $45 million or more to defeat President Trump and help death-loving Democrats take over the U.S. Senate.[38]

Catherine Davis, President of the pro-life Restoration Project, said, "One of the physicians in [a] deposition said she didn't care if the videos were released—she did nothing wrong. They profited not only from those paying for the abortion, not only from the Medicaid funds they billed the government for the abortion—they profited again from selling the parts of the children they aborted."[39] Much like the Nazis profited from the bodies of the Jewish victims they murdered.[40]

The sale or purchase of human fetal tissue is a felony punishable by up to 10 years in prison or a fine of up to $500,000. In fact, U.S. Code 280G-2 states, "It shall be unlawful for any person to knowingly acquire, receive, or otherwise transfer any human fetal tissue for valuable consideration."[41]

Investigations into the selling of fetal tissue have yielded no indictments. Yet investigative journalists David Daleiden and Sandra Merritt, who posed as fetal tissue buyers in the secretly recorded undercover videos, are facing fifteen felony charges for invasion of privacy.[42] The videos exposed the abortion industry for what it is. It should come as no surprise that the California Federal Court is censoring hundreds of hours of new information from being released through an injunction resulting from Planned Parenthood and National Abortion Federation lawsuits.[43]

While we save babies for free, the abortionists kill them for cash, rip out their organs, and sell them for more cash. But there's more behind the mask of "choice" than greed. Its repugnant roots are in racism.

The Real Racists

Guess who said this: "We don't want the word to get out that we want to exterminate the Negro population."[44]

A. President Donald Trump

B. Congressman Steve King

C. Planned Parenthood founder Margaret Sanger

The answer is C. This isn't a misquote from *The New York Times* like what they used against Congressman Steve King. There is an actual letter signed by Margaret Sanger in 1939 to fellow eugenicist Clarence Gamble describing what she called the "Negro Project." She said:

> We should hire three or four colored ministers, preferably with social-service backgrounds, and with engaging personalities. The most successful educational approach to the Negro is through a religious appeal. We don't want the word to go out that we want to exterminate the Negro population, and the minister is the man who can straighten out that idea if it ever occurs to any of their more rebellious members.[45]

Did you see that? Sanger wanted to "exterminate the Negro population," and she wanted black ministers to help her do it. It seems she thought if her organization could hire black ministers with "engaging personalities," they could manipulate the black community into thinking, as Nazi propagandist Goebbels said, they are acting on their own accord—perhaps even in their own best interests—when they decided to get abortions. That's how propaganda works best, Goebbels said, "When those who are being manipulated are confident they are acting on their own free will."[46]

Sanger got her wish. Her "Negro Project" has already exterminated 25% of the African-American population since 1973—killing more of the black community than violent crime, heart disease, AIDS, and cancer combined.[47]

Did you catch that? A *quarter* of the black population has already been wiped out, thanks to Planned Parenthood! Killed at the design of Planned Parenthood's founder who sought to exterminate the entire "Negro population." Where is the outrage?

If you believe black lives matter, it's time to stand up against the most lethal form of racism in America—abortion. Sanger knew the people she wanted to exterminate, and those who followed her made sure the crosshairs were right on the target: today 79% of Planned Parenthood's abortion facilities are in minority neighborhoods.[48]

Not surprisingly, Sanger was also a featured speaker at a meeting of the women's branch of the Ku Klux Klan, which she wrote about in her autobiography.[49] Why not? They shared the same hatred of black and minority communities. I'm sure the KKK would have held Sanger in high esteem; after all, while 3,446 black Americans were lynched in the United States between 1882 and 1968,[50] that number is surpassed every 3 days by abortion. On Sanger's board was one of her most trusted advisors, Lothrop Stoddard, Ph.D., who praised the Nazi sterilization law[51] and wrote a book titled *The Rising Tide of Color Against White World-Supremacy*.

Sanger, who sought a "cleaner race" by "weeding out the unfit,"[52] advocated requiring every American family to submit a request to the government to have a child. She told *America Weekly* in 1934 that it had "become necessary to establish a system of birth permits."[53]

She would have been right at home in communist China. Abortion is Planned Parenthood's priority. Don't believe me? Ask their director. Oh wait, she was fired. Planned Parenthood Director Leana Wen said she was terminated in July of 2019 because she "did not prioritize abortion enough."[54]

During her testimony for the Ohio Heartbeat Bill, Catherine Davis of the Restoration Project made the chilling statement that "more than

20,000,000 black lives have been lost to abortion—more than the entire black population in 1960."[55]

Mark Crutcher, president of Life Dynamics, said: "What the Ku Klux Klan could only dream about, the abortion industry is accomplishing."[56] Consider the following facts:

- Although black Americans make up 13% of the U.S. population, black women have more than 35% of the abortions.[57]
- A black baby is three times more likely to be killed in the womb than a white baby.[58]
- Almost as many African-American babies are aborted as are born.[59]
- In cities like New York, more black babies are killed by abortion than are born.[60]
- Every week more African Americans are killed by abortion than all the people killed in the Vietnam War.[61]

Where Is the Outrage?

Those who oppose conservatives are constantly calling anyone who disagrees with them "racist." Yet the greatest and most lethal form of racism is abortion.

Don't believe me? Ask Jesse Jackson. He said, "Abortion is black genocide."[62]

I ran into Mr. Jackson at an airport several years ago and asked him about it. "Rev. Jackson, do you remember when you called abortion 'black genocide'?"

He replied, "It can be."

To which I responded, "How is it that you now *favor* even partial-birth abortion?"

He claimed he didn't.

"Then you'll support the bill to ban it?"

He had to go. You see, Jesse Jackson knows in his heart that abortion kills children—and disproportionately kills black children. But in order to run for president on the Democratic ticket, one has to kiss the bloody ring and pledge allegiance to child killing. That is what Jackson did.

Rev. Jackson, if you're reading this I would also remind you of another thing you said, "What happens to the mind of a person and the moral fabric of a nation that accepts the aborting of the life of a baby without a pang of conscience?"[63]

And something Jesus said, "For what shall it profit a man, if he shall gain the whole world, and lose his own soul?" (Mark 8:36 KJV).

The other side of the story is that when Michael Schiavo was starving his estranged wife, Terri Schiavo, to death (with a public girlfriend on the side), I was there with many others fighting for her life. I had heard that Jesse Jackson made a statement in the media in favor of Terri—and so I called a number I found on a website.

Emphasizing the number of television cameras and press outside the hospice where they were starving Terri, I asked Rev. Jackson if he would come and help us. To his credit, he did.[64]

He came and prayed with the family in the same way I would have imagined Rev. Jerry Falwell might have done. His prayer was biblical, comforting, hopeful, and seemingly *heartfelt*. He then went before the press to be a voice for the woman whose voice—*and life*—was taken from her. Thank you, Rev. Jackson. I will never forget it.

Rev. Jackson called me on his way to the airport. I thanked him again for coming, and at the end of the call Jesse Jackson said, "I love you."

I replied, "I love you, too."

I hung up in a daze, telling Terri's mother, "I just told Jesse Jackson that I loved him. What alternative world are we living in?" It's a world where those who have been your friend—and then your enemy—can be your friend again. With God all things are possible.

Always keep in mind there is no one outside God's reach—*no one*. Just because they are fiercely working against you doesn't mean that God isn't moving in their hearts. When I testified for the Heartbeat Bill in the Ohio Senate Committee in 2018, a pro-abortion Democrat Senator came up to me afterward and asked me the closest thing to "What must I do to be saved?" that I have ever experienced. This woman said she used to go to a Baptist church, but after becoming a champion of abortion in the Senate, asked "How can I find my way back to God?" I didn't doubt her sincerity—she had nothing to gain by pretending; in fact, talking to me didn't win her any points with her pro-abortion friends. I prayed for her in the hallway, while a fellow Democrat senator walked by rolling her eyes. I followed up with the name of a respected Baptist church in her area, as she requested, and encouraged her to start by obeying God—and casting a vote against the shedding of innocent blood. She did not. *Yet.*

Pastor Stephen Broden, of the National Black Pro-Life Coalition, and Dr. Johnny Hunter, of Life Education and Resource Network, were among the African-American leaders who came to the Ohio Statehouse to support Ohio's Heartbeat Bill, which would protect unborn babies with a detectable heartbeat—no matter their race.

I watched these leaders lobby African-American legislators, handing them a copy of the documentary film *Maafa 21: Black Genocide in the 21st Century*. My heart broke as I heard Pastor Broden plead with black Democrats in the Ohio Senate to "be a voice for our race." They sought a champion, but found none.

I recently spoke at Merciful Ministries, a black church near Detroit, Michigan. I told them about the black pastors who pleaded with Ohio legislators, saying, "They are annihilating our race." Those legislators refused to stand and fight, but in Michigan they don't have to wait for elected officials. As I told the congregation, the people can rise up and be the voice for the voiceless with petitions that will bring the Heartbeat Bill to a vote. Dozens from the congregation came forward to become "heartbeat heroes," committing to get a thousand signatures each. When the signatures are gathered, it will go before the state legislature, where it requires a simple majority vote to become law (bypassing a veto of their pro-abortion governor).

One of the most powerful pro-life tools since *The Silent Scream* is the movie my friend Mark Crutcher produced, *Maafa 21*. It's the DVD pastors handed out in the Ohio Senate documenting the racist beginnings of abortion and the continuation of that racist agenda to this day. It was shown on Capitol Hill, and several staff members from the Congressional Black Caucus responded to the invitation to the viewing. One left in tears. She said she came with one "mindset" but left with a changed life. She hadn't realized just how committed the abortion movement was to the elimination of her race.

And while we're on the subject of racism, there is another heralded hero of the Left who was also a real white supremacist. His name was Charles Darwin.

The full title of Darwin's famous evolution book is *On the Origin of Species by Means of Natural Selection, or the Preservation of Favoured Races in the Struggle for Life*. So what are the favored races? Which race is going to occupy the inferior place nearest the ape, and which is going to occupy the superior position furthest away?

Notorious racist Madison Grant used Darwin's theory to promote what he called "scientific racism." Grant spoke of the survival of the "white master race" in his book *The Passing of the Great Race,* which was translated into German. In 1930, Grant received a letter from an aspiring politician, saying this book is "my bible."[65] The man was Adolf Hitler.

Margaret Sanger shared the same eugenic philosophy as Hitler. Sanger's *Birth Control Review* ran articles by Nazi doctors including "Eugenical Sterilization: An Urgent Need" by Ernst Rudin, head of the Nazi Society for Racial Hygiene and director of the Kaiser Wilhelm Institute, where Josef Mengele, who performed horrific "medical" experiments on Auschwitz prisoners, was employed.[66]

That article ran in April 1933, the same year Ruden worked with SS chief Heinrich Himmler to draft Germany's 1933 sterilization law calling for sterilization of all Jews and "colored" German children.[67]

Sanger didn't just share the Nazi ideals of eugenics; she shared Hitler's idea of putting those she deemed unfit into concentration camps to "corral" the "enormous part of our population" with "hereditary taints."[68] She said:

> To apply a stern and rigid policy of sterilization and segregation to that grade of population whose progeny is already tainted...to apportion farm lands and homesteads for these segregated persons where they would be taught to work under competent instructors for the period of their entire lives....[69]

Abortion and the Nazi party have this in common—racism. We know where abortion leads. We've seen where the Nazis took us. And it is all the fruit of the seed of evolution.

Inspired by Darwin

I broadcasted daily radio commentaries for nearly 20 years on over 300 networks including the Bott Radio Network and American Family Radio Network, but quit to focus on the introduction of the federal Heartbeat Bill in 2017. One commentary entitled "Inspired by Darwin" stands out to me because when I wrote it, I cried.

After telling listeners the full title of Darwin's book, I asked them what happens when people believe there is a favored, superior race. Then I gave the shocking answer. In 1906 the Bronx Zoo relied on evolution to justify caging a 23-year-old pygmy man named Ota Benga in the "monkey house."[70]

A local minister fought to release Ota and taught him English. Haunted by the dehumanizing experience, Ota repeatedly slapped his chest and declared, "I am a man. I am a man." At the age of thirty-two,

Ota shot himself in the head, dying 10 years after being put on display at the Bronx Zoo.[71]

All of this was inspired by Charles Darwin.[72]

In his book *One Blood*, Ken Ham, founder of Answers in Genesis, explains that we are all of one blood—every human being is our relative, a member of the same family, which began at creation. We could solve the racial problems by turning to the Bible.

> *And He has made from one blood every nation of men to dwell on all the face of the earth* (Acts 17:26).

The entire evolution battle is about whether God created man or if we are just part of a random mutation where the strong are free to dominate the weak. Evolution is the foundation for racism, and racism was Planned Parenthood's foundation for abortion, where the old can kill the young. Abortion has already wiped out 20 million black lives—a quarter of the black population. Each one of those black lives matter. If you believe in equality, it's time to apply that standard across the board—black and white, young and old, born and unborn. If we want to stop the prenatal lynching, we need to change the laws that allow it. As Martin Luther King, Jr. said, "Law cannot make a man love me, but it can keep him from lynching me."[73]

CHAPTER 11

A Dark Web:
The Systematic Attempt
to Silence Our Voice

"Not every item of news should be published. Rather must
those who control news policies endeavor to make
every item of news serve a certain purpose."

—Joseph Goebbels, Nazi Germany's Minister of Propaganda

The silencing of our pro-life voice begins in seemingly innocuous ways, but the deeper you look the more undeniable their objective becomes. When we were on the brink of passing the Ohio Heartbeat Bill, we needed public pressure to push it over the finish line. At that time, I tried to buy a Facebook ad that read: "Pro-Life Heartbeat Bill on Brink of Passage." Other ads had gone through, but when we were "on the brink of passage," our message was rejected. We were told, "It doesn't comply with our advertising policies."

I later learned that Facebook likes to block pro-life messages, especially those "on the brink" of a vote. Like the abortion referendum in Ireland. Facebook CEO Mark Zuckerberg actually bragged about blocking pro-life ads prior to the Ireland abortion referendum, saying, "We ended up not allowing the ads."[1]

It didn't take long to realize that this was just the tip of ideological censorship iceberg. We were beginning to see the blueprint for the systematic eradication of the pro-life voice.

No Friend in Facebook

Speaking out against late-term abortions also doesn't comply with Facebook's "community standards," as New York Pastor Tim Mercaldo found out when he tried to post an open letter to Gov. Andrew Cuomo on his Facebook page.[2]

Even Franklin Graham was banned from Facebook for 24 hours until they realized he was too high profile for them to get away with censoring him. Graham boldly called them out, saying, "Facebook is censoring free speech. The free exchange of ideas is part of our country's DNA."[3] Facebook even censored the Declaration of Independence as "hate speech" until they were called out on it and reinstated the post.[4]

Republican Senator Marsha Blackburn of Tennessee was censored when she exposed Planned Parenthood's trafficking of baby body parts.[5]

This was also exposed in videos from Project Veritas,[6] which YouTube/ Google also censored along with a video exposing Google's censorship and plan to prevent a "Trump Situation" in 2020.[7,8] Can't let that get out. Like Graham, Senator Blackburn was too high profile to be banned from Twitter, since she had other platforms through which she could expose their censorship, Twitter reversed its decision to block her.

President Trump gets it. If he wasn't president of the United States, he would also be blocked. Oops, I spoke too soon. YouTube blocked 300 of President Trump's paid political advertisements without explanation of any violated policies.[9] Then, on January 23, 2020, the day before President Trump became the first president to speak at the March for Life in Washington, D.C., Twitter blocked the President's pro-life tweet, calling it "sensitive material" forcing people to change their settings for "sensitive media selection."[10] What was this "sensitive" message Twitter blocked people from seeing? "We see it in the eyes of every new mother who cradles an innocent newborn child in her loving arms: Life is the greatest miracle of all. Let us build a culture that cherishes innocent life."[11] Cradling an innocent newborn child and building a culture that cherishes innocent life—you can see why the people at Twitter don't want *that* message to get out.

YouTube/Google disabled Right Side Broadcasting Network, which livestreams President Trump's public appearances and rallies. After 4 years of following the YouTube rules, the Right Side Broadcasting Network went from 300 million views of President Trump's rallies to losing 90% of its traffic when YouTube censored them without explanation.[12] Do we really *need* an explanation? They were broadcasting Trump rallies. But Twitter doesn't keep such a close watch on anti-Trump trends. They let the phrase "#Die Trump" trend in Turkey prior to their apology for the "mistake."[13] Sure, that's a mistake that could happen to anyone; it's not like the president is high profile or anything.

They even censored the prime minister of Israel. Facebook blocked Benjamin Netanyahu—on Election Day 2019.[14] What do you know? Prime Minister Netanyahu was censored "on the brink of a vote." Sound familiar? The prime minster rightly said, "They shut down our means of communication with our voters."[15]

Facebook blocked ads from the pro-life movie *Gosnell*[16] along with the pro-life movie *Roe v. Wade*, starring Jon Voight.[17] Google labeled *Unplanned*, about former Planned Parenthood abortion worker Abby Johnson's pro-life conversion, as "propaganda" and prohibited ads for the film.[18] On opening night for the film, Twitter suspended *Unplanned*'s account.[19]

After this was made public with the help of Shannon Bream of Fox News and celebrities like Patricia Heaton, the *Unplanned* Twitter account was reinstated—only after the number of "followers" was reduced from 200,000 to 200, essentially wiping out their speech and effectiveness.[20] If only 200 people hear what you say instead of 200,000, your voice has been diminished 1,000 fold. Meanwhile, Planned Parenthood, which kills more than 330,000 babies each year,[21] has an active Twitter account in "good standing."[22] *Unplanned* co director Chuck Konzelman told the U.S. Senate Judiciary Committee, "In a digital age, exclusion from the digital arena isn't just discriminatory—it's the most insidiously effective form of censorship imaginable."[23]

Why does this matter? Because the marketplace of ideas has become a leftist monopoly that is suppressing Christian and conservative speech. Consider the following facts:

- Google.com is the most visited website in existence.[24] Nearly nine out of ten U.S. Internet searches use Google.[25] It is the number 1 search engine in the world with 74.8% of the worldwide market share.[26] Google also owns YouTube.[27]

- YouTube.com is the second most visited webpage in existence.[28] In an average month, 1.3 billion people watch YouTube, including eight out of ten 18- to 49-year-olds.[29]

- Facebook.com is third most visited webpage in existence.[30] More than two-thirds of Americans (68 percent) are on Facebook.[31] Facebook also owns Instagram.com,[32] the sixth largest site in the world[33] with 1 billion users worldwide—including 72% of U.S. teens.[34]

- Twitter is the seventh most visited site in the world.[35] There are 330 million active Twitter users worldwide, including 68 million monthly active Twitter users in the United States 22% of all U.S. adults.[36]

New Media Blackout

In a Senate Committee addressing censorship from Google, Facebook, YouTube, and Twitter, Republican senator Ted Cruz said these new media giants "use monopoly powers to silence voices they don't like."[37] Our views are being systematically exterminated and obliterated from existence. But their idea isn't original. They are following the playbook of Joseph Goebbels, the minister of propaganda for Nazi Germany. As I noted at the beginning of this chapter, Goebbels wrote in a 1943 diary entry, "Not every item of news should be published: rather must those who control news policies endeavor to make every item of news serve a certain purpose."[38]

In a *Townhall* article entitled, "How Conservatives Are Destroyed by Facebook, Twitter and Google Without Even Realizing It," John Hawkins, whose conservative news site reached 133 million people, reported "Facebook systematically, methodically reduced the reach of all its pages with each algorithm change" destroying their reach and forcing them to shut down entirely.[39] He said, "If Facebook killed every conservative page overnight, there would be a huge outcry. On the other hand, if Facebook slowly strangled us to death, we'd fade away and would people even notice?"[40] Conservative Charles Johnson is suing Twitter because although they admitted that he didn't violate Twitter's policies, they just wanted to get rid of him.[41] Conservative pro-lifers spend years building their audience only to have Twitter pull the plug whenever they please.[42]

Former Google employees admitted that Google manipulates search results. One example is a search for President Trump's book *Great Again: How to Fix Our Crippled America* would instead display Adolf Hitler's *Mein Kampf*—a "bug" which remained for 9 months.[43] But that is just the tip of the iceberg.

Dr. Robert Epstein is a professor, author, and journalist. He earned his Ph.D. in psychology at Harvard University in 1981, was editor in chief of *Psychology Today*, and was a staunch supporter of Hillary Clinton in the 2016 presidential race. Epstein did a study comparing Google web searches of Hillary Clinton with searches from Bing and Yahoo, and he found that Google withheld negative search terms for Clinton, even when they were highly popular.[44] For example Yahoo's auto complete suggestions for "Hillary Clinton is" listed "a liar," "a criminal," "evil," and "a crook." Bing's auto complete suggestions for "Hillary Clinton is" began with "a filthy liar," "murderess," "she evil," and "lying crook." But that was not the case with Google, whose auto complete listed only: "winning" and "awesome." See the difference?

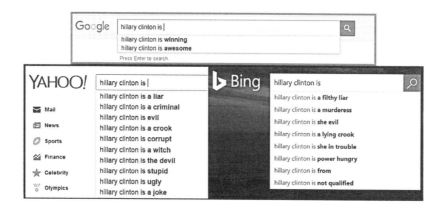

The research also found that Google's suppression of negative suggestions for Clinton was selective, yet their autocomplete of negative suggestions for Donald Trump was unhindered.[45] I'll spare you all the bar graphs and skip to what Epstein concluded:

> Research I have been conducting since 2013 with Ronald Robertson of Northeastern University has shown that high-ranking search results that favor one candidate can easily shift 20 percent or more of undecided voters toward that candidate—up to 80 percent in some demographic groups.... This is because of the enormous trust people have in computer-generated search results, which people mistakenly believe are completely impartial and objective—just as they

mistakenly believe search suggestions are completely impartial and objective.[46]

Even though Epstein was a Clinton supporter, he said he didn't believe it would have been "right for her to win the presidency because of the invisible, large-scale manipulations of a private company. That would make democracy meaningless."[47]

Epstein told Cruz, who chaired a Senate hearing on Google bias, that Google was responsible for shifting at least 2.6 million votes to Democratic candidate Hillary Clinton through bias in search results.[48]

When Cruz questioned him further, Epstein clarified: "The range [of votes manipulated by Google in the 2016 presidential election] is between 2.6 and 10.4 million votes, depending on how aggressive they were in using the techniques that I've been studying, such as the search engine manipulation effect, the search suggestion effect, the answer bot effect, and a number of others. They control these, and no one can counteract them. These are not competitive. These are tools that they have at their disposal exclusively."[49]

Epstein went on to say that "in 2020 you can bet that all of these companies are going to go all out, and the methods that they're using are invisible, they're subliminal, they're more powerful than most any effects I've ever seen in the behavioral sciences, and I've been in the behavioral sciences for almost forty years."[50]

"In 2020," Epstein said, "if all these companies are supporting the same candidate *there are 15 million votes on the line that can be shifted without people's knowledge* and without leaving a paper trail for authorities to trace."[51]

In a James O'Keefe Project Veritas sting, Twitter's Policy Manager for Twitter Trust and Safety Olinda Hassan explained, "we're trying to 'down rank'...shi--y people to not show up."[52] Twitter's former software engineer revealed the shadow ban strategy "so that you have ultimate control."[53]

"The idea of a shadow ban is that you ban someone but they don't know they've been banned, because they keep posting and no one sees their content. So they just think that no one is engaging with their content, when in reality, no one is seeing it."[54] He explained, "You just sort of turn off all the features for them. So, like, they still see everything...But at the end of the day, no one else sees what you're doing. So all that data is just thrown away."[55]

A Twitter Direct Messaging Engineer revealed on video that "machine learning" employs algorithms to screen out posts they don't like, "You look for Trump, or America, or any of, like five thousand, like keywords to describe a redneck...you assign a value to each thing, so like Trump would be, like, .5, a picture of a gun would be like 1.5, and like, if it comes up, the total comes up above, like a certain value, then it's a bot."[56]

Kevin Cernekee has an idea of Google's plans; he was one of their engineers. Cernekee stated, "They really want Trump to lose in 2020. That's their agenda. They have very biased people running every level of the company...They have quite a bit of control over the political process. That's something we should really worry about."[57]

Google once had "Don't Be Evil" within its code of conduct, but removed it in 2018.[58] *I can see why.*

More from their playbook:

> It is the absolute right of the State to supervise the formation
> of public opinion. —Joseph Goebbels[59]

Increasingly Google is working with the government, which is very troubling considering how they participated with the Chinese government to censor searches from the Chinese people about things like the 1989 Tiananmen Square massacre or references to "anticommunism."[60]

Senator Josh Hawley (R-MO) questioned Google's Vice President for government affairs and public policy, Karan Bhatia, during the Judiciary Committee Hearing in the U.S. Senate in July, 2019. Responding to Google's claim that they don't censor political views, Hawley said:

> Except for when you do it in China, right? You're happy to censor for the authoritarian Chinese regime, like for instance with Google.cn, you're happy to censor away any mention of Tiananmen Square, happy to help the Chinese government maintain control of all information within the country, happy to control the information flow to their own citizens, you're happy to do all of that. Would you call that censorship with an ideological agenda?[61]

China is now using big tech and surveillance to rate its citizens with an Orwellian "social credit score," which monitors their Internet use, postings, purchases, and behavior to categorize people and determine those deemed insufficiently loyal to the communist party.[62] Those "scores" are now used to ban people from travel, loans, schools, jobs, hotels, and even dating sites.[63,64] When Liu Hu was ordered to apologize for a series of tweets, his apology was determined by a Chinese court to be insincere.[65]

As a result Hu reported, "I can't buy property. My child can't go to a private school. You feel you're being controlled by the list all the time."[66]

Given Google's track record of suppressing free speech in China, you can get an idea of the effects it is having here. When freedom-seeking people are forbidden to search for the light of truth, they continue to be repressed in the dark. Just like when Google/YouTube/Facebook/Twitter etc. block the Christian viewpoint on life, homosexuality, and a host of other issues, people, and candidates here in America, the light of truth is suppressed, quenched, and extinguished by a dark web.

As I write these words, I'm having a hard time finding *a lot* of the stories I'm searching for on Google. They stack the pages with their leftist propaganda from Snopes, FactCheck.org, and Wikipedia. Joseph Farah of WorldNetDaily called Snopes "thoroughly unprofessional, politically biased, widely discredited and scandal-plagued."[67] I wish he was exaggerating.

It can't be addressed soon enough. Not only is this tyrannical monopoly threatening our elections and freedom of speech and thought, it threatens the *very existence* of conservative news organizations, which rely on advertising dollars and grassroots donations. This agenda-driven manipulation may be ridding the marketplace of Christian and conservative organizations altogether.

David Kupelian, award-winning journalist, author, and managing editor of *WorldNetDaily*, said that because of manipulated search algorithms, *WorldNetDaily* and other conservative news sites are being pushed "way down in search results" and starved of ad revenue that comes with web traffic. He added:

> Not a day goes by without new examples of this slow-motion revolution becoming evident, with yet another conservative, Christian or pro-life voice being banned, suspended, de-monetized, pushed way down in search rankings, or branded a "hate agent."[68]

In addition to our Heartbeat Bill ads being blocked on Facebook, I have also been personally censored by YouTube multiple times. Several years ago I was asked to host a documentary produced by Cross TV that presented scientific facts that dispel evolution entitled "Evolution vs. Creation."[69] Many of the segments were posted on YouTube, but only the ones that ridicule me and our biblical position about creation were allowed to remain.

YouTube allows several posts about it with the title "The Dodo Strikes Back, Janet Folger" parts 1–6. The only way our viewpoint is allowed to be seen on YouTube is by those who mock us and our views. Our "Evolution vs. Creation" videos were censored while "KREATOR-Satan is Real"[70] is allowed on YouTube, along with a trailer for a "Church of Satan Documentary"[71] and "Satanic Art: A Fight for Freedom."[72] YouTube believes in freedom for Satanists, just not for Christians.

YouTube also censored pro-marriage and pro-family videos, including completely removing our parody videos "Adultery Pride Parade" and "Heather Has Two Cigarettes"—which, like with the "Evolution vs. Creation" video, YouTube allows to be posted only by those who oppose us and ridicule our viewpoint.

By the way, YouTube *doesn't* censor videos whose titles refer to: "Anti-abortion idiots,"[73] "Radical anti-abortion activists,"[74] "Pro-life is anti-woman,"[75] and "The Satanic Temple's Fight to Protect Your Abortion

Rights."[76] Apparently, those videos don't violate any of YouTube's policies.

YouTube has also demonetized and censored widely popular Prager University (PragerU) 5-minute videos, putting even a Ten Commandments video on the "restricted" list. Apparently YouTube now considers "thou shalt not murder" objectionable.[77] I thought it was just the babies they favored killing. During a Senate hearing on Google censorship, Prager sarcastically offered to remove the objectionable commandment not to murder and re release the video as "the Nine Commandments."[78] Senator Cruz said, "Dennis Prager is a brilliant

According to the *Journal of Epidemiology*, homosexual behavior is up to three times more dangerous than smoking, yet we promote it in the public schools. Sadly, this scientific fact is forbidden on YouTube, who censored this video.

thinker, but nobody with any sense would describe Dennis Prager as some sort of dangerous voice that must be muzzled. But if you're a leftist, he is a very dangerous voice because he responds with facts and reason and the Left is terrified of facts and reason."[79]

At the Google hearing, Senator Cruz addressed the censorship tactic of labeling as "hate speech" content the powers that be dislike. Cruz rightly noted that "hate speech" is "an ever-changing and vague standard, meant to give censorship an air of legitimacy." It has been used as a weapon to shape culture, destroy rivals, and "ban speech."[80] Actor Sacha Baron Cohen called the big tech giants including Facebook, Google, and Twitter "the greatest propaganda machine in history."[81] While pro-life messages are blocked, 4.2 million anti-Semitic messages were posted on Twitter within a 12 month period.[82] Cohen stated, "If Facebook were around in the 1930s, it would have allowed Hitler to post 30-second ads on his 'solution' to the 'Jewish problem.'"[83]

As Cruz said, "Google is a monopoly...they *use monopoly powers to silence voices they don't like.*"[84] In our new tech-driven society, Google/ YouTube, Facebook/Instagram, and Twitter have become the new public square of speech, which our Founders pledged to protect. But now, like in communist countries—certain messages, people, and groups are disappearing from the public square.

Weaponizing Charitable Giving

Another way they silence our voice is by choking out our funding supply. The Left has weaponized charitable giving, a tactic that is currently being used against the Michigan Heartbeat Coalition. The organization, which has been gathering petitions to bring the Heartbeat Bill to a vote in Michigan, was denied access to an online giving platform because it

didn't match the "value statements" of Give Lively, a nonprofit fundraising program. Give Lively advertises that it allows "nonprofits of all sizes to fundraise online with ease"[85]—that is unless you're working to protect the rights of babies in the womb with beating hearts.

Now Google, YouTube, Facebook, and Twitter are partnering with leftist groups like the radical George Soros-funded Southern Poverty Law Center (SPLC) and Anti-Defamation League (ADL) to censor

Christian speech.[86] The SPLC and ADL treat mainstream Christian and conservative teaching about such issues as traditional marriage and the sanctity of life as "hate speech" and target them for censorship.

Amazon is prohibiting donations based on the leftist SPLC's (people we) "hate list." Amazon has used the discredited SPLC as a way to block charitable donations to groups such as Alliance Defending Freedom (ADF), which defends life, religious liberty, and traditional marriage. ADF President Michael Farris described the SPLC as a "far-left propaganda machine that slanders organizations with which it disagrees and destroys the possibility of civil discourse in the process."[87]

To give you an idea of how extreme they are, the SPLC compares conservative Christians like Republican Senator Cruz to ISIS.[88] The man who pled guilty to terrorism for the shooting at Family Research Council said he planned his attack based on the SPLC "hate map," which included the Family Research Council and the American Family Association.[89] It should be called the "people we hate list"—which includes dozens of mainstream pro-family organizations, including ours, on their site now used to discredit, censor, block donations, and target for attack.[90] But don't take my word for it. Take the word of Mark Potok, who spent 20 years as a senior fellow at the SPLC:

> Sometimes the press will describe us as monitoring hate groups. I want to say plainly that our aim in life is to destroy these groups, completely destroy them.[91]

There you have it—the SPLC wants to "completely destroy" mainstream Christian organizations and the biblical beliefs behind them.

Amazon—the fourteenth most visited website in the world[92]—isn't just blocking charitable donations of mainstream Christian groups based on the SPLC list;[93] they are broadening their censorship to a whole class of people—those who have been set free from homosexuality. You're not allowed to know about them, and you're not allowed to buy their books. My friend Anne Paulk is the executive director of the Restored Hope Network and author of *Restoring Sexual Identity: Hope for Women Who Struggle with Same-Sex Attraction*. She and former homosexual Joe Dallas, author of *Desires in Conflict*, both had their books removed from Amazon.[94] They were told their message of how Jesus transformed their lives is a "violation of our content guidelines."[95]

Want to know what isn't a violation of Amazon's content guidelines? Books about pedophilia and adult-child sex and *Daddy, This Is so... Wrong: A Big Collection of Taboo Short Stories*.[96] Just so we're clear, Amazon's content guidelines allow for books about molesting children, just not books from those set free from homosexuality.

We built our platforms on sand in their sandbox and we've been pushed out. Google/YouTube, Facebook/Instagram, Twitter, and Amazon rule the Internet like Orwellian tyrants, systematically eradicating the pro-life, pro-family, Christian, and conservative viewpoints as calculated as communist China. Freedom loving people have a very small window to take it back. If we don't use our freedom to keep our freedom *now*, Google/YouTube/Facebook/Twitter will follow their carefully laid out plan to choose our next president and *completely* silence our voice.

Here's some welcome news: state attorneys general have joined together to launch investigations into Google and Facebook's antitrust violations.[97] Senator Cruz stated: "Google is larger; it is more powerful; it has a larger market cap than AT&T was when it was broken up by the antitrust laws. It's larger and more powerful than Standard Oil was when it was broken up by the antitrust laws. Google is a monopoly, and Google is abusing its monopoly powers. We have antitrust laws to deal with that."[98]

Texas attorney general Ken Paxton, a Republican, is leading a team of dozens of law-enforcement officials who will reportedly target Facebook and Google in an antitrust investigation. Meanwhile New York Attorney General Letitia James, a Democrat, is leading a bipartisan investigation into Facebook.[99] Attorneys general from Colorado, Florida, Iowa, Nebraska, North Carolina, Ohio, Tennessee, and the District of Columbia have joined James, who announced the bipartisan effort via Twitter:[100]

> I'm launching an investigation into Facebook to determine whether their actions endangered consumer data, reduced the quality of consumers' choices, or increased the price of advertising. The largest social media platform in the world must follow the law.[101]

There are now fifty attorney generals who are opening antitrust investigations into Google.[102] The Federal Trade Commission also is investigating Facebook for antitrust violations after imposing a $5-billion fine over its privacy practices.[103] A separate investigation of Google is being launched by the U.S. Department of Justice.[104]

Senator Cruz told *Fox & Friends* that big tech media companies have "decided to be hardcore leftist, to silence, to throttle, to shadow ban conservatives, and I think if they continue to do that there is no reason they should get a special immunity from liability that nobody else does."[105]

Unless they are reigned in, Google, Facebook, and Twitter will continue to use their veto power over the First Amendment and impose their left-wing political agenda on an unsuspecting public. Why hasn't anything been done? Much like I wrote about in Chapter 6: The Enemy Within, behind-the-scenes conservative groups we thought were with us are actually fighting *against* us, on the side of Google and their fascist censorship of conservative views. Just like the "Right to Life" establishment groups provide cover for baby-killing politicians, these "conservative groups" take money from big tech and then defend the very people who are silencing our voice and our freedoms.[106]

Americans for Prosperity, funded by the Koch brothers, actually ran ads defending Google and Facebook from antitrust investigations launched by state attorneys general.[107] Why? Tucker Carlson reported that Google has given money to at least 22 right-leaning institutions also funded by the Koch network. They include the American Conservative Union, the National Review Institute, and the Heritage Foundation.[108]

Senator Josh Hawley (R-MO) introduced the "Ending Support for Internet Censorship Act," but the allegedly "limited-government conservatives" are fighting him. Hawley said, "Well, well—who is 'fine' with Big Tech censoring conservatives? People paid by Big Tech. DC is awash in money from Google and Facebook. Economists, policy groups, supposedly libertarian outfits...all taking Google and Facebook money."[109] Among those fighting Hawley's bill are the American Enterprise Institute, Americans for Prosperity, and the Cato Institute.[110]

Google was the largest donor to the Competitive Enterprise Institute dinner.[111] The Competitive Enterprise Institute then signed a letter with other "conservative" groups funded by Google expressing "grave concerns" to the U.S. Attorney General about an investigation into Google's nefarious tactics to silence the conservative voice.[112] Google silences conservatives while conservative groups take money from them—enabling the practice to continue. Carlson, who used to work at the Heritage Foundation, said, "Heritage no longer represents the interests of conservatives, at least on the question of tech."[113] Heritage issued a white paper defending Google's special privileges, urging Congress not to intervene against their online bias that controls the new public square.[114] Carlson said, "It's embarrassing. But Heritage isn't embarrassed."[115] He added, these "conservative" groups in Washington "make deals with people who hate you, they secretly sell out your interests" and then ask for your money.[116]

Our views are being systematically exterminated and obliterated from existence. The new public square was supposed to be the free exchange of ideas and information—to let all ideas be heard so the best ones could win. What the Left couldn't achieve with logic and facts, they are taking with tyranny. Just like fake "Right to Life" groups enable baby-killers, "conservative" establishment groups are enabling the systematic destruction of our views in the new public square. But the only way they can win is if we let them.

Media Censorship

Beyond the Left's control of the Internet, the overt bias and censorship in the media has long been the standard. It is obvious and undeniable. I have a word of advice for those on the front lines in the battle for life, liberty, and the kingdom of God: Don't take every interview that comes your way. Just because they're a big name with a broad reach doesn't mean you should talk to them. First pray about it. If it's a hostile member of the press, I usually ask them to email me their questions. If I see they have no intention of being fair, I don't waste my time responding. If you feel led to consent to an interview with a hostile reporter, *make sure* you video record it—even with your phone. After what *The New York Times* did to Congressman King, I wasn't about to violate this rule.

When *The New York Times* asked if they could fly into town to interview me about the Heartbeat Bill, I agreed under the condition that I would be recording the interview. But when they showed up at the door and saw the video camera, they refused to allow it. They refused to allow me to video even my own responses—without them appearing on camera. A huge *red flag*—if the interview was legit, this wouldn't be a problem. So I politely thanked them for coming and showed them to the door. They will report whatever they please, but we don't have to participate in a smear.

For those who think what they see on the news is real, think again. In 1983, fifty companies controlled 90% of U.S. media companies. By 2011, that 90% was controlled by six companies, and today five dominate the industry—Time Warner, Disney, Murdoch's News Corporation, Bertelsmann of Germany, and Viacom. *Business Insider* points out that the recent consolidation of media companies creates the "illusion of choice."[117] It's why the networks all share the same taking points.

And what about the "choice" we have? Apart from those behind the news, here's a personal insight about what you're really watching. Because I will always be a voice for the innocent, I volunteered to be a spokesperson for Judge Roy Moore's U.S. Senate Campaign in 2017. In addition to scores of other hostile programs, I was asked to appear on CNN's *Anderson Cooper 360* to address the now discredited accusations against Judge Moore.

They called and claimed that it had to be "taped," to which I replied, "No thanks."

"What do you mean?" I couldn't *possibly* be turning down the opportunity of a lifetime to appear on their show.

I responded, "I'm gonna take a pass. Thanks anyway."

The representative from the show reiterated how much they really wanted me, but there was "no possible way" they could do the show live.

I let them know that I appreciated their offer but wasn't interested in being taped. You see, I know what happens when you are taped by media outlets that disagree with your beliefs. They edit you. That's what happened when I appeared on *Nightline*. They *selectively* edited what I said.[118]

When I was the national director of the Center for Reclaiming America, we initiated a "Truth in Love" campaign (which many national groups joined) featuring former homosexuals expressing "hope for change" for those who wanted out of the homosexual lifestyle. On *Nightline* my opponent tried to discredit the campaign by accusing me of working with someone who advocated the death penalty for homosexuals. I responded, "Not only is that *not* what I believe, I've *never heard of* the guy you say I'm working with."

Here's what *Nightline* did. They left the accusation in, but took my response out—making it appear to viewers that I was avoiding the question because it "must have been true."

So now you know why I won't be taped. And wouldn't you know it? Minutes after telling me that it was "impossible" for Anderson Cooper to have me on the program live, they decided if that was the only way they could have me, they would do it.

Unless it's live, what you see on the news is likely a chopped up, edited version of what was said—as CNN did twice in this single interview with Anderson Cooper.

They told me the interview was going to be 7 minutes, but it went closer to 15.[119] Afterward my husband and I went back to our hotel in Alabama and turned on CNN—something I *never* do. On the screen it said, "Coming up, Roy Moore's spokesperson." I looked to my husband and said, "That must be a mistake." After all, I was just on the program live for a quarter hour.

Nope. Turns out as soon as I appeared on the program live, they went back to their original plan of selectively editing the interview to make it look like I didn't answer any of his questions. As if that weren't enough, they spent the *night* editing it even more to play an even worse version on the news the *next* night.

When I saw Judge Moore the next day at campaign headquarters, I told him, "I think I'm done with fake news for a while."

Speaking of fake news, after reporting for 2 years on the Russia collusion hoax, CNN lost a "jaw-dropping 47 percent of its primetime audience and 41 percent of its total day viewers."[120] MSNBC lost 28 percent of its viewers with their day total down 20%.[121]

According to a Nielsen Media Research report in June of 2019, Fox News had more viewers than CNN and MSNBC combined[122]—2.3 million viewing Fox (between 8 p.m. and 11 p.m. ET from June 10-16) versus 1.5 million viewing MSNBC. CNN, on the other hand, finished fourteenth, behind HGTV, A&E, USA, Discovery, TNT, the Food

Network, TLC, Investigation Discovery, TBS, Hallmark Channel, and the History Channel.[123] More people are watching the Hallmark Channel than are watching CNN. Both are fiction, but at least Hallmark has a happy ending.

In November 2019, MSNBC lost about 35% of its audience, but CNN hit a 3-year low.[124] During the impeachment hearings, CNN was unable to attract even one-fourth of 1% of the American population.[125] Their viewership consists primarily of the "captive" audience force-fed anti-Trump fake news at airports.

What seemed like just an ill-timed Google ad refusal when our Heartbeat Bill was "on the brink of passage" revealed what was really happening on the other side of our screens—insidious, systematic, ideological censorship. It has affected our Heartbeat Bill, abortion referendums, Prime Minister Netanyahu's election, and it threatens every election from this point forward. As Dr. Epstein stated, upwards of "15 million votes" are in jeopardy if the tyrannical information monopoly continues unchecked. Our freedom of speech, freedom of religion, and freedom of expression are being threatened like never before, as beliefs are blocked and our support suppressed.

What happens if we don't break the tyrannical reign over our information? Those who control the Internet will elect those who agree with them, Christianity will become criminalized and our freedom extinct. We cannot let a dark web extinguish the light of truth. We must seize this narrow window of opportunity to break their stronghold and abolish their plans to silence our voice, or as Reagan said, "We will spend our sunset years telling our children and our children's children what it was once like in the United States where men were free."[126]

CHAPTER 12

Pick Up the Sword

"Pick up the sword and lead the way." —Dutch Sheets

Monica Boyer was a daily listener of my Faith2Action radio program for years. She became a pro-life activist, and we became friends. Monica told me that I needed to meet her friend Amy Schlichter and asked if it would it be OK if they drove from Indiana to Ohio for a visit. On the long drive, Amy, "filling time" and "making conversation," told Monica about a dream she had the previous night.

In the dream, Amy sensed a real and immediate danger from an outside attacker. She put her children behind her to keep them safe while she braced herself for a certain, oncoming attack. She looked up to see some daggers and swords, so she reached out to grab one to protect herself and her children. She saw a large sword like the kind thirteenth-century Scottish freedom fighter William Wallace used that had a silver plate on it. But she thought, "That's too big for me," so she made a quick decision to instead grab a small antique dagger for protection. Amy ran back to

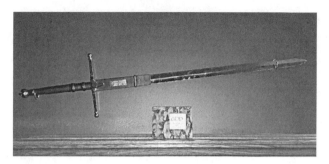

My "Defender of Life" William Wallace sword from Allan Parker and the Justice Foundation.

guard her children and realized she had taken the wrong weapon—what she had was inadequate for the task. And then she woke up.

When she got to our home, Amy stood in shock, nudging Monica as they stared above our fireplace. Hanging above the mantle was my William Wallace sword—with a silver plate on it, the exact sword from her dream. Years earlier I had been given the sword as an award from Allan Parker of the Justice Foundation. Inscribed on the silver plate are the words "Defender of Life."

After Amy told me her dream, I took the sword off the wall and laid it on the floor. I told her, "You've been given a divine do-over. Pick up the sword."

Amy looked at me like I was a bit crazy.

Unfazed, I told her again, "Pick up the sword."

And so she picked it up and held it over her head. I told Amy God gave her a dream with my sword for a reason. The next week she met with her state senator, who introduced a Heartbeat Bill in Indiana.

It wasn't until I was writing this book and reviewed the videos of some of our Heartbeat Bill rallies that I stumbled across these words that national prayer leader Dutch Sheets, who was born and raised in Ohio, said when he opened our September 20, 2011 rally at the Ohio Statehouse:

> It was in 2005 that I was traveling around the nation ministering in all fifty states on a very important assignment from the Lord. And when we arrived in Ohio, I felt the Lord impress me with the story of Gideon. And to my surprise, I found myself saying, "The assignment on the state of Ohio is to pick up the sword. Though you be a small army at this point, God is going to empower you to turn the nation." And so we said, "Ohio, pick up the sword and lead the way." And here we are today.[1]

The message isn't just for Ohio or Indiana. We've all been given a divine do-over to pick up the sword to *end* abortion instead of merely regulating it. Amy had a burden to be a voice for life but didn't feel adequate. I explained to her that I once was in that same place. I was the shy girl, afraid to give a speech, inadequate to the task of defending the defenseless. But it's not about us. It's about the God in us, who lacks nothing.

The only ability you need to serve God is availability. Remember, it's not about our knowledge, talent, connections, or anything we lack. It's about obeying God and letting Him make up for all that is missing. As I mentioned, stepping out in faith is a risk. Remember what Winston Churchill said, "Great success always comes at the risk of enormous failure."[2]

True leadership is willing to go where success is not guaranteed. It is ceasing to call God a liar and acting like God's Word is true. Fear is faith in the enemy, instead of the One who already defeated the enemy. True leadership is when obeying God matters more than whether or not you look foolish. Because true leadership can't be swayed by doubters or defeatists, by credit or by criticism.

When passing a Heartbeat Bill in your state or doing anything that advances the kingdom of God, there will be obstacles you must overcome along the way. We've talked about several of them in this book. But there are other obstacles you must overcome before you even begin. While we have little control over the external obstacles standing in the way of victory, the internal obstacles, such as disappointment, fear, and compromise, can be overcome. But only you can do it.

Disappointment

One of the most pervasive obstacles standing in the way of us winning the war (on any issue) is disappointment. We get so beaten down by disappointment and hope deferred that we lose heart. That happened to me. It took 9 years to pass our Heartbeat Bill in Ohio. We had to introduce it *five times*. In fact, I watched Heartbeat Bills pass in five other states before it passed in my own in April 2019. Even though I kept going and finally experienced the long-awaited victory, my heart is only now recovering from year after year of devastating disappointment.

Sometimes the dreams in our heart get beaten out of us. Talk to any preschooler. If you ask them what they want to be, they'll tell you—an artist, an astronaut, a baseball player, an inventor—sometimes all at the same time. Then they go to school and see that other kids are smarter, more artistic, or more athletic, and they lower the bar.

I used to be the girl who couldn't wait to do the impossible. In fact, 20 years ago the *Cleveland Plain Dealer* published a cover story about my work that began with the words, "Janet loves the word 'impossible'...there are people around the country who can't wait to see what Janet Folger [Porter] is going to do next."

That is what I used to be like. I actually *loved* to hear the word *impossible* just so I could point people to the God of the impossible and see their faces when the impossible happened. And it happened again and again and again. (You can read many of those stories in my other books.)

Like the time my husband told me we needed a new roof but couldn't afford it. He said we should just sell the house *now*—moving us from Ohio and my mission to pass the Heartbeat law. Unmoved, I said, "I'm going to pray for a new roof, and you should join me." He just looked at me like I was naïve. I didn't care. I prayed. I had seen God come through so many times before, on this day I didn't even doubt.

A week or 2 later there was a storm. It uprooted trees in our neighborhood and blew some shingles off our roof. Not really a big deal. But a day or 2 later the phone rang with a solicitor on the other end. I was just about to hang up but something in me said not to. So I kept listening. It was a roofing company calling to see if they could inspect our roof to see if the storm caused any damage. I said yes. They took some pictures of a few shingles that were missing, but they all but said the idea of the insurance company paying for a new roof was "doubtful at best." So I prayed. Actually, the roofing guy, my mom, and I all prayed together. After all, what's "doubtful" for us is easy for the God of the impossible.

God answered that prayer. Our new roof is beautiful, and it cost us nothing. I trusted God to take care of what we needed and wasn't surprised when He did.

Then one day I realized something had changed. My husband and I were visiting a friend, Sue Trombino, founder of WIN: Women Impacting the Nation. She gave us a tour of her office, and as she told us how they acquired the facility and furnished it, one thing after another was a "miracle." She said, "We didn't have enough money for this office, yet here we are!" And on and on it went: "God provided this impossibility! And over here *that* impossibility!"

My husband kept nudging me, "Who does *that* sound like?" He meant me, but I realized that I hadn't been living like that in *years*. Years of disappointment, of hitting brick walls and not seeing breakthrough had crushed my faith and hope. Sure, I kept fighting for the Heartbeat Bill. I kept believing it would pass. But that spark, the childlike faith for God to move mountains all around me, wasn't there like it used to be.

I remember telling my husband I used to be like David—seeing giants fall, miracles happen, favor on everything I touched. But I told him, "In this battle, I feel more like Saul, like God's hand has been lifted, and the favor is gone." His answer: "Sometimes the impossible takes a little longer." The late Jerry Falwell, founder of Liberty University and a tireless advocate for the unborn, once said, "A man's greatness is measured not by his talent or his wealth, but by what it takes to discourage him."[3]

Revelation 19:10 says, "For the testimony of Jesus is the spirit of prophecy." Sue's testimony of victory prophesied to mine. And my testimony of victory prophesies to *yours*. After all the crushing blows, the heartbreaking disappointments, the narrow defeats, I am here to tell you that *it can be done*. You can be used by God to see the impossible bow to the name of Jesus. *And despite everything, it's worth it.*

Can you imagine getting to heaven and finding out there was much *more* for us to accomplish that we never bothered to even try? I don't want that to happen to me.

Fear

As I mentioned previously, I was the girl who was afraid to give a speech. But fear is just a feeling that stands in the way of the destiny God has for you. I've often heard it said that fear stands for "false evidence appearing real." Fear is lying to you, making you think whatever you're dealing with is too big for God. If you had a friend who lied to you as much as fear did, you would get a restraining order and block their calls.

Most of us know the story of the talents. If you haven't read it, the parable is kind of like *America's Got Talent* but instead of three or four judges there's only one. The ones who made use of the talents were commended and rewarded—whether they had much or whether they had little. But the one who was afraid and hid his talent was called wicked and lazy. (See Matthew 25:14-26.) And what happens to the fearful is harsher than any rebuke from Simon Cowell on *America's Got Talent*:

> *But from him who does not have, even what he has will be taken away. And cast the unprofitable servant into the outer darkness. There will be weeping and gnashing of teeth* (Matthew 25:29-30).

Those are words that describe hell. Here's another scary thought for those overcome by fear. In Revelation 21:8, guess who are the first ones thrown into the lake of fire? It's not the murderers; it's not the rapists; it's the *cowards*.

> *But the cowardly, unbelieving, abominable, murderers, sexually immoral, sorcerers, idolaters, and all liars shall have their part in the lake which burns with fire and brimstone, which is the second death.*

We must take what God has given us and put it to use. The ones who made use of what God gave them got rewarded. But the ones who were "afraid," made excuses, and buried their talents—let's just say, you don't want to be one of those.

Compromise

My friend Evan Parker once convicted me about listening to secular music. I fought him, thinking he was being ridiculous, "Come on, these songs are fun!" Then he asked me to pay attention to the lyrics. "Jan, if you want to drive 20 miles per hour, it doesn't matter what gas you put in your tank. But if you want to soar at 20,000 feet, you can't use the cheapest octane."

I quit listening to secular music about 15 years ago. I want to soar. My mom said the same thing applies to the food we put in our body. I'm still working on that one.

To get to your destiny, you have a choice. There's a very popular and appealing broad road, and there is a narrow road. The broad road is filled with all kinds of immediate pleasures much like taking drugs—a fleeting high followed by a life of addiction and premature death. Keep in mind that Satan *never* gives you anything for free.

We can follow the crowd, but the broad road isn't going to take us where we want to go. The highway of holiness may not be easy, but the alternative is a path to nowhere:

> *For they have left the highway of holiness and walk in the ways of darkness. They take pleasure when evil prospers and thoroughly enjoy a lifestyle of sin. But they're walking on a path to nowhere, wandering away into deeper deception* (Proverbs 2:13-15 TPT).

I don't want to walk on a "path to nowhere." I want a life of purpose—God's purpose. One huge obstacle standing in the way of the destiny God has for us is *compromise*.

God is merciful, longsuffering, and gracious, but He is also "holy," which is the only attribute of God that is mentioned three times in a row. That's why the message of cheap grace—do anything you want because you're forgiven—flies in the face of God's command in 1 Peter 1:16: "Be holy, for I am holy."

Again and again, in both the Old and New Testaments, the Bible calls us to holy living:

> *Who may ascend into the hill of the Lord? Or who may stand in His holy place? He who has clean hands and a pure heart* (Psalm 24:3-4).

If I had not confessed the sin in my heart, the Lord would not have listened (Psalm 66:18 NLT).

Hudson Taylor said, "Christ is either Lord of all or He is not Lord at all."[4]

I attended a church where the pastor did something I have never seen done before. After a message about following God and living a holy life, he asked couples who were living together outside of marriage to come forward and repent.

I cringed, thinking, "He's really putting people on the spot here." And you know what happened? Hundreds of couples went to the altar to repent before God for violating His command. They vowed to separate until they were married and pledged to wholeheartedly follow God and His plan for their lives. They decided to start their lives together God's way, and I'm confident God blessed them for it.

Another of the most courageous altar calls I have ever seen was given by Cindy Jacobs. During the Obama administration in a racially diverse crowd, she flat-out told people that if they cast a vote for a pro-abortion candidate they needed to repent before God. She told the crowd of people they had put race over God, and she called them forward to repent.

Oh wow. Were we about to see a revolt? I couldn't believe what I witnessed—people of all races and backgrounds, sobbing and repenting for casting a vote to kill babies. They were restored to God, pledging not to violate His word again on the critical issue of shedding innocent blood. Thank you, Cindy.

Churches across America remain silent on abortion. Some because they don't want members to be offended. More often, it's because they don't want it to affect the weekly offering. Others won't mention abortion because they don't want to appear to judge those who've participated in one. But it's not about judgment—it's about *restoration*. While sin opens the door to destruction, repentance heals and restores.

When I was the national director of the Center for Reclaiming America, we launched the Truth in Love campaign to let those engaging in homosexual activity know that there was "hope for change." Shortly afterward, 300 people picketed Dr. D. James Kennedy's Coral Ridge Presbyterian Church (which I attended) across from my office. They were angry that we would suggest there was such a thing as a *former* homosexual; after all, they claimed they were "born that way." So we prayed for them. It was a simple, "God, please speak the truth to their hearts in a way they will hear it."

Two years later I was speaking to a group of ex-homosexuals who were finding healing and deliverance from unwanted same-sex attractions. Afterward, I was approached by a man named Robert. He said, "I was one of the people who stood outside the church picketing you and Dr. Kennedy. I just wanted to say thank you for having the courage to stand in the face of all the attacks and hostility so that people like me could hear the truth." He then told me that he was now free from homosexuality and same-sex attraction, his marriage was restored, and he was back home with his wife and children.

If in your heart you repent and choose to follow Jesus, He can help you turn from sin, and if you fall He will pick you back up. In fact, Proverbs 24:16 says, "For though the righteous fall seven times, they rise again, but the wicked stumble when calamity strikes" (NIV). The key is a heart of *repentance.*

Dietrich Bonhoeffer put it this way, "Cheap grace is the grace we bestow on ourselves. Cheap grace is the preaching of forgiveness without requiring repentance."[5]

William Booth, the founder of the Salvation Army, once said: "The chief dangers which confront the coming century will be religion without the Holy Ghost, Christianity without Christ, forgiveness without repentance, salvation without regeneration, politics without God, and heaven without hell."[6]

International preacher Bobby Connor has suggested that our timidity may be a sign of our carnality. He points to Proverbs 28:1, which states, "The wicked flee when no one pursues, but the righteous are bold as a lion." He suggests that the foremost reason for the lack of power in the church is a lack of holiness.[7]

Financial advisor Dave Ramsey said, "If you will live like no one else, later you can live like no one else."[8] That's not just for living debt free. Want the book of your life to read like the miraculous pages of the Bible? Want the movie of your life to be an action adventure that changes the course of history? It's not always easy but it's always worth it. "But the people who know their God will display strength and take action" (Daniel 11:32 NASB). That is how our life is meant to be. If it's not, there's something you can do about it. Remove the obstacles of disappointment, fear, and compromise, and step out to end abortion and change the world.

If a Heartbeat Bill has passed where you live, great—join us in the effort to pass the federal Heartbeat Bill, or support the effort to end abortion elsewhere physically or financially. If a Heartbeat Bill hasn't passed in your state or nation, you have an unprecedented opportunity. God has given us a tool in the Heartbeat Bill that can save more lives than everything we've done so far—*combined*. And passing a bill in your state or nation may be easier than you realize. Here are the basic steps to pick up the sword and lead the charge:

1. Recruit a team.

The first step is to assemble a core team of two to five people who are willing to do "whatever it takes." These are people you would trust with your life and the lives of millions of children. The enemy loves to infiltrate so you must have key people you can trust. I could write a chapter about people in our "inner circle" who shouldn't have been there, but sometimes you find out too late. You need a "Lori Viars"—the one who backs you even in the fire and won't retreat when it gets hot. You also need people of great faith who aren't intimidated by giants and huge walls of resistance.

2. Pray for the right sponsor.

The model Heartbeat Bill—posted at Faith2Action.org and Heart-BeatBill.com—will serve as a starting place for your state representatives and senators to draft heartbeat legislation specific to your state and nation. But before you give the model bill to just any pro-life lawmaker, first pray about who would be best to lead the charge. Research the pro-life leaders in your state legislature. You will need to find those who really want to end abortion, and not just those who sponsor the incremental regulation bills supported by the establishment.

3. Don't be impressed by rank.

When we were drafting the first Heartbeat Bill in 2010, I was so excited to have a Heartbeat Bill sponsor who was the chairman of the committee hearing the bill that I didn't even pray about it. It seemed too good to be true. I overrode other suggestions because the guy we were asking used to be "anti-establishment." He used to be a fighter. But when the establishment pushed back, he toed their line. When picking a sponsor, find the one with nothing to lose. Forget about optics. You don't need a chairman or a female—you need a champion. Thankfully, the first female we chose to lead became a champion, but it took some time for her to see the establishment Republicans she was beholden to were lying through their teeth.

4. Line up your cosponsors.

Before you announce to the world what you are about to do, do the hard work first. Every time we introduced the Heartbeat Bill in Ohio, we had a majority of House (and Senate in 2019) members as cosponsors. Get as many cosponsors as you can to make the strongest case possible that your bill has support and can pass if brought to the floor. It's also much harder to talk someone into voting against the bill if their name is on top of it.

5. Get allied groups to stand with you.

Don't rule out your state Right to Life groups. Some of them really want to end abortion and will help you. But because of the influence of National Right to Life, many become predisposed toward sabotage, so I would save asking them until last. Don't discount smaller or local pro-life and pro-family groups and pastors. Pastors are key, especially if they will let you speak at their church. Even a 5-minute announcement can help build an army of activists and prayer warriors. Some even take a collection to help with the educational part of the campaign to keep hearts beating. If those you ask won't help, ask if they will lend their name to your list of supporters. A large list of supporters means a lot to legislators; it has always been one of our first hand-outs in meetings. Then, you can do what I did—print it on an enormous board and hold it over your head for all to see at your Heartbeat Bill rally! Legislators find courage when they know they are not alone.

6. Build your website, email, and media lists.

If you don't have a website, get one. We can even link to it from HeartbeatBill.com. Then, build an email list through a site like Constant Contact or Mailchimp so you can keep people involved with how they can help. You can inform them of your press conferences, rallies, or the phones that need to ring. You can also use social media (until they block you) driving them to your website or the call to action.

Then, build a list of the media you want to target (you can find this information online) and write a press release to announce your press conference that introduces your bill. Don't forget Christian radio, television, and print. Reserve a room for your press conference at the Statehouse or a hotel near your capitol that's convenient for the Statehouse press to attend. In addition to the media (reached through your press release and follow-up phone calls), you should also invite the bill sponsors, select cosponsors, and supportive groups that call for its passage. Get a sign-in table outside the room so you know who is coming and what media they represent. If pro-abortion groups try to get in, politely but firmly tell them, "Sorry, this is a media-only event by invitation only." Then ask your allied groups to reach people through email blasts, social media posts, phone calls, and meetings.

Once you have laid this groundwork, it's time to start moving the bill through the legislature. Every state will have unique procedures, but this general overview applies to all states:

- ♥ **Assemble Prayer Warriors.** You want a team of faith-filled prayer warriors to persistently pray throughout the effort from the very beginning until your victory (banners optional).

- ♥ **Introduce the bill** in your House or Senate—wherever you have the most support—with as many cosponsors as possible.

- ♥ **Get a committee hearing scheduled**. Bring in witnesses for the bill, including doctors, lawyers, group leaders, post-abortive women, pastors, concerned citizens, and an unborn child via mobile ultrasound or video. For the committee vote, stack the room with supporters who will arrive early to fill the seats. You don't want to be moved to an overflow room; you want your supporters in the main room praying.

- ♥ **Wear red**. I recommend supporters show their numbers in unity by wearing red. You want the committee members to look out to audience and see how many people stand with you—even if they aren't testifying for the bill. Buttons are also good, but keep them positive. The abortion supporters usually wear a clashing pink or purple with negative messaging. Let the representatives and senators see the stark contrast.

♥ **Secure the needed support to pass the bill in committee.**
If you are the leader, your job is to count the votes. Do
not schedule a vote and "hope for the best." Work with
the Heartbeat Bill sponsor and committee chairman to
schedule the vote when you know you have the votes. This
is not something you can ever take for granted. A "yes"
2 weeks ago isn't necessarily a "yes" vote today. Check
back just prior to the vote to make sure *everyone* is still
committed to keep hearts beating.

♥ **Secure the needed support and schedule a floor vote.**
Again, as a leader of the battle, your job is to count the
votes. There was only one time we lost in the Ohio House—
it was when they scheduled a floor vote without telling us,
and we were not able to do the necessary groundwork to
make sure we had the votes. We had a plurality, but not a
majority. If the members don't keep you informed about
what's happening, you can't help deliver the votes. Stay in
constant communication with them.

♥ **Repeat in the other chamber.** Nebraska is the only
unicameral state, with a one-body legislative system. All
others have two: both a House and a Senate. Unless you
live in Nebraska, once you get your floor vote in either your
House or Senate, you must repeat the process in the other
body, ending with a passing floor vote. If no changes are
made to the bill passed in the second chamber, it goes right
to the governor for a signature. If changes are made, it will
have to go back to the other body to approve them first.

♥ **Get the governor's signature or bypass him.** If you get a
signature, your bill becomes a law. Prepare for the challenge
in the courts to prevent the law from going into effect. If
the governor vetoes the bill, go back to your legislature and
seek the votes to override the veto. Once you have enough
votes, have your bill sponsor to go to the legislature's
leadership to call the vote. Any obstruction along the
way must be called out. This is when your senators' and
representatives' phones must ring like crazy—to secure
their support and build the case for leadership to call for a
vote to override the veto. Push for a vote to override a veto
even if the votes aren't there. Why? First, some who tell
you "no" will vote "yes" when put on the spot. They don't
want to be featured as a heartless pro-abort in the next
election. Second, we want people on record to find out
who we need to challenge in the next election. And third,
you have nothing to lose by trying.

A few months ago, I was speaking at the Trump International Hotel
in Washington, D.C., at an event hosted by Cindy Jacobs, cofounder of
a ministry called Generals International. There I ran into a dear friend
from Arizona named Deb Welch. Our paths had crossed many years ago,
when we often prayed together for the end of abortion.

But I noticed something different about Deb. She wasn't saying, "You
go out there and get 'em while we cover you in prayer." She wanted the
model Heartbeat Bill to get it passed in Arizona. She wasn't about to be
one of the states without a Heartbeat law! She told me she understands
how much is on the line in the next election and said she wouldn't even

let her prayer meeting participants leave without first registering them to vote. A great idea—one we should also implement in churches!

She is now a precinct committeewoman, attending the GOP events. I just returned from meeting with her prayer warriors, and an Arizona legislator working to introduce the Arizona Heartbeat Bill. What happens when the prayer movement joins with the *action* movement? What happens when the church joins with those of us on the front lines? I'll tell you what happens—we *win*.

Psalm 133 says that God commands a blessing when there is unity among us:

> *Behold, how good and how pleasant it is for brethren to dwell together in unity! ...For there the Lord commanded the blessing—life forevermore* (Psalm 133:1,3).

If you have been on the sidelines, blocked by disappointment, fear, and compromise, this is your moment. Today is a new day. You have been given a divine do-over. Lock shields with your allies and prepare for battle because your victory awaits. This is your moment to pick up the sword.

But don't expect to cross your finish line without a fight. You have to remember, like with football, when you are a touchdown away from victory at the 5-yard line, that is when every defensive player is standing as a blockade wall between you and the goal line. If your battle is anything like ours, expect to have to fight to the very last inch.

The Ohio Senate gutted the Heartbeat Bill before passing it 2019. By requiring only external ultrasounds instead of the bill's original language, which required "standard medical practice," they made sure only babies from 12 weeks were protected instead of as early as 6 weeks. That was just over 3,000 babies instead of 20,000 babies each year.

I didn't throw a huge fit in the Senate, because we were happy to get anything through what had been our biggest obstacle. Our plan was to fix the bill back to its original form in the House. The fact that House leadership was holding a meeting about our bill without so much as inviting me was not a good sign. It's moments like these when whom you choose as a prime sponsor really matters.

Heartbeat Bill sponsor Ron Hood said, "If you're not going to that meeting, then there won't be a meeting." Yeah, I picked the right guy. Heartbeat Bill joint sponsor Candice Keller backed him up and brought me into the meeting as if I had been invited. I told them that the ultrasound issue was a "deal-breaker," and I think they could tell that I meant it. I told them we didn't fight for 9 years to save a handful of babies. We need to save them all, and they could tell I was prepared to go to war over it. I was shocked when they agreed to the change we needed.

I shouldn't have been shocked when they reneged on their word. On a conference call with the chairman and the speaker's office, they let us know that change wasn't going to be made. I threw a fit.

"What do you mean? That essential change was agreed to by everyone in our meeting!"

They didn't argue that they agreed to it, just the matter of keeping their agreement. Be prepared, for the final 5% is a fight to the finish.

On Monday night, the day before the committee vote, I was on the phone with my friend Mark Harrington of Created Equal. We had already called our sponsor, Rep. Ron Hood, and the governor's office to enlist their help. While Mark and I were planning the Statehouse press conference for the next day to scream bloody murder, I got a call from the chairman and the speaker's office.

The call began with four words, said with more than a hint of disdain, *"What do you want?"*

I gave up a few small items on our list and said, "I want the *external* ultrasound language out so we can protect all the babies whose heartbeats can be detected."

This really isn't a controversial issue. The abortionists use transvaginal ultrasounds. Abby Johnson testified in committee for the Kentucky Heartbeat Bill that "A transvaginal ultrasound is standard procedure inside of every National Abortion Federation clinic which includes every Planned Parenthood." She added, "That transvaginal ultrasound is done for primarily one reason: to determine how far along a woman is in her pregnancy so that we knew how much to charge her for the abortion."[9]

Transvaginal ultrasounds are standard in abortion clinics. But when it comes to detecting the baby's heartbeat, people scream that it's "intrusive." No, it's "standard medical practice," which is all the Heartbeat Bill requires. For those who say this is intrusive to women should take a look at abortion—a real intrusion to a woman's body—and the body of her growing child.

They agreed to my demand, but as we learned from Ronald Reagan, I told them I would, "Trust, but verify." I explained that I would need to see the language before we signed off on it. After all, it's not like they kept their word the last time.

Mark Harrington and I were there at the Statehouse, as instructed, at 9:00 a.m. waiting to see the language. We waited. And waited. Finally, less than 10 minutes before the committee hearing where the language

Mark Harrington, Heartbeat Sponsor Rep. Candice Keller and Janet Porter after the final committee vote to pass the Ohio Heartbeat Bill.

was to be voted on, we were handed the amendment. I took a picture of it as we briskly walked to the hearing, emailing it to our co counsel Walter Weber, of the American Center for Law and Justice. Three minutes before the hearing started, we got the green light from Walter. They had, in fact, kept their word this time. The bill was voted out with babies as early as 6 weeks protected. But we still had to clear the full House and Senate floor vote.

We heard from two sources—a senator and an email from the Senate President's Chief of Staff—that the Senate President wasn't happy about the change.[10] We were warned that he would try to gut the bill again by taking it to conference committee. It was Wednesday morning the day of the vote. That is when I called the governor on his cell phone and filled him in on what was happening. He promised to "look into it."

Given the information we had hours before the vote, the only move we had was to alert our members to what was happening. I knew that ringing the senate president's phone off the hook was going to upset him. But our goal was to save babies—as many as we possibly could. If the senate president was planning to gut the Heartbeat Bill again, I wanted him to know that he was going to be held accountable—by *very informed* constituents.

I called Lori Viars before I hit "send." She agreed—given what we were told, we had no choice but to send the email. This is the email I sent to tens of thousands of our members before my husband and I headed to the Statehouse for the House and Senate final vote:

> **Is the Senate planning to gut the Heartbeat Bill today?**
>
> Ask Ohio Senate President Larry Obhof to pass the stronger House version of the Heartbeat Bill today without gutting it with an amendment that would kill more than 15,000 babies each year.
>
> **Please Call Senate President Larry Obhof Now**

The Ohio House was voting before the Senate that day, and so while Obhof's phones rang, Lori and I worked the house members to make sure they weren't going to try to weaken the bill. Thankfully, they did not. The session began while the pro-aborts screeched outside the chambers non stop for hours. Legislators described them as demonic, and I couldn't disagree. The moment the vote was cast, the pro-aborts unfurled banners from the balcony of the House chamber while their mob made a scene outside the chamber doors. That was a tactical error on their part. If they were smarter, they would have sent their people over to the Senate whose vote was still needed to seal the victory.

Our team ran to the Senate, where people were already saving our seats and praying. The pro-aborts were still too busy protesting in the House to show up. We needed to make sure the Senate would concur with the House-passed version of the Heartbeat Bill. I sat in my usual place on the front row next to Lori Viars, my mom, Beth Folger, and my husband, David Porter, where we had access to the senators on the floor and right where the Senate President could see us. Our prayer warriors and activists filled every seat we could save—nearly all of them.

Senate President Obhof was there early, probably to escape the sound of his ringing phones. He slammed down the gavel before most of the members even arrived. After Senator Roegner's floor speech and customary Democrat attempts to amend it, the vote was cast and the bill passed unscathed. We were going to protect *all* the children with detectable heartbeats and not just a few thousand of them! With the promised signature from Governor DeWine, this vote meant our victory was final, children with beating hearts would live and not die! *Finally.*

Just after the victory, I spent time alone with God. I had spent years asking Him for the victory and my heart was bursting with gratitude and praise. The daily reading in my One-Year NIV Bible that day included Jeremiah 50:21b: *"Do everything I have commanded you."* And, for the first time in the fierce and lengthy 9-year battle to keep hearts beating, I was able to take my pen and make a check mark on the page. Praise be to God!

When you expose the Republican Senate President's plan to gut the Heartbeat Bill for a second time, you won't be the most popular person in Republican circles. Especially after you challenged him in the primary. You might even be banned from the bill signing of your own bill.

I talked with the Governor the morning of the vote to inform him of the reports that the Senate President was planning to gut the bill again and was told he was going to "look into it." I don't know for certain what happened next, but if the "deal" was that we would get the full protection of children if I was disinvited to the bill signing, I will take that deal any day. *Any day.*

I would do it all again, in a heartbeat.

April 10, 2019 after the final passage of the Ohio Heartbeat Bill through the House and Senate.[11] This core group of champions, standing next to the plaque where Abraham Lincoln stood, met after the final House and Senate victory in the Statehouse Atrium—where we had rallied and prayed many times.

Yes, there are always people at the finish line who never ran the race. That was never more true than in Ohio on April 11, 2019.[12] Not only were there people smiling for the photo op who did nothing to pass the bill, there were those who fought us for years including the President and Executive Director of Ohio Right to Life, who lobbied and testified against the Heartbeat Bill for 8 years, and called for its veto not once but *twice*.

Also missing from the bill signing: Lori Viars, whom I awarded the Heartbeat MVP award, and former Rep. Christina Hagan, a champion of the Heartbeat Bill for years.

The day of the bill signing my husband and I saw the movie *Unplanned*. The girl at the ticket counter recognized me from speaking at her church during my campaign for senate, still recalling the horrific slander against me. As I told her that day, I might have lost, but the babies won. During the film, I turned to my husband and said, "We just stopped *this*."

There is something *far* better than being well liked by the establishment, invited to the balls, receptions, and photo ops—that's *ending abortion*. It can be done and you can be the one to do it.

The battleground is your state and nation. The arrow is crafted. The target is fixed. The strategy secure. Heartbeat Bills spread like wildfire across the country beginning with Heartbeat Laws in Arkansas and North Dakota in 2013 and Iowa in 2018. But it was in 2019 that Heartbeat Bills became law in Mississippi, Kentucky, Georgia, Missouri, Louisiana, and...Ohio, where it all began.

The movement that is sweeping across America is now getting attention around the globe. I have met with pro-life leaders in Asia and Israel along with leaders from New Zealand and Panama. Pro-life leaders are now working to bring a Heartbeat Bill to Japan. The Heartbeat Bill wildfire will soon ignite around the world!

On January 22, 2020 President Trump declared the anniversary of *Roe v. Wade* "Sanctity of Life Day" and stated, "We will never tire of defending innocent life."[13] We must return him to office to finish the job. Take heart. This is our moment to forget about the fear of man and start acting like the word of God is true. To step out and do "whatever it takes," no matter the cost to defeat the enemies without and the enemies within. To speak the truth even if the ground shakes. To stand up to the bullies, science deniers, C-list celebrities, Internet censors, and speech police. We will topple the giants, pick up our sword, and fight until we win.

When we began the Heartbeat effort back in 2010, ending abortion seemed impossible; it is now inevitable. As the first president to speak at the March for Life in January 2020, President Trump said, "We are fighting for those who have no voice...And we will win because we know how to win."[14]

The Heartbeat Bill is the way to win.

Our testimony is your prophecy; our victory will soon become yours.

Together, we're gonna end abortion. Write it down—the collapse of *Roe v. Wade* is a heartbeat away.

All glory to the God of the impossible!

From start to finish prayer paved the way to victory.

Take the Land

"Take possession of the land and settle in it, because I have given it to you to occupy." —Numbers 33:53 NLT

I once spent the night working on a project at a FedEx Kinkos where I met some self-described Satanists. I asked, "You're not *really* Satanists, are you? It's just a gimmic for your music, right?"

No, they told me they were the real deal. So I asked them another question, "How did you find out about Satan? I mean, how do you know he even exists—through the *Bible*, right?"

One of them answered, "Among other places."

I said, "So, if you read the Bible to find out about your hero, Satan, what you'll find is he's not just out to steal, kill, and destroy your enemies, he's out to steal, kill, and destroy...*you*. And if you read the end of the book, you'll find that those who follow him don't end up so good."

The *author* of life, who knit you together in your mother's womb, is *God*. His existence isn't determined by whether or not you believe in

Him. Like gravity, some things are true whether you believe them or not. Likewise, our opinion about God doesn't alter the truth.

Even more basic than "live baby: good, dead baby: bad" is:

- God is good.
- Satan is bad.
- Both are real.

It's God who is good. Yet it astounds me how many people get that wrong and blame God for the results of our bad choices and all the evil in the world.

Reverend Billy Graham was asked, "If Christianity is valid, why is there so much evil in the world?" He responded, "With so much soap, why are there so many dirty people in the world? Christianity, like soap, must be personally applied if it is to make a difference in our lives."[1]

Before I discuss conquering other giants who occupy our land, let me address the most important part of this book and of life. Even more important than the right to life is where you will spend *eternal* life. You see, everyone gets eternal life. The question is where will you spend it? It may not mean much to you now, but one day it's going to mean *every-thing*. Because not only is heaven real, even though hardly anyone talks about it, so is *hell*. Another basic truth:

- Heaven is good.
- Hell is bad.
- Both are forever.

Even though you never hear anyone talk about hell, Jesus did. If you only read the red letters in scripture, you would find that Jesus talked about hell more than any one else in the Bible.[2] In Matthew 10:28 Jesus said: "And do not fear those who kill the body but cannot kill the soul. But rather fear Him who is able to destroy both soul and body in hell."

William Booth, the founder of the Salvation Army, said, "Most Christians would like to send their recruits to Bible college for 5 years. I would like to send them to hell for 5 minutes. That would do more than anything else to prepare them for a lifetime of compassionate ministry."[3]

Hell is a literal place, but not where all your friends will go to party. If you know anyone still considering it as an eternal destination, here are some descriptions of hell from the Bible for the travel brochure:

- Lake of fire (Revelation 20:14)
- Eternal punishment (Matthew 25:46)
- Eternal fire prepared for the devil and his angels (Matthew 25:41)
- Unquenchable fire (Mark 9:43)
- Punishment of eternal destruction (2 Thessalonians 1:9)
- Pits of darkness (2 Peter 2:4)
- Fiery furnace (Matthew 13:50)
- There will be weeping and gnashing of teeth (Matthew 13:50)
- Judgment by fire (2 Peter 3:7)
- Fire and brimstone (Revelation 20:10)

- Where their worm does not die and the fire is not quenched (Mark 9:48)

The bad news is hell is real, but the good news is you don't have to go there. The people you love don't have to go there.

Because of sin, hell is the default destination; heaven is by reservation only. So, before you do *anything else*, let me first urge you to get your name (and the name of everyone you care about) on heaven's list. It's more of a *book*, actually. But belief in God isn't what reserves your place. Even the devil believes in God, and, well, he's not going to heaven. Being a "good person" won't get you there, since the Bible says even "our righteousness" is "like filthy rags" (Isaiah 64:6).

Being pro-life won't cut it. Being a conservative or a Republican won't get you through the gate. Neither will funding every environmental or social program in existence.

So how do we get our name on Heaven's reservation list? What would Dr. D. James Kennedy, founder of Evangelism Explosion, say?

While working for Dr. Kennedy at the Center for Reclaiming America, I filmed a pro-life television commercial. In studio was Norma McCorvey, the "Roe" of *Roe v. Wade*, Sandra Cano, the "Doe" of the companion decision *Doe v. Bolton,* and former abortionist Bernard Nathanson, the founder of NARAL then called the National Association for the Repeal of Abortion Laws.[4] Norma McCorvey, the plaintiff in *Roe*, admitted she lied about being gang-raped, the lie upon which *Roe* was based.[5] She called her case, which legalized abortion on demand, "the biggest mistake of my life."[6]

Sandra Cano never wanted an abortion and was used by pro-abortion lawyers as a pawn. Her companion case removed all abortion limits since "health of the mother" was defined to include "all factors—physical emotional, psychological, familial, and the woman's age."[7] In other words, you can kill a child in the womb for any reason at all. The commercial pointed to the fact that the rulings on abortion were based on lies, just as NARAL's founder, Bernard Nathanson, admitted he lied about the number of women who died from illegal abortions,[8] The real numbers were a tiny fraction of the thousands he claimed. Nathanson later said, "I confess that I knew the figures were totally false, but...it was a useful figure, widely accepted, so why go out of our way to correct it with honest statistics?"[9] The year we ran the commercial, the first question asked at the NARAL press conference was about their founder's admission that their organization is based on a lie. Money well spent.

Here I was with Dr. Kennedy at lunch with the three people most responsible for abortion in America. What would Dr. Kennedy say? He explained the Gospel to our guests—*with silverware*. He pointed to the knife next to the plate stating, "That's every religion in the world: 'I' *must*, 'I' *need*, 'I' *should*...." He stated that every religion says that we must *do* something to earn our way to heaven—with *one exception*. He then placed his fork over the knife in the shape of a cross stating, "Christianity is the only religion about what God did for us—so we could be with Him." I believe all four of them are now together with God who reached down from heaven to provide a way to save us.

God's hand is not too short to save *anyone*—even Bernard Nathanson who performed 5,000 abortions and oversaw another 60,000.[10] But the problem most have isn't that they think they've sinned *too much* for God to forgive them; most think they haven't sinned at all.

You hear it all the time from those who are busy making God in their own image: "*I'm a good person, I'm not a murderer or a rapist, of course I'm going to heaven.*" But what God said is, "For *all* have sinned and fall short of the glory of God" (Romans 3:23). All means—*all*. And, big or small, the price for sin is *death*. Not because I said it but because God did. "For the wages of sin is death, but the gift of God is eternal life in Christ Jesus our Lord" (Romans 6:23).

So here's the choice facing you and all of mankind, given that we are all sinners and the price for sin is death. The question everyone must answer is:

Who do you want to pay for it?

A. You

B. Jesus

I don't know about you, but I choose "B." I pick Jesus. He already paid the price of death for our sins so we don't have to; that's what the cross was all about. That's why the Gospel is called the "good news." Baptist Pastor Dr. Steve Lawson put it this way: "Salvation is not a reward for the righteous, it is a gift for the guilty."[11]

Evangelist Reinhard Bonnke stated Jesus wasn't "raised on the cross just to raise our standard of living. He died to seek and to save those who are lost."[12]

For those who think that there are lots of ways to heaven, think again. Jesus said He was the only way and I believe Him:

> *Jesus said to him, "I am the way, the truth, and the life. No one comes to the Father except through Me"* (John 14:6).

Think about it for a minute, if there were lots of ways, then Jesus wouldn't have had to be tortured to death on the cross, right? He even asked God the Father if there was any *other* possible way for us to be saved, to do *that* instead:

> *He went a little farther and fell on His face, and prayed, saying, "O My Father, if it is possible, let this cup pass from Me; nevertheless, not as I will, but as You will"* (Matthew 26:39).

The answer was *no*.

Jesus paid the mandatory price for sin when He died on the cross in our place. But you have to do more than just *know* that in your head. I can know that my father gave me a new Ferrari, but until I take the keys from him I haven't *received* it. That's what we have to do with Jesus—receive Him; He's the key to our salvation. Faith is the outstretched hand, the instrument to *receive* the salvation Jesus paid for when He took the punishment our sins deserved.

I remember the picture that hung in my grandparents' dining room with the verse from Acts 16:31a: "Believe on the Lord Jesus Christ, and you will be saved, you and your household."

Growing up, my mother called that her "fire insurance." She believed—did that mean she was saved? She told me it wasn't until she understood that the word translated "believe" really means: "to rely upon, to cling to, to trust in completely, on a continual basis" that she knew what that verse really meant.[13,14]

Rely upon, cling to, and trust completely—like a loving father with his toddler son. Here's the picture I once heard Pastor Jentezen Franklin describe. Imagine a 2-year-old lost in the mall. He is scared. Crying. Wandering around lost. Well-meaning people try to console him, "Here, have some ice cream, little boy." That takes his mind off his lost condition for a moment, but just for a moment. He cries again, longing for his daddy. People then try and distract him with a shiny toy car. "Look! Play with this, little boy!" And so the little boy plays with the toy car for a moment, but that doesn't satisfy the longing in his heart. Strangers say he's a good boy, but that's not what he longs for—he wants to be picked up by his father and feel his father's love, his affirmation, his protection. Only God can fill the deepest longing of our heart.

God's plan has always been for a family. God the Father looked down on a planet of orphans and wanted to adopt us into His family, but we had already been lured into the trap of sin. Knowing the price for our escape, the Father sent His Son on a rescue mission. Jesus agreed—He would rather die than live without you. He traded His life for ours so we could be a part of His family forever. After living a sinless life, Jesus paid for our rescue and adoption with His blood, the most powerful substance in existence.

But God doesn't *force* anyone into His family; the choice remains yours. Rev. Billy Graham put it this way, "God will never send anybody to hell. If man goes to hell, he goes by his own free choice."[15]

You have a decision to make. No decision is also a decision. Jesus already signed your adoption papers with His blood. If you want to be a part of God's family and reserve your place in heaven, pray this prayer with your heart and your voice. Then you can sign the adoption papers, too.

> **All have sinned.**
> **The price for sin is death.**
> **Who do you want to pay for it?**
>
> **A. You**
> **B. Jesus**

Father, I'm sorry for sinning against You and I ask You to forgive me. I believe You died on the cross and rose from the dead to pay the price for every sin I have committed. I trust You alone to be my Savior and ask You to become the Lord in charge of my life. Help me turn away from sin and follow You to fulfill the future and destiny You have planned for me. In Jesus' name, amen.

Name _____

Date _____

If you prayed that prayer and meant it in your heart, welcome to the family of God. God said, "if you confess with your mouth the Lord Jesus and believe [rely upon, cling to, and trust completely] in your heart that God has raised Him from the dead, you will be saved" (Romans 10:9). We don't have to wonder about it, we can know for sure.

> *These things I have written to you who believe in the name of the Son of God, that you may know that you have eternal life, and that you may continue to believe in the name of the Son of God* (1 John 5:13).

You weren't just getting "fire insurance" to escape eternal death when you signed God's adoption papers; you become a true son or daughter of God. And, according to Galatians 4:7: "Therefore you are no longer a slave [to sin] but a son, and if a son, then an heir of God through Christ." That means you have access to not just everlasting life, but to *everything* God has promised us in His word. Salvation is *just the beginning*.

God's best-selling book is your roadmap. It's filled with more than 7,000 amazing promises for your life that are yours for the asking.[16] Because God is a loving Father, He doesn't recommend we play in the middle of the highway. He put up ten main guard rails to keep us from getting hit by a truck or falling off a cliff. As I mentioned, being a Christian isn't really about the stuff we're not supposed to do—it's about the amazing destiny we were *created* to do! History is *His*-story. As Pastor Bill Johnson declared, "If you'll make history with God, He'll make history through you."[17]

Like taking the keys to the Ferrari, if you prayed the prayer to enter into God's family and meant it in your heart, you have received the gift of God's salvation through Jesus. That is when your real life begins. The Christian life, as it was meant to be, is the opposite of a boring, humdrum life of barely making it and "what not to do." It's exchanging the burden of guilt and shame for mercy, forgiveness, freedom, and power. It's where we get to take the keys to the Ferrari and actually *drive* it. And like the German Autobahn, there are no limits.

The Real War

For years, I bought the lie that we need to leave God out of our public discussion of issues because some don't believe in God or His word. I would always debate the issue of life on the foundation of science, which proves human life, and the role of government, which is to protect human life. I was wrong. I no longer believe we should keep God and His word out of any discussion. In my documentary *Light Wins,* Ken Ham from Answers in Genesis and the Creation Museum gave the clearest explanation I've heard as to why:

> Imagine two knights fighting and one knight says to the other, "Before we begin, throw down your sword." Now, you would say, the other knight's not going to do that, that would be a stupid idea. So we throw away the Bible—in other words we give up our sword—because God's word is the sword of the Spirit. When we give up our sword, we've really conceded defeat. You've already said "We can deal with this without God."

In order to advance the kingdom of God, we need to quit pretending like we can do it without Him. Doing the impossible takes more than a quick prayer, and "I'll take it from here." If we're going to see the impossible bow to the name of Jesus, we need to quit leaving Jesus out of the discussion and out of room.

That's because what we're facing is bigger than what we can see. While most don't realize it, we were born on a battlefield. That's why Ephesians 6:12-17 tells us to put on that armor:

For we do not wrestle against flesh and blood, but against principalities, against powers, against the rulers of the darkness of this age, against spiritual hosts of wickedness in the heavenly places. Therefore take up the whole armor of God, that you may be able to withstand in the evil day, and having done all, to stand.

Stand therefore, having girded your waist with truth, having put on the breastplate of righteousness, and having shod your feet with the preparation of the gospel of peace; above all, taking the shield of faith with which you will be able to quench all the fiery darts of the wicked one. And take the helmet of salvation, and the sword of the Spirit, which is the word of God.

We know we're in a spiritual battle, but what does that mean? The Bible told us that things that are seen are made from things that are unseen (see Heb. 11:3). Before the invention of the microscope that seemed ridiculous. How can what we see be made from the invisible? Once again, the Bible was proven true over the pre-microscope world of "science."

Because we've all looked through a microscope, we understand our bodies are made of cells, which are invisible to the naked eye. And yet, for some reason, it seems hard for us to understand an unseen spiritual world actually affecting our physical world. It begins with an accurate understanding of who we are. Here's a basic question most don't consider.

Q: Are you a body or a spirit?

A: We are a spirit, we have a soul (mind, will, and emotions), and we live in a body.

My former boss Dr. D. James Kennedy explained it this way. Just as we can learn about an artist from their art, we can see hints of the Creator in creation. God is a trinity—Father, Son, and Holy Spirit. We see God's fingerprint in how he made us—also a trinity: body, soul, and spirit. God's triune fingerprints are seen in His creation. The universe consists of space, time, and matter; space consists of length, breadth, and height; and time consists of the past, present, and future.[18]

We know what a body is. We have all been to funerals where the body of a person is there but "they"—the real them—is not (see Dan. 7:15). Their spirit has left (see Eccles. 12:7). We get that.

But we seldom think of ourselves as a spirit housed within a body. Because we are spirits, we are more connected to the invisible spiritual realm than we thought.

There's a door that connects our spirits to God. His name is Jesus. He called himself "the door" that leads to salvation (see John 10:9). But there is also a bridge to the unseen world called faith. It's the bridge by which God's promises are delivered to us. Faith is what connects us to the invisible realities of God and His Word, bringing the unseen into the seen.

Now faith is the assurance [the confirmation, the title deed] of the things [we] hope for, being the proof of things [we] do not see and the conviction of their reality [faith perceiving as real fact what is not revealed to the senses] (Hebrews 11:1 AMPC).

With faith we have the "assurance," "confirmation," "proof," "reality," "real fact," and the "title deed" for the things for which we hope. If our prayers are grounded in God's word, faith is the "confirmation" of the answer that's on the way. The "title deed" for what we own but haven't yet seen. The victory we have not yet experienced. Through faith we can see victory and overcome the world: "For whatever is born of God overcomes the world. And this is the victory that has overcome the world—our faith. Who is he who overcomes the world, but he who believes that Jesus is the Son of God?" (1 John 5:4-5).

How do you get faith? It comes by hearing, so turn off the distractions and immerse yourself in the word of God (Romans 10:17). Let it seep into your heart.

How do you get boldness? Seek God's face like we're told in the 2 Chronicles 7:14 checklist (right after humbling our self and praying and right before the part where we turn from our wicked ways). The more time you spend with God the less impressed you'll be with the giants. So turn off the "giant report" and immerse yourself in the presence of God like Peter and John did. Even though they were ordinary men, people were amazed by their boldness and recognized they had been with Jesus (see Acts 4:13).

Jesus told us to "occupy" until He returns. *He meant that.* God said, "Ask of Me, and I will give You the nations for Your inheritance, and the ends of the earth for Your possession" (Psalms 2:8). Every time I read that verse, I ask for America. It's a *starting* place.

If you want the book of your life to read like the miraculous pages of the Bible, and the movie of your life to be an action adventure that changes the course of history, spend time with the director and find out what He has for you in the next scene. Once you know what that is, you can step out of your comfort zone with confidence. You can move mountains. You will slay giants.

The Goliath of abortion is teetering. He's just been pummeled with ten rocks to the head, with many more being loaded into slings. Nine Heartbeat Laws and Alabama's complete protection law were just the beginning. As in David's day, there are more giants who occupy our land. Giants who also must fall.

Four More Giants

To advance the kingdom of God, we must move from defense to offense, starting with the key battlefronts where the threat is the greatest to life, liberty, and the family. We must take back ground instead of reacting, responding, and defending a shrinking piece of real estate. Take the land and occupy it instead of complaining about the giants who rule because we have let them. With a change in strategy comes a change in results. As in David's day, more giants will fall.

These four were born to the giant in Gath, and fell by the hand of David and by the hand of his servants (2 Samuel 21:22).

Goliath had four gigantic brothers who occupied the land who were next to fall. It is time for history to repeat itself. So pick your giant, but not just any giant. How do we decide which giants to slay first? Martin Luther provides direction I have always used:

> Though we be active in the battle, if we are not fighting where the battle is the hottest, we are traitors to the cause. —Martin Luther[19]

The battle is the hottest where the threat is the greatest to life, liberty, and the family. We must first conquer the giants who are the biggest threats. To take the land there are four giants who currently occupy our centers of power and influence and threaten our freedoms, our elections, our children, and our values. For us to advance, these giants must fall: 1. Internet Monopoly, 2. Voter Fraud, 3. Government School Monopoly, and 4. Fake News and Evil Entertainment.

1. Internet Monopoly

As Chapter 11 explains, the public square is now found online and the giant who occupies it controls our information and our votes. This Internet giant hates us and everything we believe and is using its power to squash, silence, and remove us from the public square entirely. The big tech monopolies strangling our free exchange of ideas and information must be broken before a dark web extinguishes the light of truth.

Urge those who represent you in Congress to pass legislation like Senator Josh Hawley's (R-MO) "Ending Support for Internet Censorship Act." Start by using an alternative search engine that doesn't track your every move such as DuckDuckgo.com. Stop feeding this giant and fueling their agenda; don't buy on Amazon. Call out and push back against the censorship. To keep our freedoms, this giant must fall—before the next election is decided without us.

2. Voter Fraud

Next, without fair and free elections our democracy is dead. Here's an idea: let's kill the giant of voter fraud, instead. Stalin said, "It's not the people who vote that count, it's the people who count the votes."[20]

- "Judicial Watch's state-by-state results yielded 462 counties where the registration rate exceeded 100 percent. There were 3,551,760 more people registered to vote than adult U.S. citizens who inhabit these counties."[21]

- According to *Zerohedge* (which was banned by Twitter[22] and Facebook),[23] the man who controls the voting machines in 16 states is tied to leftist billionaire George Soros.[24]

- *The Hill* reported that a group from Princeton needed only 7 minutes to hack a voting machine to transfer votes from one candidate to another.[25]

- There are 18 states where voters do not need any sort of ID in order to cast a vote. They are California, Illinois, Iowa, Maine, Maryland, Massachusetts, Minnesota, Nebraska, Nevada, New Jersey, New Mexico, New York, North Carolina, Oregon, Pennsylvania, Vermont, West Virginia, Wyoming, and Washington, D.C.
- Elections in Colorado and Washington are held by mail, meaning voter ID laws won't impact most voters.[26]

If you live in a state without voter ID, change it through those who represent you at your Statehouse. Meet with your Secretary of State to clean up the voter rolls so at least the reported 1.8 million dead people aren't voting again in this election.[27] Electronic and early voting gives the corrupt more time and opportunity to cheat. This, too, can be fixed. Phil Evans is an electrical engineer who developed mathematical election analysis methods to uncover anomalies—the fingerprint of election fraud. Evans says "The only system that can be trusted is hand-marked paper ballots collected into a transparent Plexiglas box under high-definition surveillance from precinct opening until the last vote is hand-counted." Let's do it before another election is stolen. For us to have free and fair elections, the giant of voter fraud must fall.

3. Government School Monopoly

Another giant who occupies our land is the government school monopoly—indoctrinating our children to march in lockstep with their godless giant agenda. This giant's demise is *long* overdue. Every year the government monopoly controls our education, another class of America-hating socialists receive their diplomas to hang right next to their participation trophies.

Two words to immediately solve your child's education crisis—*homeschool*. They outperform government-educated students across the board.[28] I have often said that I would prefer a 14-year-old homeschooler to be nominated to the U.S. Supreme Court over most graduates of Yale—at least you know they've *read* the Constitution. Homeschooling has grown 7% in the last 10 years, with 1.5 million children currently homeschooled in the United States.[29] In a study of 12,000 homeschool students from all fifty states, three standardized achievement tests—the California Achievement Test, the Iowa Test of Basic Skills, and the Stanford Achievement Test—were given from fifteen independent testing services and found homeschoolers topped the charts. Homeschoolers scored:

- Reading: 89th percentile
- Language: 84th percentile
- Science: 86th percentile
- Social Studies: 84th percentile[30]

The average public school student taking these tests scored in the 50th percentile in each subject area.[31] Remember the words to solve your child's education crisis right now—*homeschool*.

What can be done for those who remain in government schools? One idea is to pass the "Education Emancipation Act" creating a tax exemption so parents with children in public schools can afford to educate their children elsewhere. My friend, former Texas School Board member

Cynthia Dunbar, had this bill drafted to give parents their own money back via tax exemption from the property tax designated for their school district. Dunbar explains that the public schools won't suffer a financial loss since "Savings granted to the school for not having to educate those students will always be greater than the tax exemption that is allowed to the taxpayer." She added, "Tax exemptions have no governmental control strings attached since the dollars are viewed as belonging to the taxpayer and simply stay in the taxpayer's pocket as money exempt from taxation."

By preventing double dipping, the tax exemption helps enable school choice, forcing the public schools to compete, like in the private market, which provides a better education for all. Ask your state representative to introduce the "Education Emancipation Act" and blaze the trail for others to follow to education freedom. If you are a church, start a school.

We also need to make sure our children's foundation in God is rock solid so they can defend their faith in even the most hostile environments. It's time Christians quit sending their children to college as believers and have them return as brainwashed Marxists. It begins by slaying the giant of the government school monopoly, and it can't happen soon enough.

4. Fake News and Evil Entertainment

A fourth giant seeks complete control of our news and entertainment. Every effective pro-life conservative is a target (and future victim) of assault from a maligning media and agenda-driven press. The leftist media pour a stream of sewage into our homes each night disguised as news and harmless entertainment. As Pastor Mark Batterson in his book *Chase the Lion* rightly stated, "Too often the church complains about the culture rather than creating it." It's time for that to change. If we are to take the land, we need to take back the news and entertainment. Not just a good movie here and there—we need to be the ones producing the news, the drama, the movies, and the sitcoms. While you assemble a team to write, produce, and distribute your quality programs, shut down the sewage source flooding your home. If we can't yet slay this giant, we can quit feeding him. Quit Netflix. Somebody figure out how to free airport travelers from being forced to watch CNN. In the meantime, check out Pureflix, One America News Network (OAN), AFA's One News Now, Breitbart, and the Bongino Report. It's time to take this land and occupy it.

Is There Not a Cause?

As David said, "Is there not a cause?" There are other giants who must fall and fall they will when "the people who know their God stand firm and take action" (Daniel 11:32b ESV). We can see God heal our land when we follow His checklist in 2 Chronicles—which includes His command to "turn from our wicked ways." That begins by stopping the shedding of innocent blood. That's what the Heartbeat Bill is designed to do.

The teetering giant of abortion will soon fall. Then, we must slay his brothers. We must take back our freedoms of speech and religion in the public square—beginning with the Internet. We must ensure free and fair elections and restore voter integrity, break the government school monopoly, and take back the news media and our entertainment across the board. That's not everything, but it's a start.

To those who signed the adoption papers into God's family, remember you are now a son or daughter of the one who created the heavens and the earth. The one who is good and the one who is for you. In addition to all the promises in His word, in Him we are "more than conquerors." But to see victory we must do more than react, respond, and defend a shrinking piece of real estate.

Winning requires more than our customary defense. We are here to *advance* the kingdom of God. That requires a change in how we think and a change in what we do. We must also put on the armor of God and engage in the real war that can't be seen, It's time for the people of God to stop calling God a liar and start doing what He says. To quit complaining about the giants who occupy our land and start picking up rocks. It's time to put our faith to action, to raise our shields and pick up our swords. It's time to take the land.

Remember, with God *all things* are possible.

Heartfelt thanks to everyone who prayed, called, encouraged, emailed, faxed, wrote letters, mailed postcards, signed petitions, testified, lobbied, spoke, donated, drafted, distributed fliers, ran for office, campaigned, sponsored, cosponsored, voted, attended rallies, hearings, floor votes, banquets, kept praying, made copies, saved seats, wore red, blew up balloons, aired programs, kept giving, ran ads, wrote articles, delivered roses, heart candy, heart cookies, teddy bears with beating hearts, and helped in any way to keep hearts beating.

I know many of your names, God knows all of your names.

Thank you from the bottom of my heart.

Notes

Introduction

1. https://tinyurl.com/tbk5x76

2. War Archives, "President Franklin D. Roosevelt Declares War on Japan (Full Speech) | War Archives," YouTube, August 26, 2011, https://www.youtube.com/watch?reload=9&v=lK8gYGg0dkE.

3. "Remembering Pearl Harbor: A Pearl Harbor Fact Sheet," The National WWII Museum, October 2, 2019, https://www.census.gov/history/pdf/pearl-harbor-fact-sheet-1.pdf.

4. "Our History," Planned Parenthood of Indiana and Kentucky, Inc., October 2, 2019, https://www.plannedparenthood.org/planned-parenthood-indiana-kentucky/about/history.

5. Steven Ertelt, "Planned Parenthood Is America's Biggest Abortion Business: Operates 45% of All Abortion Clinics," LifeSiteNews, January 28, 2015, https://www.lifenews.com/2015/01/28/planned-parenthood-is-americas-biggest-abortion-business-operates-45-of-all-abortion-clinics/.

6. Randall O'Bannon, "Abortions Kill More People Every Year Than Heart Disease or Cancer," LifeSiteNews, August 9, 2016, https://www.lifenews.com/2016/08/09/abortions-kill-more-people-every-year-than-heart-disease-or-cancer/.

7. Ronnie Floyd "Abortion Is the World's Leading Cause of Death," Washington Examiner, January 22, 2019, https://www.washingtonexaminer.com/opinion/op-eds/abortion-is-the-worlds-leading-cause-of-death.

8. Nese F. DeBruyne, "American War and Military Operations Casualties: Lists and Statistics," Congressional Research Service, April 26, 2017, https://www.census.gov/history/pdf/wwi-casualties112018.pdf.

9. https://www.multpl.com/united-states-population/table/by-year

Chapter 1: The Spark that Ignited the Heartbeat Revolution

1. Dave Andrusko, "NRLC's 6th Annual 'State of Abortion in America, 2019,' a Must-Read for Pro-Life Activists: Part One," National Right to Life News, January 30, 2019, https://www.

nationalrighttolifenews.org/2019/01/nrlcs-6th-annual-state-of-abortion-in-america-2019-a-must-read-for-pro-life-activists-part-one/.

2. https://thefederalist.com/2017/02/14/fact-check-abortion-not-safest-medical-procedure-america/

3. Andrusko, "NRLC's 6th Annual 'State of Abortion in America, 2019,' a Must-Read for Pro-Life Activists: Part One."

4. https://www.nytimes.com/2019/05/29/us/louisiana-abortion-heartbeat-bill.html

5. Gregory J. Roden, "Unborn Children as Constitutional Persons," *Issues in Law & Medicine* 25, no. 3 (Spring 2010).

6. Ibid.

7. https://www.nytimes.com/2013/03/27/us/north-dakota-governor-signs-strict-abortion-limits.html

8. Black's Law Dictionary, s.v. "fetus," September 12, 2019, https://thelawdictionary.org/search2/?cx=partner-pub-2225482417208543%3A5634069718&cof=FORID%3A11&ie=UTF-8&q=fetus&x=0&y=0.

9. Merriam-Webster, s.v. "fetus," September 12, 2019, https://www.merriam-webster.com/dictionary/fetus.

10. Cambridge Dictionary, s.v. "fetus," September 12, 2019, https://dictionary.cambridge.org/us/dictionary/english/fetus.

11. https://www.merriam-webster.com/dictionary/gravida

12. https://www.wgal.com/article/pennsylvania-lawmakers-introduce-heartbeat-bill-that-would-restrict-abortion/29539813#

13. https://www.foxnews.com/politics/heartbeat-bills-gaining-momentum-in-several-states

14. George Barna Survey of 1,002 adults, sampling error of +/- 3.1 percentage points, conducted January 19-27, 2017.

15. https://townhall.com/tipsheet/townhallcomstaff/2019/11/16/louisiana-saturday-night-election-media-thinks-trump-is-running-n2556610

16. Ibid.

17. https://www.nationalreview.com/news/pennsylvania-governor-promises-to-veto-abortion-heartbeat-bill/

18. https://www.cnn.com/2019/03/07/health/georgia-heartbeat-bill-abortion/index.html

19. https://www.youtube.com/watch?v=wSfrOLdiC2A

20. https://www.cnn.com/2019/03/21/health/mississippi-heartbeat-bill-law-bn/index.html

21. Ibid.

22. https://www.nwmissourinews.com/news/article_b28b03e8-4073-11e9-8ee4-0fb8cfcd3eb5.html

23. "Abby Johnson—The Supreme Court and Michigan the Heartbeat Bill," YouTube, 4:39, Michigan Heartbeat Coalition, September 28, 2019, https://www.youtube.com/watch?v=r0rl4MyaZGo.

24. https://www.owensborotimes.com/features/community/2019/03/fetal-heartbeat-bill-becomes-law-in-kentucky/

25. https://www.owensborotimes.com/features/community/2019/03/fetal-heartbeat-bill-becomes-law-in-kentucky/

26. https://www.nwmissourinews.com/news/article_b28b03e8-4073-11e9-8ee4-0fb8cfcd3eb5.html

27. https://www.wgal.com/article/pennsylvania-lawmakers-introduce-heartbeat-bill-that-would-restrict-abortion/29539813#

28. https://www.philstar.com/entertainment/2019/11/05/1966195/abortion-not-option-miss-universe-philippines-2019-gazini-ganados-reacts-georgias-heartbeat-bill

29. Never Give In!: The Best of Winston Churchill's Speeches by Winston S. Churchill, https://www.goodreads.com/book/show/24988.Never_Give_In_

30. https://thehill.com/policy/healthcare/abortion/442515-louisiana-latest-state-to-advance-heartbeat-abortion-ban

31. https://www.lifesitenews.com/news/full-text-trumps-2020-march-for-life-speech

Chapter 2: The Enemy Has Overplayed His Hand

1. https://www.azquotes.com/author/2886-Winston_Churchill/tag/enemy

2. https://www.governor.ny.gov/news/governor-cuomo-directs-one-world-trade-center-and-other-landmarks-be-lit-pink-celebrate-signing

3. Donald Trump, 2019 State of the Union Address, https://www.whitehouse.gov/briefings-statements/president-donald-j-trumps-state-union-address-2/

4. https://www.ajc.com/news/state--regional-govt--politics/georgia-senate-passes-anti-abortion-heartbeat-bill/lAHF2bfwndc7vrsgiQG9yL/

5. https://www.npr.org/sections/thetwo-way/2018/05/05/608738116/iowa-bans-most-abortions-as-governor-signs-heartbeat-bill

6. Rebecca Downs, "9/11 Memorial Recognized Unborn Children," Live Action, September 15, 2012, https://www.liveaction.org/news/911-memorial-recognizes-unborn-children/.

7. Barbara Simpson, "Astounding Legislation Protects Cows but Not Babies," LifeNews.com, January 27, 2019, https://www.wnd.com/2019/01/astounding-legislation-protects-cows-but-not-babies/.

8. Micaiah Bilger "New Jersey Gov. Signs Bill Protecting Animals from Abuse, But Aborting Babies Is Fine," May 8, 2019 https://www.lifenews.com/2019/05/08/new-jersey-gov-signs-bill-protecting-animals-from-abuse-but-aborting-babies-is-fine/.

9. https://www.opensecrets.org/pacs/pacgot.php?cmte=C00314617

10. https://www.cbsnews.com/news/planned-parenthood-announces-record-high-election-spending-ahead-of-2020/

11. https://www.christianpost.com/news/7-states-already-allow-abortion-up-to-birth-not-just-new-york.html

12. Ben Sasse, "Sen. Ben Sasse: Do You Support Infanticide? Every Senator Must Choose Whether They Do or Not," FOX News Network, LLC, February 25, 2019, https://www.foxnews.com/opinion/sen-ben-sasse-do-you-support-infanticide-every-senator-must-choose-whether-they-do-or-not.

13. https://www.foxnews.com/politics/senate-to-vote-on-born-alive-bill-to-protect-infants-who-survive-a-failed-abortion

14. Ibid.

15. https://www.breitbart.com/politics/2020/02/04/trump-every-child-miracle-of-life/

16. https://www.lifenews.com/2020/02/07/pete-buttigieg-says-infanticide-is-not-a-thing-cdc-shows-hundreds-of-babies-left-to-die-after-failed-abortions/

17. Andrew Kugle, "Northam on Abortion Bill: Infant Could Be Delivered and Then 'Physicians and the Mother' Could Decide If It Lives," Washington Free Beacon, January 30, 2019, https://freebeacon.

com/issues/northman-on-40-week-abortion-bill-infant-would-be-delivered-and-then-a-discussion-would-ensue-between-the-physicians-and-the-mother/.

18. Kugle, "Northam on Abortion Bill."

19. Susan Berry, "Virginia Democrat Proposes Bill Allowing 'Abortion' as Woman Is 'Dilating,'" Breitbart, January 29, 2019, https://www.breitbart.com/politics/2019/01/29/virginia-democrat-proposes-bill-allowing-abortion-as-woman-is-dilating/.

20. https://www.redstate.com/alexparker/2019/01/31/kathy-tran-infant-murder-abortion-cankerworm-house-bill-2495/

21. Donald Trump, 2019 State of the Union Address, https://www.whitehouse.gov/briefings-statements/president-donald-j-trumps-state-union-address-2/

22. Kugle, "Northam on Abortion Bill," emphasis added.

23. https://www.billboard.com/articles/news/politics/8496194/ralph-northam-michael-jackson-blackface-virginia-governor

24. https://www.nytimes.com/2019/02/01/us/politics/ralph-northam-yearbook-blackface.html

25. Grace Carr, "Gov Northam: 'I Don't Have Any Regrets' About Infanticide Comments," Daily Caller, January 31, 2019, https://www.dailycaller.com/2019/01/31/ralph-northam-no-regrets-abortion/.

26. https://www.breitbart.com/politics/2020/02/04/trump-every-child-miracle-of-life/

27. Ibid.

28. Ibid.

29. https://thehill.com/policy/healthcare/abortion/442515-louisiana-latest-state-to-advance-heartbeat-abortion-ban

30. Anna North, "While Some States Try to Ban Abortion, These States Are Expanding Access," Vox Media, Inc., June 20, 2019, https://www.vox.com/identities/2019/6/12/18662738/abortion-bill-illinois-maine-laws-new-york.

31. Chris Enloe, "WATCH: Democrats in Two States Proudly Introduce Horrifying Bills That Would Allow Abortions up to Birth," Blaze Media LLC, January 30, 2019, https://www.theblaze.com/news/virginia-rhode-island-abortion-birth.

32. Scott Klusendorf, "Peter Singer's Bold defense of Infanticide," Christian Research Institute, April 16, 2019, https://www.equip.org/article/peter-singers-bold-defense-of-infanticide/.

33. Klusendorf, "Peter Singer's Bold Defense of Infanticide."

34. Abbey Crain and Mike Cason, "'Kill Them Now or Kill Them Later': Alabama Lawmaker Defends Controversial Abortion Comments," AL.com, updated May 6, 2019, https://www.al.com/news/2019/05/kill-them-now-or-kill-them-later-alabama-lawmaker-defends-controversial-abortion-comments.html.

35. Susan Berry, "Ohio Democrat Proposed Amendment to Heartbeat Bill to Allow 'Slavery' Exemption for Black Women," Breitbart, April 15, 2019, https://www.breitbart.com/politics/2019/04/15/ohio-democrat-proposed-amendment-to-heartbeat-bill-to-allow-slavery-exemption-for-black-women/.

36. "Summary of Vital Statistics 2016 the City of New York," New York City Department of Health and Mental Hygiene, July 2018, https://www1.nyc.gov/assets/doh/downloads/pdf/vs/2016sum.pdf.

37. https://www.lifesitenews.com/news/full-text-trumps-2020-march-for-life-speech

38. https://www.thenewamerican.com/culture/faith-and-morals/item/34235-michael-bloomberg-the-radical-abortion-candidate

39. Novielli, "Planned Parenthood Forum."

40. https://www.politico.com/story/2019/06/27/julian-castro-debate-abortion-1385950

41. Ben Johnson, "Democrats Adopt Most Pro-Abortion Platform in History in 2016," LifeSiteNews. com, July 27, 2016, https://www.lifesitenews.com/news/democrats-adopt-most-pro-abortion-platform-in-history-in-2016.

42. Ibid.

43. https://www.pressofatlanticcity.com/opinion/commentary/candidates-say-all-democrats-must-support-abortion-says-cynthia-m/article_75dd2750-7651-58af-81f3-ba8d2c20be12.html

44. Ibid.

45. https://www.liveaction.org/news/democrats-for-life-pete-buttigieg/

46. Ibid.

47. Ibid.

48. Consider Revelation 3:16, "So then, because you are lukewarm, and neither cold nor hot, I will vomit you out of my mouth."

49. Steven Ertelt, "Trump Defunds Planned Parenthood, Abortion Biz Loses $60 Million in Taxpayer Dollars," LifeNews.com, August 19, 2019, https://www.lifenews.com/2019/08/19/trump-defunds-planned-parenthood-abortion-biz-will-lose-60-million-in-taxpayer-dollars/

50. https://www.breitbart.com/politics/2019/08/21/planned-parenthood-still-receives-over-500-million-in-taxpayer-funding-annually/

51. https://www.latimes.com/california/story/2020-02-22/trump-conservative-judges-9th-circuit

52. https://www.msn.com/en-us/news/politics/trump-has-flipped-the-9th-circuit-e2-80-94-and-some-new-judges-are-causing-a-shock-wave/ar-BB10hC2f

53. Ibid.

54. https://www.lifesitenews.com/news/full-text-trumps-2020-march-for-life-speech

55. Ben Johnson, "2016 Republican Party Platform Hailed as Most Pro-Life, Pro-Family Ever," LifeSiteNews.com, https://www.lifesitenews.com/news/2016-republican-party-platform-the-most-pro-life-ever

56. "Republican Platform 2016," Republican National Convention, September 13, 2019, https://prod-cdn-static.gop.com/media/documents/DRAFT_12_FINAL[1]-ben_1468872234.pdf.

57. Emily Shugerman, "Heartbeat Abortion Bills Were Once a Fringe Idea. Could They Overturn *Roe v. Wade*?," Daily Beast, March 29, 2019, https://www.thedailybeast.com/heartbeat-abortion-legislation-championed-by-janet-porter-was-once-a-fringe-idea-now-could-it-overturn-roe-v-wade.

58. David French, "In Missouri, Another Supermajority Passes Another Heartbeat Bill," *National Review*, May 17, 2019, https://www.nationalreview.com/corner/missouri-passes-heartbeat-bill-supermajority/.

Chapter 3: From the Basics to the Impossible

1. https://tinyurl.com/tbk5x76

2. https://quillette.com/2019/10/16/i-asked-thousands-of-biologists-when-life-begins-the-answer-wasnt-popular/?fbclid=IwAR3KssXpj-7HM3eXZjECZa5c16fKK3KyCbIO32NfiMx9LFGe1g8K4fQM-60

3. Ibid.

4. Ibid.

5. Ibid.

6. https://thefederalist.com/2018/11/02/im-not-pro-abortion-wouldnt-outlaw-parallels-stephen-douglass-argument-slavery/

7. Ibid.

8. https://www.youtube.com/watch?v=g67z_xBe07Q&list=PL6hk_NIkW85VJKKeoYnJscNKrRGQzCTWR&index=47

9. https://bethelmusic.com/blog/bill-johnson-quotes/

10. https://tinyurl.com/tbk5x76

11. Henry T. Blackaby, *Created to Be God's Friend* (Nashville: Thomas Nelson, 1999).

12. Mark Batterson, *Chase the Lion* (New York: Multnomah, 2019), 201.

13. https://www.faithstrongtoday.com/annmainse/fear-not-is-the-most-repeated-command-in-the-new-testament

14. https://www.azquotes.com/quote/478114

15. https://www.azquotes.com/quote/811927

16. Evangelist Reinhard Bonnke–Official Page (@evangelistreinhardbonnke), "Is Christianity boring? So is television if we don't plug in. For the best programs, switch on–it makes quite a difference. So does switching on to God." Facebook, October 1, 2011, https://www.facebook.com/evangelistreinhardbonnke/posts/is-christianity-boring-so-is-television-if-we-dont-plug-in-for-the-best-programs/10150832619100258/.

17. "An Appeal to Heaven," Jamestown-Yorktown Foundation, May 15, 2014, https://www.historyisfun.org/blog/appeal-to-heaven/, emphasis added.

18. "An Appeal to Heaven," Jamestown-Yorktown Foundation.

Chapter 4: Crafting the Arrow

1. David Forte, "Life, Heartbeat, Birth: A Medical Basis for Reform," Cleveland State University, September 20, 2019, https://engagedscholarship.csuohio.edu/cgi/viewcontent.cgi?referer=https://search.yahoo.com/&httpsredir=1&article=1660&context=fac_articles.

2. Forte, "Life, Heartbeat, Birth."

3. *Gonzales v. Carhart,* 550 U.S. 124 (2007).

4. Parenthood Federation of *America v. Ashcroft,* 320 F.Supp.2d 957 (2004).

5. Federal Rules of Civil Procedure, The Committee on the Judiciary House of Representatives, December 1, 2014, https://www.uscourts.gov/sites/default/files/Rules%20of%20Civil%20Procedure.

6. *Gonzales v. Carhart.*

7. Federal Rules of Evidence, The Committee on the Judiciary House of Representatives, December 1, 2018, https://www.uscourts.gov/sites/default/files/ev_rules_eff._dec._1_2018_0.pdf.

8. Planned Parenthood of Southeastern Pa. v. Casey, 505 U.S. 833, 870 (1992).

9. Heartbeat Protection Act of 2017, H.R.490, 115th Cong. (2017-2018), September 20, 2019, https://www.congress.gov/bill/115th-congress/house-bill/490/text.

10. Erik Eckholm, "Anti-Abortion Groups Are Split on Legal Tactics," *New York Times*, December 4, 2011, https://www.nytimes.com/2011/12/05/health/policy/fetal-heartbeat-bill-splits-anti-abortion-forces.html.

11. John Yoo, "Does the Constitution Protect against Sex Discrimination?," National Review, January 5, 2011, https://www.nationalreview.com/corner/does-constitution-protect-against-sex-discrimination-john-yoo/.

12. Jacob Gershman and Arian Campo-Flores, "Antiabortion Movement Begins to Crack, After Decades of Unity," *Wall Street Journal*, July 17, 2019, https://www.wsj.com/articles/antiabortion-movement-begins-to-crack-after-decades-of-unity-11563384713?shareToken=stc10b245e0db14919b683973fd405b8a3&reflink=article_email_share.

13. Calvin Freiburger, "National Right to Life Testifies Against Tennessee Bill to Ban All Abortions," LifeSiteNews.com, August 19, 2019, https://www.lifesitenews.com/news/national-right-to-life-testifies-against-tennessee-bill-to-ban-all-abortions.

14. Eckholm, "Anti-Abortion Groups Are Split on Legal Tactics."

15. Calvin Freiburger, "U.S. Congressman: National Right to Life Is Preventing Vote on Bill Banning Nearly All Abortions," LifeSiteNews.com, March 27, 2018, https://www.lifesitenews.com/news/u.s.-congressman-national-right-to-life-is-preventing-vote-on-bill-banning.

16. "The Constitution: Amendments 11–17," National Archives, September 20, 2019, https://www.archives.gov/founding-docs/amendments-11-27.

17. https://mail.google.com/mail/u/0/#inbox/WhctKJVqqqWZxqxHzrLlwcmhQBVPpfSthgkhcmKGKKZQMlMsqLhbsNHXDgPvCxVZrTwXXDG?projector=1&messagePartId=0.1

18. https://www.youtube.com/watch?v=xPBeaFQalIw

19. https://biotech.law.lsu.edu/cases/la/health/embryo_rs.htm

20. https://www.nytimes.com/1982/03/22/opinion/l-unborn-children-recognized-by-courts-698203.html

21. State Laws on Fetal Homicide and Penalty-Enhancement for Crimes Against Pregnant Women," National Conference of State Legislatures, May 1, 2018, http://www.ncsl.org/research/health/fetal-homicide-state-laws.aspx.

22. "State Laws on Fetal Homicide and Penalty-Enhancement for Crimes Against Pregnant Women," National Conference of State Legislatures.

23. Laura Baigert, "Andy Schlafly: It's Terrible to See Such a Misuse of the 'Right To Life' Name," *Tennessean Star*, June 13, 2019, https://tennesseestar.com/2019/06/13/andy-schlafly-its-terrible-to-see-such-a-misuse-of-the-right-to-life-name/.

24. Baigert, "Andy Schlafly."

25. Roden, "Unborn Children as Constitutional Persons."

26. https://www.kalb.com/content/news/House-passes-fetal-heartbeat-bill-in-Louisiana-510584081.html

27. Ibid.

28. "Rebecca Kiessling Video Testimony Ohio Heartbeat Bill—House," YouTube, 7:02, Rebecca Kiessling, March 21, 2019, https://www.youtube.com/watch?v=QcVVarR2200.

29. "Rebecca Kiessling Video Testimony Ohio Heartbeat Bill—House," YouTube.

30. David C. Reardon, "Rape, Incest, and Abortion: Searching Beyond the Myths," AbortionFacts.com, September 20, 2019, https://www.abortionfacts.com/reardon/rape-incest-and-abortion-searching-beyond-the-myths.

31. "(HR490) Written Testimony of Rachelle Heidlebaugh, November 1, 2017," https://docs.house.gov/meetings/JU/JU10/20171101/106562/HHRG-115-JU10-20171101-SD003.pdf.
32. Reardon, "Rape, Incest, and Abortion."
33. https://www.rainn.org/articles/rape-kit
34. Amy Sobie, "Suicide Rate for Women Having Abortions Is Six Times Higher Than Women Giving Birth," LifeSiteNews.com, December 19, 2014, https://www.lifenews.com/2014/12/19/suicide-rate-for-women-having-abortions-is-six-times-higher-than-women-giving-birth/.
35. David C. Reardon, "Abortion and Suicide," AbortionFacts.com, September 20, 2019, https://www.abortionfacts.com/reardon/abortion-and-suicide.
36. Sobie, "Suicide Rate for Women Having Abortions Is Six Times Higher Than Women Giving Birth."
37. Ibid.
38. Ibid.
39. https://www.wsj.com/articles/antiabortion-movement-begins-to-crack-after-decades-of-unity-11563384713?shareToken=stc10b245e0db14919b683973fd405b8a3&reflink=article_email_share
40. Allan Parker, in personal communication with the author.
41. *MKB Management Corp. v. Wayne Stenehjem.*
42. Roden, "Unborn Children as Constitutional Persons."

Chapter 5: Creative Strategies

1. https://www.memphisdailynews.com/news/2018/jan/24/anti-abortion-heartbeat-bill-revived-despite-like-minded-opposition//print
2. https://www.youtube.com/watch?v=RD9WAXo9Bdc
3. https://www.cleveland.com/open/2016/12/ohio_senate_unexpectedly_passe.html
4. "Ohio Senators Hear 'Heartbeat' Abortion Bill," *Desert News*, December 7, 2011, https://www.deseret.com/2011/12/8/20236730/ohio-senators-hear-heartbeat-abortion-bill.
5. H.R. 490, The Heartbeat Protection Act of 2017: Hearing Before the Subcommittee on the Constitution and Civil Justice of the Committee on the Judiciary House of Representatives 115th Cong. (2017), September 21, 2019, https://www.govinfo.gov/content/pkg/CHRG-115hhrg32354/pdf/CHRG-115hhrg32354.pdf; "Ashland Team Testifies on Capitol Hill for Federal Heartbeat Bill," Ashland Care Center, November 2017 https://www.ashlandcarecenter.org/upload/donor_site/documents/newsletters/2017/acc_newsletter_nov_2017-_final.pdf.
6. https://www.catholicnewsagency.com/news/abortion-survivor-testifies-before-senate-committee-as-bishops-back-bill-51502
7. https://theabortionsurvivors.com/abortion-survivors-and-their-stories/melissa-ohden/
8. https://www.nationalrighttolifenews.org/2019/02/melissas-birth-mother-didnt-know-she-had-survived-the-abortion-then-they-met-face-to-face/
9. "Abortion Survivor Testifies for Heartbeat Bill," YouTube, 2:51, faith2action, September 21, 2019, https://www.youtube.com/watch?v=xi948ZXkWZM.
10. "Kids for the Heartbeat Bill," YouTube, 2:51, CreatedEqualFilms, January 12, 2012, https://video.search.yahoo.com/search/video?fr=mcafee&p=kids+for+heartbeat+bill#id=1&vid=4d1c1b37e7f410c6538ecc49ba8b87a8&action=click.

11. "Kids for the Heartbeat Bill," YouTube.

12. "School Bus Ad for Heartbeat Bill," YouTube, 0:29, faith2action, November 18, 2011, https://www.youtube.com/watch?v=-HwLEGr4sL0.

13. Ally Boguhn, "Janet Porter: The Architect of Ohio's 'Heartbeat' Bills," Rewire.News, December 19, 2018, https://rewire.news/article/2018/12/19/janet-porter-architect-heartbeat-bill/.

14. https://www.wnd.com/2009/11/117088/

15. https://www.wnd.com/2009/11/116729

Chapter 6: The Enemy Within

1. Paula Bolyard, "Ohio Right to Life and NARAL Team Up Against OH Heartbeat Bill," RedState.com/Salem Media, March 12, 2011, https://www.redstate.com/diary/paulkib/2011/03/12/ohio-right-to-life-and-naral-team-up-against-oh-heartbeat-bill/.

2. C:\\Janet\\Documents\\001 FAITH2ACTION\\HEARTBEAT BILL\\MIKE ON NARAL SITE.htm.

3. "Pro-Life Legislation We Supported," 2019 Legislative Session, Louisiana Right to Life, September 22, 2019, https://prolifelouisiana.org/session.

4. Julie Carr Smyth, "Bill Advances in Ohio to Bar 'Heartbeat' Abortions," Seattle Times, March 30, 2011, https://www.seattletimes.com/nation-world/bill-advances-in-ohio-to-bar-heartbeat-abortions/.

5. Eckholm. "Anti-Abortion Groups Are Split on Legal Tactics."

6. https://www.cleveland.com/politics/2018/12/gov-john-kasich-vetoes-anti-abortion-heartbeat-bill-legislative-pay-raises.html

7. "Ohio Right to Life Supports a Pathway Forward for Ohio's Heartbeat Legislation," press release, Ohio Right to Life, December 27, 2018, https://www.ohiolife.org/ohio_right_to_life_supports_a_pathway_forward_for_ohios_heartbeat_legislation, emphasis added.

8. https://www.thenation.com/article/janet-porter-abortion-ban/

9. Mary Mogan Edwards, "Abortion Foe Janet Porter's Zealous Tactics Divide, Inspire," *Columbus Dispatch*, updated December 11, 2016, https://www.dispatch.com/content/stories/local/2016/12/11/1-janet-porter-abortion-foes-zealous-tactics-divide-inspire.html

10. Eckholm. "Anti-Abortion Groups Are Split on Legal Tactics."

11. From endorsement.

12. "Clearing Up Confusion About Heartbeat vs. Dismemberment," Right to Life of Michigan, May 20, 2019, https://rtl.org/heartbeat-dismemberment-confusion/.

13. "Clearing Up Confusion About Heartbeat vs. Dismemberment," Right to Life of Michigan.

14. "A Bill," faith2action, September 23, 2019, http://f2a.org/images/Model_Heartbeat_Bill_Apr._2019_version.pdf.

15. Gershman and Flores, "Antiabortion Movement Begins to Crack, After Decades of Unity."

16. Laura Baigert, "Ohio's Right to Life Organization Supported a 'Heartbeat Bill,' While Tennessee's Opposed It," *Tennessee Star*, April 15, 2019, https://tennesseestar.com/2019/04/15/ohios-right-to-life-organization-supported-a-heartbeat-bill-while-tennessees-opposed-it/.

17. Ibid.

18. Ibid.
19. "Sixth Circuit Provides Hope for Heartbeat Bill," Family Action Council of Tennessee, Inc., April 9, 2019, https://factn.org/fact-report-sixth-circuit-provides-hope-heartbeat-bill/.
20. Stockard, "Anti-Abortion 'Heartbeat Bill' Revived Despite Like-Minded Opposition."
21. https://www.memphisdailynews.com/news/2018/jan/24/anti-abortion-heartbeat-bill-revived-despite-like-minded-opposition//print
22. Laura Baigert, "Tennessee Right to Life PAC Rejected Sponsors of Unborn Child Heartbeat and 20-Week Abortion Ban Bills in 2018 Elections," *Tennessee Star*, August 1, 2019, https://tennesseestar.com/2019/08/01/tennessee-right-to-life-pac-rejects-sponsors-of-unborn-child-heartbeat-and-20-week-abortion-ban-bills-in-2018-elections/.
23. Baigert, "Ohio's Right to Life Organization Supported a 'Heartbeat Bill,' While Tennessee's Opposed It."
24. Baigert, "Andy Schlafly."
25. Baigert, "Tennessee Right to Life PAC Rejected Sponsors of Unborn Child Heartbeat and 20-Week Abortion Ban Bills in 2018 Elections."
26. Baigert, "Ohio's Right to Life Organization Supported a 'Heartbeat Bill,' While Tennessee's Opposed It."
27. Sarah Pulliam Bailey, "The Surprising Battle Over 'Heartbeat Bills' Among Activists Who Oppose Abortion," *Washington Post*, April 12, 2019, https://www.washingtonpost.com/religion/2019/04/12/surprising-battle-over-heartbeat-bills-among-activists-who-oppose-abortion/?utm_term=.7559caef716e.
28. Mark Batterson, *Chase the Lion* (New York: Multnomah, 2019), 87.
29. https://www.lifesitenews.com/news/national-right-to-life-testifies-against-tennessee-bill-to-ban-all-abortions
30. https://www.foxnews.com/politics/tennessee-governor-heartbeat-bill-restrict-abortions
31. https://tennesseestar.com/2018/01/31/letter-to-the-editor-the-heartbeat-bill-should-wait/
32. DeNeen L. Brown, "Martin Luther King Jr.'s Scorn for 'White Moderates' in His Birmingham Jail Letter," *Washington Post*, January 15, 2018, https://www.washingtonpost.com/news/retropolis/wp/2018/01/15/martin-luther-king-jr-s-scathing-critique-of-white-moderates-from-the-birmingham-jail/?utm_term=.63078c0f31a9.
33. Bailey, "The Surprising Battle Over 'Heartbeat Bills' Among Activists Who Oppose Abortion."
34. Laura Baigert, "Tennessee Right to Life Special Counsel Will Testify at the Summer Study that the Heartbeat Bill Is 'Ill Advised,'" *The Tennessean*, July 26, 2019, https://tennesseestar.com/2019/07/26/tennessee-right-to-life-special-counsel-will-testify-at-the-summer-study-that-the-heartbeat-bill-is-ill-advised/.
35. https://www.vox.com/2019/8/22/20826982/abortion-tennessee-laws-2019-alabama-georgia-ohio
36. "A Bill," faith2action.
37. Bailey, "The Surprising Battle Over 'Heartbeat Bills' Among Activists Who Oppose Abortion."
38. Susan Michelle-Hanson, "Ohio Governor John Kasich Vetoes Pro-Life Heartbeat Bill," Live Action News, December 21, 2018, https://www.liveaction.org/news/ohio-kasich-vetoes-heartbeat-bill/.
39. "Statement of the Reasons for the Veto of Items in Amended Substitute House Bill 493," State of Ohio Executive Department Office of the Governor, December 13, 2016, https://www.dispatch.com/assets/pdf/archive/veto_message.pdf.
40. Gershman and Flores, "Antiabortion Movement Begins to Crack, After Decades of Unity."

41. Bolyard, "Ohio Right to Life and NARAL Team Up Against OH Heartbeat Bill," emphasis added.

42. Freiburger, "U.S. Congressman."

43. Jason Scott Jones, "The Pro-Life Movement Isn't Cracking. It's Becoming Anti-Fragile," The Stream, July 24, 2019, https://stream.org/the-pro-life-movement-isnt-shattered-its-becoming-anti-fragile/?fbclid=IwAR2NVwR7EerbHC0V7ADjZ4zqnX4_TlJ_pX_pL6Ai9I8n8gwWsfzV_lz9zbM.

44. https://aclj.org/pro-life/aclj-presents-testimony-pro-life-heartbeat-bill

45. Eckholm, "Anti-Abortion Groups Are Split on Legal Tactics."

46. Gershman and Flores, "Antiabortion Movement Begins to Crack, After Decades of Unity."

47. https://www.texasgop.org/priorities/

48. Stephen Young, "Texas Lawmakers Leading the Anti-Abortion Effort Take a Gentler, More Tactical Approach," *Dallas Observer*, May 22, 2019, https://www.dallasobserver.com/news/texas-lawmakers-arent-going-soft-on-abortion-theyre-going-tactical-11669327.

49. Tony Guajardo, "Texas Heartbeat Bill Dies in the House," The Texan, May 9, 2019, https://thetexan.news/texas-heartbeat-bill-on-life-support-stalled-in-the-house/.

50. https://www.texastribune.org/2019/05/10/texas-anti-abortion-groups-arent-leading-charge-overturn-roe-v-wade/

51. David Crary, "States Pushing Near-Bans on Abortion, Targeting Roe v. Wade," April 10, 2019, https://www.apnews.com/3a9b3bc0e14d47aa8691aca84c32f391.

52. https://www.texasrighttolife.com/texas-house-tanks-pro-life-priorities-ignores-grassroots-supporters-and-the-cries-of-the-unborn/

53. https://www.houstonchronicle.com/news/houston-texas/houston/article/Anti-abortion-group-accuses-Texas-Republicans-of-13879848.php

54. Recorded phone interview, February 6, 2020.

55. Ibid.

56. https://www.pop.org/project/heartbeat/

57. https://800wvhu.iheart.com/featured/the-tom-roten-morning-show/content/2019-11-08-what-do-gop-leadershipwv-for-life-have-against-the-heartbeat-bill/

58. Ibid.

59. Ibid.

60. Personal recorded interview with Idaho Rep. Tammy Nichols, January 17, 2020.

61. Ibid.

62. Gershman and Flores, "Antiabortion Movement Begins to Crack, After Decades of Unity."

63. Eckholm, "Anti-Abortion Groups Are Split on Legal Tactics."

64. http://stevetothfortexas.com/

65. "National Right to Life Mission Statement," National Right to Life, September 23, 2019, https://www.nrlc.org/about/mission/.

66. "Tennessee Legislators Discuss Abortion Bill in Hopes of Overturning Roe v Wade," CNA, August 13, 2019, https://www.catholicnewsagency.com/news/tennessee-legislators-discuss-abortion-bill-in-hopes-of-overturning-roe-v-wade-41882.

67. "National Right to Life Betrays Babies–Blocks Congressional Vote on Pro-Life Heartbeat Bill," Christian Newswire, January 18, 2018, http://christiannewswire.com/news/5288680634.html.

68. https://www.prochoiceamerica.org/wp-content/uploads/2017/01/5.-Personhood-Measures-Extreme-and-Dangerous-Attempts-to-Ban-Abortion.pdf

69. Ibid.

70. "National Right to Life Betrays Babies–Blocks Congressional Vote on Pro-Life Heartbeat Bill," Christian Newswire.

71. Eckholm, "Anti-Abortion Groups Are Split on Legal Tactics."

72. Tom DeLay, "Saving Every Baby Whose Heart Is Beating," *Washington Times*, January 17, 2018, https://m.washingtontimes.com/news/2018/jan/17/abortion-legislation-currently-before-congress-wil/.

73. "King Asks: Is Something Wrong Within National Right to Life?," press release, Congressman Steve King, February 6, 2018, https://steveking.house.gov/media-center/press-releases/king-asks-is-something-wrong-within-national-right-to-life

74. "King Asks," press release, Congressman Steve King.

75. "Dietrich Bonhoeffer," AZ Quotes, September 23, 2019, https://www.azquotes.com/quote/813685.

76. "King Asks," press release, Congressman Steve King.

77. Jamie Whitlock, "The Power of Belief or What I Learned from a Barracuda," EzineArticles, October 14, 2007, https://ezinearticles.com/?The-Power-Of-Belief-Or-What-I-Learned-from-A-Barracuda&id=781776.

78. https://abolishabortiontx.org/2018/06/19/why-we-oppose-regulating-murder-via-heartbeat-bills/

79. http://www.forerunner.com/blog/why-personhood-florida-does-not-support-pro-life-heartbeat-bills

80. https://www.mdjonline.com/opinion/ginny-ehrhart-my-bad-breakup-with-georgia-right-to-life/article_ad786aea-a8c8-11e9-b584-8fb898ff3ba2.html

81. Greg Bluestein and Maya T. Prabhu, "Georgia Republicans Face High-Stakes Pressure Over Anti-Abortion Bill," *Atlanta Journal-Constitution*, March 27, 2019, https://www.ajc.com/news/state--regional-govt--politics/georgia-republicans-face-high-stakes-pressure-over-anti-abortion-bill/X7uXblQnoEAFnVzpDJtfNM/.

82. Eckholm, "Anti-Abortion Groups Are Split on Legal Tactics."

Chapter 7: Whatever It Takes

1. Morton C. Blackwell, "The Laws of the Public Policy Process," Leadership Institute, March 19, 2015, https://www.leadershipinstitute.org/writings/?ID=30.

2. Janet Porter, "'Republicans' Block Nation's Strongest Pro-Life Bill," WND, May 21, 2012, https://www.wnd.com/2012/05/republicans-block-nations-strongest-pro-life-bill/.

3. "'A Time for Choosing' by Ronald Reagan," YouTube, 29:32, Reagan Foundation, April 2, 2009, https://www.youtube.com/watch?v=qXBswFfh6AY&t=8s.

4. Sen. Jason Rapert (@RapertSenate), "Speak the truth even if the ground shakes." Facebook, June 21, 2019, https://www.facebook.com/267072741303/posts/the-man-makes-great-points-i-love-a-man-with-courage-and-enough-backbone-to-spea/10156420355841304/.

5. https://www.liveaction.org/news/mississippi-legislature-bans-abortion-heartbeat/

6. Bill Johnson (@BillJohnsonMinistries), "If you don't live by the praises of men you won't die by their criticisms." Facebook, May 15, 2011, https://www.facebook.com/BillJohnsonMinistries/posts/if-you-dont-live-by-the-praises-of-men-you-wont-die-by-their-criticisms/10150181003393387/.

7. In interview with the author.

8. In personal text with the author.

9. "Our Mission," The South Carolina Family Caucus, September 27, 2019, https://scfamilycaucus.org/.

10. The South Carolina Family Caucus, September 27, 2019, https://scfamilycaucus.org/.

11. In interview with the author.

12. "South Carolina House Passes Fetal Heartbeat Abortion Bill," *Washington Times*, April 24, 2019, https://www.washingtontimes.com/news/2019/apr/24/south-carolina-fetal-heartbeat-abortion-bill-pass-/.

13. Caleb Parke, "South Carolina Governor Pledges to Sign State's 'Heartbeat' Abortion Ban," FOX News Network, LLC, May 21, 2019, https://www.foxnews.com/politics/abortion-south-carolina-governor-heartbeat/

14. In a personal, recorded phone call with the author.

15. https://www.youtube.com/watch?v=DuhciTnXd7I

16. "John Kasich–Ohio Heartbeat Bill," YouTube, 1:15, Heartbeat Films, October 8, 2014, https://www.youtube.com/watch?v=-Lss_KQejyc.

17. "What's a Girl to Do? Trailer," YouTube, 1:10, faith2action, November 22, 2016, https://www.youtube.com/watch?v=CZ0OObJpj9c.

18. "Alice Paul," A&E Television Networks, LLC, updated August 21, 2018, https://www.history.com/topics/womens-history/alice-paul.

19. "Alice Paul," A&E Television Networks, LLC.

20. https://myemail.constantcontact.com/Ohio-just-lost-a-pro-life-hero.html?soid=1101796939293&aid=zir-j3yxnt0

21. Laurel Thatcher Ulrich, *Well-Behaved Women Seldom Make History* (New York: Vintage Books, 2005).

22. Martin Luther King Jr., "A Letter From Birmingham Jail, Ebony 18, no. 10 (August 1963), 26, emphasis added.

23. Morton C. Blackwell. "The Laws Of The Public Policy Process," Leadership Institute, March 19, 2015, https://www.leadershipinstitute.org/writings/?ID=30.

24. James Aubry (@JamesAubryNBC4), 2018, "I sat down with @Bill_Beagle after his "no" vote to override @JohnKasich veto of the Heartbeat Abortion Bill and in this clip he explains why he decided to vote the way he did. Beagle had previously voted to pass the bill in committee and on the floor of the Senate." Twitter, December 27, 2018, 12:33 p.m., https://twitter.com/JasonAubryNBC4/status/1078388317631250432.

25. Light Wins.

Chapter 8: The Federal Heartbeat Bill

1. https://www.c-span.org/video/?c4754024/nancy-pelosi-wrap-up-smear

2. https://www.nytimes.com/2020/02/20/us/politics/russian-interference-trump-democrats.html

3. https://www.lifesitenews.com/news/full-text-trumps-2020-march-for-life-speech

4. "Memo: Fact Checking the New York Times Misquote of Steve King."

5. https://slate.com/news-and-politics/2019/01/gop-strips-iowa-steve-king-judiciary-agriculture-committee-assignments-white-supremacy-comments.html

6. https://www.youtube.com/watch?v=CFfw4302EaI

7.   http://freerepublic.com/focus/f-news/1374139/posts

8.   https://www.rushlimbaugh.com/daily/2013/09/19/tom_delay_exonerated_after_smear/

9.   Tom DeLay, "Saving Every Baby Whose Heart Is Beating," *Washington Times*, January 17, 2018, https://www.washingtontimes.com/news/2018/jan/17/abortion-legislation-currently-before-congress-wil/.

10. http://f2a.org/full_article.php?record=108

11. https://www.azquotes.com/quote/530616

12. http://f2a.org/full_article.php?record=127

13. "Protecting the Pre-born: Heartbeat Bills in America Part 1," May 6, 2019, Family Talk, transcript, https://drjamesdobson.org/broadcasts/transcript/2019/may/protecting-the-pre-born-heartbeat-bills-in-america-part-1/.

14. Susan Davis and Richard Wolf, "U.S. Senate Goes 'Nuclear,' Changes Filibuster Rules," *USA TODAY*, November 21, 2013, https://www.usatoday.com/story/news/politics/2013/11/21/harry-reid-nuclear-senate/3662445/.

15. Alicia Cohn, "Pence Became Ultimate Tie-Breaker in 2017," *The Hill*, December 31, 2017, https://thehill.com/homenews/administration/366811-pence-became-ultimate-tie-breaker-in-2017.

16. Cohn, "Pence Became Ultimate Tie-Breaker in 2017."

17. https://www.lifesitenews.com/news/full-text-trumps-2020-march-for-life-speech

18. "Heartbeat Bill Press Conference (Clips)," YouTube.

19. President Trump (@POTUS), 2017, "No dream is too big. No challenge is too great. Nothing we want for our future is beyond our reach." Twitter, January 22, 2017, 8:03 p.m., https://twitter.com/POTUS/status/823380672463208448.

Chapter 9: Courageous Truth

1.   Alan Blinder, "Louisiana Moves to Ban Abortions After a Heartbeat Is Detected," *New York Times*, May 29, 2019, https://www.nytimes.com/2019/05/29/us/louisiana-abortion-heartbeat-bill.html.

2.   George Orwell, *1984* (New York: New American Library, 1961), 4.

3.   Jacqueline Kantor and Reis Thebault, "Louisiana's Democratic governor just defied his party and signed an abortion ban into law," *Washington Post*, May 30, 2019, https://www.washingtonpost.com/nation/2019/05/29/louisiana-passed-an-abortion-ban-its-democratic-governor-plans-defy-his-party-sign-it/?fbclid=IwAR2Bp9w8EMuK_JlhEHSdsspiO51mUte07PRrDN8-aO0P4hg_tABVUTCKXpA.

4.   "Heartbeat bill," Wikipedia, September 23, 2019, https://en.wikipedia.org/wiki/Heartbeat_bill.

5.   Alexandra Hutzler, "These Are All the States That Have Passed Anti-Abortion Laws in 2019," *Newsweek*, May 31, 2019, https://www.newsweek.com/state-abortion-laws-2019-list-1440609.

6.   https://www.breitbart.com/the-media/2019/06/13/the-guardian-to-enforce-pro-abortion-language/

7.   Ibid.

8.   William C. Shiel Jr., "Medical Definition of Pulse," December 27, 2018, https://www.medicinenet.com/script/main/art.asp?articlekey=5131, emphasis added.

9.   "Prenatal Form and Function—The Making of an Earth Suit," The Endowment for Human Development, Inc., September 24, 2019, https://www.ehd.org/dev_article_unit7.php#4chamberheart.

10. Walter M. Weber, "Federal Court Follows the NARAL/Planned Parenthood Instruction Manual on How to Write a Pro-Abortion Opinion," American Center for Law and Justice, October 5, 2019, https://aclj.org/pro-life/federal-court-follows-the-naral/planned-parenthood-instruction-manual-on-how-to-write-a-pro-abortion-opinion.

11. Orwell, *1984*, 81.

12. Francis H. Hardy, "Lessons From the American Election," *The Eclectic Magazine of Foreign Literature, Science and Art* 65, no. 1 (1897), 3.

13. https://townhall.com/tipsheet/mattvespa/2017/03/15/even-soldiers-are-eating-from-the-trash-in-the-socialist-utopia-of-venezuela-n2298561

14. https://pjmedia.com/election/biden-chooses-beto-take-your-ar-15-orourke-to-take-care-of-the-gun-problem-with-me/

15. https://nypost.com/2020/01/10/the-telling-tale-of-glacier-national-parks-gone-by-2020-signs/

16. https://www.realclearpolitics.com/video/2019/01/22/ocasio-cortez_the_world_is_going_to_end_in_12_years_if_we_dont_address_climate_change.html

17. https://www.answers.com/Q/Did_Goebbels_really_say_%27Tell_a_lie_often_enough_and_it_becomes_the_truth%27

18. Adolf Hitler, *Mein Kampf*, trans. James Murphy (self-pub., CreateSpace, 2017), 101, emphasis added.

19. "Dehumanizing the Vulnerable: When Word Games Take Lives," by Dr. William Brennan, PhD. (Loyola University Press, 1995, 3441 North Ashland Avenue, Chicago Illinois 60657 1800-621-1008.

20. "Dehumanizing the Vulnerable: When Word Games Take Lives," by Dr. William Brennan, PhD. (Loyola University Press, 1995, 3441 North Ashland Avenue, Chicago Illinois 60657 1800-621-1008.

21. https://www.lincolndiocese.org/op-ed/life-insight/1766-verbal-engineering-always-precedes-social-engineering

22. Hitler, *Mein Kampf*, trans. James Murphy, 99.

23. *Light Wins*, directed by Janet Porter (North Royalton, OH: Faith2ActionFilms, 2015), DVD.

24. https://www.breitbart.com/tech/2020/02/07/project-veritas-twitter-suspended-james-okeefe-to-prevent-the-next-trump-situation/

25. https://pjmedia.com/trending/bombshell-video-shows-bernie-sanders-field-organizer-advocating-for-riots-and-gulags/

26. https://tennesseestar.com/2020/01/20/sanders-field-organizer-kyle-jurek-bailed-out-after-arrest-still-no-comment-from-campaign-over-gulag-rants-caught-on-camera/

27. https://pjmedia.com/trending/bombshell-video-shows-bernie-sanders-field-organizer-advocating-for-riots-and-gulags/

28. https://iotwreport.com/why-hasnt-bernie-sanders-fired-iowa-staffer-kyle-jurek-yet/

29. "How Do You Deal With Painful Truths? Left vs. Right #4," YouTube, 5:10, PragerU, December 12, 2015, https://www.youtube.com/watch?v=IC7ZU5vGPy0.

30. "Does Free Speech Offend You?," YouTube, 5:20, PragerU, December 12, 2015, https://www.youtube.com/watch?v=9vVohGWhMWs.

31. *Sweezy v. New Hampshire*, 354 U.S. 234 (1957).

32. "The Least Free Place in America," YouTube, 5:48, PragerU, January 27, 2014, https://www.youtube.com/watch?v=dJaM8IOev7E.

33. "The Least Free Place in America," YouTube.

34. Janet L. Folger (Porter), *The Criminalization of Christianity*, Multnomah Publishers, Inc., 2005, pg. 95.

35. https://www.answers.com/Q/What_did_Thomas_Jefferson_mean_by_the_price_of_freedom_is_eternal_vigilance

36. "Report of the Committee on Freedom of Expression," University of Chicago, September 24, 2019, https://provost.uchicago.edu/sites/default/files/documents/reports/FOECommitteeReport.pdf.

37. John Ellison, letter to incoming students, University of Chicago, September 24, 2019, https://news.uchicago.edu/sites/default/files/attachments/Dear_Class_of_2020_Students.pdf.

38. "Chicago Statement: University and Faculty Body Support," FIRE, August 15, 2019, https://www.thefire.org/chicago-statement-university-and-faculty-body-support/.

39. Jessica Chasmar, "Gov. Brian Kemp Rips 'C-List Celebrities' Threatening to Boycott Georgia Over Anti-Abortion Law," *Washington Times*, May 20, 2019, https://www.washingtontimes.com/news/2019/may/20/brian-kemp-rips-c-list-celebrities-threatening-to-/.

40. Matt Donnelly, Gene Maddaus, and Elaine Low, "Netflix the Only Hollywood Studio to Speak Out in Attack Against Abortion Rights," Variety Media, LLC, May 29, 2019, https://variety.com/2019/film/features/abortion-laws-hollywood-studios-netflix-1203225843/.

41. https://www.breitbart.com/entertainment/2019/05/13/dean-cain-rips-hollywood-left-for-imposing-their-values-on-georgia-voters-with-heartbeat-law-boycott/

42. Ibid.

43. Donnelly, Maddaus, Low, "Netflix the Only Hollywood Studio to Speak Out in Attack Against Abortion Rights."

44. Greg Bluestein, "Kemp Mocks 'C-List Celebrities' Threatening Boycott Over Anti-Abortion Law," *Atlanta Journal-Constitution*, May 18, 2019, https://www.ajc.com/blog/politics/kemp-mocks-list-celebrities-threatening-boycott-over-anti-abortion-law/kS7Podf6NnCGI4BevKOcUK/#.

45. Emily Wax-Thibodeaux and Ariana Eunjung Cha, "Georgia Governor Signs 'Heartbeat Bill,' Giving the State One of the Most Restrictive Abortion Laws in the Nation," *Washington Post*, May 7, 2019, https://www.washingtonpost.com/national/health-science/georgia-governor-signs-heartbeat-bill-giving-the-state-one-of-the-most-restrictive-abortion-laws-in-the-nation/2019/05/07/d53b2f8a-70cf-11e9-8be0-ca575670e91c_story.html?noredirect=on.

46. Bluestein, "Kemp Mocks 'C-List Celebrities' Threatening Boycott Over Anti-Abortion Law."

47. https://www.wnd.com/2019/05/parsing-alyssa-milanos-call-for-a-sex-strike/

48. https://townhall.com/columnists/abbyjohnson/2019/05/12/sexstrike-hollywood-finally-embraces-abstinence-n2546194

49. https://townhall.com/columnists/abbyjohnson/2019/05/12/sexstrike-hollywood-finally-embraces-abstinence-n2546194

50. Aaron Colen, "Hollywood Boycotts of Georgia Over Abortion Law Have Not Materialized as Major Companies Stay Put," Blaze Media LLC, September 4, 2019, https://www.theblaze.com/news/film-and-tv-studios-stay-in-georgia-after-threatening-boycott-over-abortion-law.

51. https://dailystockdish.com/boycott-backfires-film-and-tv-shows-stay-in-georgia-after-protest-of-heartbeat-bill/

52. Carney, "Price Tag for Netflix's Horrible Week: $23 Billion Dollars."

53. Feiner, "Here's Why Netflix Says It Lost US Paid Subscribers for the First Time in Eight Years."

54. https://www.netflix.com/title/80057918

55. https://www.lifesitenews.com/news/netflix-streams-blasphemous-christmas-video-depicting-gay-jesus-adulterous-virgin-mary

56. Donnelly, Maddaus, Low, "Netflix the Only Hollywood Studio to Speak Out in Attack Against Abortion Rights."

57. https://www.azquotes.com/author/12140-Ronald_Reagan

58. Spencer Kornhaber, "How Madonna Gave Trump Ammo With a Cry for Peace," *The Atlantic*, January 23, 2017, https://www.theatlantic.com/entertainment/archive/2017/01/madonna-trump-blow-up-the-white-house-womens-march-speech/514106/.

59. Ian Schwartz, "Ashley Judd At D.C. Women's March: 'I Am a Nasty Woman; A Loud, Vulgar, Proud Woman,'" RealClearHoldings, LLC, January 21, 2017, https://www.realclearpolitics.com/video/2017/01/21/ashley_judd_at_dc_womens_march_i_am_a_nasty_woman_a_loud_vulgar_proud_woman.html.

60. Diana Pearl, "'Pussyhats' Galore: Inside the Pink Toppers Thousands Will Wear to the Women's March on Washington," Meredith Corporation, January 21, 2017, https://people.com/politics/pussyhats-galore-inside-the-pink-toppers-thousands-will-wear-to-the-womens-march-on-washington/.

61. "Tamika Mallory and Bob Bland Discuss Women's March Controversy," YouTube, 8:42, *The View*, January 14, 2019, https://www.youtube.com/watch?v=iRzOS7SNKmY.

62. "Farrakhan Again Describes Hitler as a 'Very Great Man,'" *New York Times*, July 17, 1984, https://www.nytimes.com/1984/07/17/us/farrakhan-again-describes-hitler-as-a-very-great-man.html.

63. Josefin Dolsten, "Farrakhan's Anti-Semitic Tweet Gets Deleted After Twitter Policy Change," The Forward Association Inc., July 10, 2019, https://forward.com/fast-forward/427327/louis-farrakhan-s-2018-tweet-comparing-jews-to-termites-is-gone-after/.

64. Chris Perez, "Ilhan Omar Blasted Over Latest 'Anti-Semitic' Tweet About Israel," *New York Post*, March 3, 2019, https://nypost.com/2019/03/03/ilhan-omar-blasted-over-latest-anti-semitic-tweet-about-israel/.

65. https://townhall.com/tipsheet/bethbaumann/2019/05/12/seriously-rashida-tlaib-gets-a-warm-feeling-when-thinking-about-the-holocaust-n2546210

66. Ibid.

67. https://www.theguardian.com/us-news/2019/sep/25/trumps-phone-call-with-ukraines-president-read-the-full-transcript

68. https://www.politico.com/story/2019/01/04/dems-livid-tlaib-impeachment-comment-1081370

Chapter 10: Behind the Mask: Greed and Racism

1. https://www.linkedin.com/pulse/so-we-mourn-catherine-davis/?trackingId=hYWhGxf2Qmal6b1qsvZAiQ%3D%3D; Salvation Army founder William Booth, said, "God loves with a great love the man whose heart is bursting with a passion for the impossible." Booth added, "I am not waiting for a move of God, I am a move of God!"

2. "Abortion Cost," CostHelper, Inc., October 3, 2019, https://health.costhelper.com/abortion.html.

3. Garrett Johnson, "Documentary: The Business of Abortion "'Blood Money,'" Catholic Links, January 17, 2018, https://catholic-link.org/documentary-business-abortion-blood-money/.

4. Abortion Is Big Business for Planned Parenthood," LifeSiteNews, April 15, 2002, https://www. lifesitenews.com/news/abortion-is-big-business-for-planned-parenthood.

5. Howard Fischer, "House Speaker Bowers Says Schools Chief "Radicalizing' Children Through Sex Education," Arizona Daily Star, September 17, 2019, https://tucson.com/news/local/house-speaker-says-schools-chief-radicalizing-children-through-sex-education/article_e4227e91-dce1-58a4-8c55-abcbd0f70967.html.

6. Jerrod MacDonald-Evoy, "House Speaker Bowers Calls Hoffman "Radical' for Pushing Comprehensive Sex Ed," Arizona Mirror, September 17, 2019, https://www.azmirror. com/2019/09/17/house-speaker-bowers-calls-hoffman-radical-for-pushing-comprehensive-sex-ed/.

7. "The Business of Abortion 'Blood Money' (a documentary)," YouTube.

8. Ibid.

9. Ibid.

10. https://www.lifenews.com/2019/08/30/former-planned-parenthood-instructor-we-pushed-sex-ed-on-kids-to-create-a-market-for-abortion/?fbclid=IwAR2kCcuUPyMNeKL10ote8U1tgi8fFpmhHJ0MNitvnM2G22h6CPiV-xOUP-k

11. Ibid.

12. Ibid.

13. https://www.lifenews.com/2015/01/28/planned-parenthood-is-americas-biggest-abortion-business-operates-45-of-all-abortion-clinics/

14. "100 Years 2016-2017 Annual Report," Planned Parenthood, October 4, 2019, https:// www.plannedparenthood.org/uploads/filer_public/d4/50/d450c016-a6a9-4455-bf7f-711067db5ff7/20171229_ar16-17_p01_lowres.pdf, 31. See also Randall O'Bannon, "Planned Parenthood Makes Almost $1.3 Billion Killing 324,000 Babies in Abortions," LifeSiteNews, January 7, 2016, https://www.lifenews.com/2016/01/07/planned-parenthood-makes-almost-1-3-billion-killing-324000-babies-in-abortions/.

15. "A Balance Sheet of Death: Planned Parenthood's Abortion Business Profits Continue to Soar as Prenatal and Miscarriage 'Services' Precipitously Dwindle," ACLJ, October 4, 2019, https://aclj.org/pro-life/a-balance-sheet-of-death-planned-parenthoods-abortion-business-profits-continue-to-soar-as-prenatal-and-miscarriage-services-precipitously-dwindle.

16. https://www.afa.net/the-stand/culture/2019/08/planned-parenthood-minus-60-million-per-year/

17. Ibid.

18. O'Bannon, "Planned Parenthood Makes Almost $1.3 Billion Killing 324,000 Babies in Abortions."

19. "Recognized as Top-Ranking Nonprofit by Philanthropic Experts," Planned Parenthood, January 30, 2014, https://www.plannedparenthood.org/about-us/newsroom/press-releases/planned-parenthood-recognized-top-ranking-nonprofit-philanthropic-experts.

20. Sarah McCammon, "With Abortion Rights on the Line, Planned Parenthood Announces 2020 Push," NPR, October 9, 2019, https://www.npr.org/2019/10/09/768399183/with-abortion-rights-on-the-line-planned-parenthood-announces-2020-push; https://www.breitbart.com/politics/2019/10/09/planned-parenthood-to-spend-45m-to-beat-trump-flip-senate/

21. "Second Planned Parenthood Senior Executive Haggles Over Baby Parts Prices, Changes Abortion Methods," The Center for Medical Progress, July 21, 2015, http://www.centerformedicalprogress.org/2015/07/second-planned-parenthood-senior-executive-haggles-over-baby-parts-prices-changes-abortion-methods/.

22. Ibid.

23. Ibid.

24. "Human Capital–Episode 3: Planned Parenthood's Custom Abortions for Superior Product," YouTube, 10:37, The Center for Medical Progress, August 19, 2015, https://www.youtube.com/watch?v=FzMAycMMXp8&has_verified=1.

25. Ibid.

26. Ibid.

27. Ibid.

28. Ibid.

29. Ibid.

30. Steven Ertelt, "Video Catches Planned Parenthood Abortionist Joking About Eyeballs From Aborted Babies 'Rolling Into Our Laps,'" LifeSiteNews, May 25, 2017, https://www.lifenews.com/2017/05/25/video-catches-planned-parenthood-abortionist-joking-about-eyeballs-from-aborted-babies-rolling-into-our-laps/.

31. "Obeying Orders," Facing History and Ourselves, October 4, 2019, https://www.facinghistory.org/holocaust-and-human-behavior/chapter-10/obeying-orders.

32. Ibid.

33. Ibid.

34. Ibid.

35. "Planned Parenthood Baby Parts Buyer StemExpress Wants 'Another 50 Livers/Week,'" YouTube, 9:42, The Center for Medical Progress, August 25, 2015, https://www.youtube.com/watch?v=cz1gRNPgMvE.

36. "Second Planned Parenthood Senior Executive Haggles Over Baby Parts Prices, Changes Abortion Methods," The Center for Medical Progress.

37. Steven Ertelt, "Full, Unedited 8th Video Confirms Planned Parenthood Sells Fully Intact Aborted Babies," LifeSiteNews, August 28, 2015, https://www.lifenews.com/2015/08/28/full-unedited-8th-video-confirms-planned-parenthood-sells-fully-intact-aborted-babies/.

38. https://www.lifesitenews.com/news/planned-parenthood-to-spend-45-million-to-defeat-trump-retake-congress

39. Catherine Davis, "So, We Mourn," LinkedIn Corporation," September 8, 2019, https://www.linkedin.com/pulse/so-we-mourn-catherine-davis-/?trackingId=hYWhGxf2Qmal6b1qsvZAiQ%3D%3D

40. https://www.nytimes.com/1996/12/14/world/swiss-acknowledge-profiting-from-nazi-gold.html

41. "42 U.S. Code § 289g—2. Prohibitions Regarding Human Fetal Tissue," Legal Information Institute, October 4, 2019, https://www.law.cornell.edu/uscode/text/42/289g-2.

42. Micaiah Bilger, "Planned Parenthood Admits in Court That It Sold Body Parts From Aborted Babies," LifeSiteNews, September 4, 2019, https://www.lifenews.com/2019/09/04/planned-parenthood-admits-in-court-that-it-sold-body-parts-from-aborted-babies/.

43. "Undercover Journalist David Daleiden Wants Planned Parenthood to Produce Evidence," Thomas Moore Society, July 19, 2018, https://www.thomasmoresociety.org/tag/daleiden/page/2/.

44. Becky Yeh, "7 Incredibly Shocking Quotes From Planned Parenthood Founder Margaret Sanger," LifeSiteNews, February 23, 2015, https://www.lifenews.com/2015/02/23/7-shocking-quotes-from-planned-parenthood-founder-margaret-sanger/

45. Yeh, "7 Incredibly Shocking Quotes From Planned Parenthood Founder Margaret Sanger," emphasis added.

46. "Joseph Goebbels," AZ Quotes, October 1, 2019, https://www.azquotes.com/quote/823348.

47. "Two Movements, One Vision," Priests for Life, October 1, 2019, http://www. civilrightsfortheunborn.org/about.htm.

48. "Planned Parenthood Targets Minority Neighborhoods," Protecting Black Life, October 1, 2019, https://www.protectingblacklife.org/pp_targets/index.html.

49. Margaret Sanger, *The Autobiography of Margaret Sanger* (Mineola, NY: Dover Publications, 2004), 366.

50. "History of Lynchings," NAACP, October 1, 2019, https://www.naacp.org/history-of-lynchings/.

51. "Nazism and Planned Parenthood," Restoring America, October 4, 2019, http://www. restoringamerica.org/nazism_planned_parenthood.htm.

52. Yeh, "7 Incredibly Shocking Quotes From Planned Parenthood Founder Margaret Sanger."

53. "America Needs a Code for Babies," Margaret Sanger Project, March 27, 1934, https://www.nyu.edu/ projects/sanger/webedition/app/documents/show.php?sangerDoc=101807.xml.

54. Leana S. Wen, "Leana Wen: Why I Left Planned Parenthood," New York Times, July 19, 2019, https://www.nytimes.com/2019/07/19/opinion/sunday/leana-wen-planned-parenthood.html.

55. Catherine Davis, "So, We Mourn," LinkedIn Corporation," September 8, 2019, https://www.linkedin. com/pulse/so-we-mourn-catherine-davis/?trackingId=hYWhGxf2Qmal6b1qsvZAiQ%3D%3D

56. Klan Parenthood home page, Life Dynamics, October 1, 2019, https://www.klannedparenthood. com/.

57. Ibid.

58. Ibid.

59. Ibid.

60. Tessa Longbons, "More African-American Babies Are Aborted Than Born Alive in New York City," LifeSiteNews, December 21, 2018, https://www.lifenews.com/2018/12/21/more-african-american-babies-are-aborted-than-born-alive-in-new-york-city/.

61. "Two Movements, One Vision," Priests for Life.

62. George Neumayr, "Jesse Jackson: 'Abortion Is Black Genocide,'" The American Spectator, September 30, 2005, https://spectator.org/1188_jesse-jackson-abortion-black-genocide/

63. Ibid.

64. Abby Goodnough, "Jesse Jackson Takes Up Cause of Schiavo's Parents," New York Times, March 30, 2005, https://www.nytimes.com/2005/03/30/us/jesse-jackson-takes-up-cause-of-schiavos-parents. html.

65. Timothy W. Ryback, "A Disquieting Book From Hitler's Library," *New York Times*, December 7, 2011, https://www.nytimes.com/2011/12/08/opinion/a-disquieting-book-from-hitlers-library.html.

66. "The Nazis and Abortion," Christian Patriots For Life, October 4, 2019, https://www.cpforlife.org/ the-nazis-and-abortion.

67. Ibid.

68. Ibid.

69. Ibid.

70. Pamela Newkirk, "The Man Who Was Caged in a Zoo," *The Guardian*, June 3, 2015, https://www. theguardian.com/world/2015/jun/03/the-man-who-was-caged-in-a-zoo.

71. Beth Hale, "Caged in the Human Zoo: The Shocking Story of the Young Pygmy Warrior Put on Show in a Monkey House—and How He Fuelled Hitler's Twisted Beliefs," *Daily Mail*, October 30, 2009,

http://www.dailymail.co.uk/news/article-1224189/Caged-human-zoo-The-shocking-story-young-pygmy-warrior-monkey-house--fuelled-Hitlers-twisted-beliefs.html#ixzz455eFRo5P.

72. Ibid.

73. http://archive.jsonline.com/greensheet/martin-luther-king-packs-the-auditorium--in-1964-b99656814z1--366636381.html

Chapter 11: A Dark Web:
The Systematic Attempt to Silence Our Voice

1. Breck Dumas, "Mark Zuckerberg Brags That Facebook Blocked Pro-Life Ads Ahead of Ireland's Vote," Blaze Media, LLC, July 9, 2019, https://www.theblaze.com/news/ready-mark-zuckerberg-brags-about-facebook-blocking-pro-life-ads-ahead-of-irelands-vote.

2. Timothy J. Mercaldo, "Here we go again… will not let this rest…I will continue to post the letter to NY Gov. FB keeps flagging me with no response their review. Waiting…," Facebook, January 29, 2019, https://www.facebook.com/photo.php?fbid=10156195962386275&set=a.109665661274&type=3&theater

3. Franklin Graham, "Facebook is censoring free speech. The free exchange of ideas is part of our country's DNA," Facebook, December 28, 2018, https://www.facebook.com/FranklinGraham/posts/2265315136857988.

4. Sam Wolfson, "Facebook Labels Declaration of Independence as 'Hate Speech,'" Guardian News & Media Limited, July 5, 2018, https://www.theguardian.com/world/2018/jul/05/facebook-declaration-of-independence-hate-speech.

5. "Pro-life Groups Call on Twitter to Stop Blocking Them From Advertising," Blunt Force Truth, October 14, 2017, https://bluntforcetruth.com/news/pro-life-groups-call-on-twitter-to-stop-blocking-them-from-advertising/; Hayley Tsukayama, "Twitter Blocked a Congresswoman's Antiabortion Ad Over 'Baby Body Parts.' But It Allowed an Identical Tweet," *Washington Post*, October 10, 2017, https://www.washingtonpost.com/news/the-switch/wp/2017/10/10/twitter-blocked-a-congresswomans-antiabortion-ad-over-baby-body-parts-but-it-allowed-an-identical-tweet/.

6. Project Veritas, "Shocking and appalling new footage obtained by David Daleiden's Center for Medical Progress exposing yet another high level Planned Parenthood executive…," Facebook, July 21, 2015, https://www.facebook.com/projectveritas/posts/shocking-and-appalling-new-footage-obtained-by-david-daleidens-center-for-medica/864413990310787/. See also The Center for Medical Progress, ·Second Planned Parenthood Senior Executive Haggles Over Baby Parts Prices, Changes Abortion Methods, YouTube, July 21, 2015, https://www.youtube.com/watch?t=31&v=MjCs_gvImyw&fbclid=IwAR18fg83PhblLQb_iNvXrOV34UFgICGoex8UmCU0HDLnkXUwJXXQZl9DuQA.

7. https://www.reddit.com/r/conspiracy/comments/c50cak/googleyoutube_has_censored_the_project_veritas/

8. https://www.infowars.com/google-censors-project-veritas-video-exposing-googles-censorship/

9. https://www.thenewamerican.com/usnews/politics/item/34203-report-youtube-blocked-more-than-300-of-trump-s-ads

10. https://twitter.com/DonaldJTrumpJr/status/1220723778382106624/photo/1?ref_src=twsrc%5Etfw%7Ctwcamp%5Etweetembed%7Ctwterm%5E1220723778382106624&ref_

url=https%3A%2F%2Fwww.thegatewaypundit.com%2F2020%2F01%2Ftwitter-attaches-warning-to-president-donald-trumps-historic-speech-at-march-for-life%2F

11. https://www.thegatewaypundit.com/2020/01/twitter-attaches-warning-to-president-donald-trumps-historic-speech-at-march-for-life/

12. "Google Is Evil: YouTube Censors Top Trump Media Outlet Right Side Broadcasting Network—Removes Live-Stream Capabilities," The Gateway Pundit, September 16, 2019, https://www.thegatewaypundit.com/2019/09/google-is-evil-youtube-censors-top-trump-media-outlet-right-side-broadcasting-network-removes-live-stream-capabilities/; RSBN (@RSBNetwork), 2019, "After 300 million + views of President @realDonaldTrump rallies and 4 years following the rules on YouTube, our live streaming ability was taken away with no explanation. We have ZERO copyright or community violations on our account. We are shocked. Why, @YouTube? #FreeRSBN," Twitter, September 15, 2019, 5:52 p.m., https://twitter.com/RSBNetwork/status/1173399137129250816.

13. https://www.breitbart.com/tech/2019/10/07/twitter-apologizes-for-allowing-die-trump-to-trend-in-turkey/

14. "Facebook Briefly Blocks Netanyahu Chatbot on Election Day," Reuters, September 17, 2019, https://uk.reuters.com/article/uk-israel-election-facebook/facebook-briefly-blocks-netanyahu-chatbot-on-election-day-idUKKBN1W21PE.

15. "Facebook Briefly Blocks Netanyahu Chatbot on Election Day," Reuters.

16. "Pastor Says Facebook Blocked His Pro-Life Post for Going Against Community Standards," Christian Today, February 1, 2019, https://www.christiantoday.com/article/pastor-says-facebook-blocked-his-pro-life-post-for-going-against-community-standards/131633.htm.

17. "Facebook Blocks Ads for Pro-Life Movie 'Roe V. Wade' Starring Jon Voight," Christian Today, January 21, 2019, https://www.christiantoday.com/article/facebook-blocks-ads-for-pro-life-movie-roe-v-wade-starring-jon-voight/131522.htm.

18. Jim McNeff, "Google Labels the Movie 'Unplanned' as 'Propaganda,'" Badge 145, April 12, 2019, https://badge145.com/google-labels-the-movie-unplanned-as-propaganda/.

19. Paul Bond and Katie Kilkenny, "Anti-Abortion Movie's Twitter Account Briefly Suspended," The Hollywood Reporter, March 30, 2019, by https://www.hollywoodreporter.com/news/unplanned-movie-twitter-account-briefly-suspended-1198343.

20. "Stifling Free Speech: Technological Censorship and the Public Discourse," Committee on the Judiciary, April 10, 2019, https://www.judiciary.senate.gov/imo/media/doc/Konzelman%20Testimony.pdf.

21. 2017–2018 Annual Report, Planned Parenthood, September 29, 2019 https://www.plannedparenthood.org/uploads/filer_public/4a/0f/4a0f3969-cf71-4ec3-8a90-733c01ee8148/190124-annualreport18-p03.pdf.

22. "Stifling Free Speech," Committee on the Judiciary.

23. "Stifling Free Speech," Committee on the Judiciary.

24. Adi Domocos, "Top 30 Most Visited Websites in the World—2018 Edition," Hot in Social Media, July 9, 2018, https://hotinsocialmedia.com/top-30-most-visited-websites-in-the-world/.

25. "Sen. Cruz: Google Subjects the American People to Overt Censorship and Covert Manipulation," U.S. Senator for Texas Ted Cruz, press release, July 16, 2019, https://www.cruz.senate.gov/?p=press_release&id=4589.

26. Gagan Bhangu, "Ten of the Most Popular Search Engines in the World," otechworld.com, updated April 29, 2019, https://otechworld.com/most-popular-search-engines-in-world/.

27. "Google to Acquire YouTube for $1.65 Billion in Stock," Google Media, October 9, 2006, https://googlepress.blogspot.com/2006/10/google-to-acquire-youtube-for-165_09.html.

28. "Sen. Cruz: Google Subjects the American People to Overt Censorship and Covert Manipulation," U.S. Senator for Texas Ted Cruz.

29. "36 Mind Blowing YouTube Facts, Figures and Statistics—2017 (re-post)," Videonitch, December 13, 2017, http://videonitch.com/2017/12/13/36-mind-blowing-youtube-facts-figures-statistics-2017-re-post/.

30. Domocos, "Top 30 Most Visited Websites in the World—2018 Edition."

31. Ashley Rae Goldenberg and Dan Gainor, "CENSORED! How Online Media Companies Are Suppressing Conservative Speech," Media Research Center, April 16, 2018, https://www.newsbusters.org/blogs/culture/ashley-rae-goldenberg/2018/04/16/censored-how-online-media-companies-are-suppressing.

32. Nathan Reiff, "Top Companies Owned by Facebook," Dotdash, updated June 25, 2019, https://www.investopedia.com/articles/personal-finance/051815/top-11-companies-owned-facebook.asp.

33. Domocos, "Top 30 Most Visited Websites in the World—2018 Edition."

34. Todd Clarke, "22+ Instagram Stats That Marketers Can't Ignore This Year," Hootsuite Inc., March 5, 2019, https://blog.hootsuite.com/instagram-statistics/.

35. Domocos, "Top 30 Most Visited Websites in the World—2018 Edition."

36. "Twitter by the Numbers: Stats, Demographics & Fun Facts," Omnicore Agency, updated September 5, 2019, https://www.omnicoreagency.com/twitter-statistics/.

37. "Sen. Cruz: Google Is a Monopoly That Is Abusing Its Power," U.S. Senator for Texas Ted Cruz, press release, July 16, 2019, https://www.cruz.senate.gov/?p=press_release&id=4586.

38. "The Goebbels Diaries," *Life* 24, no. 13 (March 29, 1948), https://tinyurl.com/y24m9lzp.

39. https://townhall.com/columnists/johnhawkins/2018/01/13/how-conservatives-are-being-destroyed-by-facebook-twitter-and-google-without-even-realizing-it-n2433962

40. Ibid.

41. Ibid.

42. Ibid.

43. https://www.thenewamerican.com/usnews/politics/item/34203-report-youtube-blocked-more-than-300-of-trump-s-ads

44. "Sputnik Exclusive: Research Proves Google Manipulates Millions to Favor Clinton," Sputnik, September 14, 2016, https://sputniknews.com/us/201609121045214398-google-clinton-manipulation-election/.

45. Ibid.

46. Ibid.

47. Ibid.

48. "Sen. Cruz Questions Victims of Censorship on Google's Bias," YouTube, 12:08, Senator Ted Cruz, July 18, 2019, https://www.youtube.com/watch?v=IzF7nBmwPso.

49. Ibid.

50. Ibid.

51. Ibid.

52. https://tinyurl.com/trfovhv

53. https://www.realclearpolitics.com/video/2018/01/12/project_veritas_hidden_camera_twitter_and_reddit_do_shadow_ban_certain_political_opinions.html

54. Ibid.

55. Ibid.

56. Ibid.

57. Victor Garcia, "Google wants Trump to lose in 2020, former engineer for tech giant says: 'That's their agenda,'" Fox News, August 3, 2019, https://www.foxnews.com/media/fired-google-engineer-fears-company-will-try-and-influence-2020-election-they-really-want-trump-to-lose

58. Kate Conger, "Google Removes 'Don't Be Evil' Clause From Its Code of Conduct," G/O Media Inc., May 18, 2018, https://gizmodo.com/google-removes-nearly-all-mentions-of-dont-be-evil-from-1826153393.

59. https://www.azquotes.com/quote/566433

60. https://theintercept.com/2018/08/01/google-china-search-engine-censorship/

61. https://www.youtube.com/watch?v=_yzIYZbS8b8

62. https://newyork.cbslocal.com/2018/04/24/china-assigns-every-citizen-a-social-credit-score-to-identify-who-is-and-isnt-trustworthy/

63. https://tinyurl.com/ruukgsn

64. https://www.bbc.com/news/world-asia-china-34592186

65. https://newyork.cbslocal.com/2018/04/24/china-assigns-every-citizen-a-social-credit-score-to-identify-who-is-and-isnt-trustworthy/

66. https://newyork.cbslocal.com/2018/04/24/china-assigns-every-citizen-a-social-credit-score-to-identify-who-is-and-isnt-trustworthy/

67. Joseph Farah, "Everything you need to know about Snopes," WND, September 11, 2018, https://www.wnd.com/2018/09/everything-you-need-to-know-about-snopes/.

68. In personal communication with the author.

69. https://www.crosstv.com/uploads/1/2/5/5/125556243/wpcatalog2013.pdf

70. https://www.youtube.com/watch?v=mUv8GxrqXPk

71. https://www.youtube.com/watch?v=UaEA6bu8kew

72. https://www.youtube.com/watch?v=NrnW6-pjQa0

73. https://www.youtube.com/watch?v=r_RY3byWdnQ

74. https://www.youtube.com/watch?v=vk_i0ouWvrA

75. https://www.youtube.com/watch?v=ScWDC0dZ-NQ

76. https://www.youtube.com/watch?v=1r98-33BrMk

77. https://www.prageru.com/video/google-is-censoring-the-10-commandments/

78. "Google and Censorship Through Search Engines," Committee on the Judiciary, July 16, 2019, https://www.judiciary.senate.gov/meetings/google-and-censorship-though-search-engines.

79. "Sen. Cruz: Google Is a Monopoly That Is Abusing Its Power," U.S. Senator for Texas Ted Cruz.

80. "Sen. Cruz: Google Subjects the American People to Overt Censorship and Covert Manipulation," U.S. Senator for Texas Ted Cruz.

81. https://www.breitbart.com/tech/2019/11/22/sacha-baron-cohen-calls-silicon-valley-greatest-propaganda-machine-in-history-for-hate-groups/

82. https://www.abbyjohnson.org/abbyjohnson/2019/3/29/transcript-abby-johnson-sb9-testimony-kentuck

83. https://news.yahoo.com/baron-cohen-facebook-let-hitler-post-anti-semitic-215843464.html

84. "Sen. Cruz: Google Is a Monopoly That Is Abusing Its Power," U.S. Senator for Texas Ted Cruz, emphasis added.

85. "Give Lively," Stripe, September 29, 2019, https://stripe.com/partners/give-lively.

86. Goldenberg and Gainor, "CENSORED! How Online Media Companies Are Suppressing Conservative Speech."

87. Christine Rousselle, "Alliance Defending Freedom Booted From Amazon Smile Program Over 'Hate Group' Label," CAN, May 7, 2018, https://www.catholicnewsagency.com/news/alliance-defending-freedom-booted-from-amazon-smile-program-over-hate-group-label-12911.

88. Tyler O'Neil, "Southern Poverty Law Center Compares Conservative Christians Like Ted Cruz to ISIS," PJ Media, September 14, 2017 https://pjmedia.com/faith/2017/09/14/southern-poverty-law-center-compares-mainstream-christians-like-ted-cruz-to-isis/.

89. Paul Bedard, "Southern Poverty Law Center Website Triggered FRC Shooting," Washington Examiner, February 6, 2013, https://www.washingtonexaminer.com/southern-poverty-law-center-website-triggered-frc-shooting.

90. "In 2018, 36 Hate Groups Were Tracked in Ohio," The Southern Poverty Law Center, September 29, 2019, https://www.splcenter.org/states/ohio.

91. Tyler O'Neil, "Southern Poverty Law Center: 'Our Aim in Life Is to Destroy These Groups, Completely,'" PJ Media, September 1, 2017 https://pjmedia.com/trending/2017/09/01/southern-poverty-law-center-our-aim-in-life-is-to-destroy-these-groups-completely/.

92. Domocos, "Top 30 Most Visited Websites in the World—2018 Edition."

93. Bre Payton, "Amazon Boots Christian Nonprofit From Donations Program Because of SPLC's 'Hate List,'" The Federalist, May 3, 2018, https://thefederalist.com/2018/05/03/amazon-boots-christian-nonprofit-from-donations-program-because-of-splcs-hate-list/.

94. Brandon Showalter, "Christian Authors Blast Amazon for Banning Their Books, Selling Pedophilia Titles," Christian Post Inc., August 30, 2019, https://www.christianpost.com/news/christian-authors-blast-amazon-banning-their-books-selling-pedophilia-titles-232747/.

95. Showalter, "Christian Authors Blast Amazon for Banning Their Books, Selling Pedophilia Titles."

96. Ibid.

97. John D. McKinnon, "States to Launch Google, Facebook Antitrust Probes," *Wall Street Journal*, updated September 6, 2019, https://www.wsj.com/articles/states-to-launch-google-facebook-antitrust-probes-11567762204.

98. "Sen. Cruz: Google Is a Monopoly That Is Abusing Its Power," U.S. Senator for Texas Ted Cruz.

99. Emily Crane, "Dozens of State Attorney Generals Set to Begin Their Anti-Trust Investigation Into Google and Facebook NEXT WEEK–Adding to the Scrutiny the Tech Giants Are Already Facing in a Federal Probe," *Daily Mail*, September 6, 2019, https://www.dailymail.co.uk/news/article-7435191/States-begin-antitrust-probe-Google-Facebook.html.

100. Crane, "Dozens of State Attorney Generals Set to Begin Their Anti-Trust Investigation Into Google and Facebook NEXT WEEK."

101. NY AG James (@NewYorkStateAG), 2019, "I'm launching an investigation into Facebook to determine whether their actions endangered consumer data, reduced the quality of consumers' choices, or increased the price of advertising. The largest social media platform in the world must

follow the law," Twitter, September 6, 2019, 4:58 a.m., https://twitter.com/NewYorkStateAG/status/1169942938023071744.

102. Lauren Feiner, "Google Faces a New Antitrust Probe by 50 Attorneys General," CNBC, September 9, 2019, https://www.cnbc.com/2019/09/09/texas-attorney-general-leads-google-antitrust-probe.html.

103. Feiner, "Google Faces a New Antitrust Probe by 50 Attorneys General."

104. Ibid.

105. "Sen. Cruz: Google Is a Monopoly That Is Abusing Its Power," U.S. Senator for Texas Ted Cruz.

106. https://video.foxnews.com/v/6117450381001#sp=show-clips

107. https://thehill.com/policy/technology/460931-koch-group-targets-attorneys-general-with-ads-defending-tech-giants

108. https://video.foxnews.com/v/6117450381001#sp=show-clips

109. https://www.breitbart.com/tech/2019/07/03/josh-hawley-supposedly-libertarian-tech-groups-swamped-in-google-facebook-cash/

110. Ibid.

111. https://video.foxnews.com/v/6117450381001#sp=show-clips

112. https://video.foxnews.com/v/6117450381001#sp=show-clips

113. Ibid.

114. Ibid.

115. Ibid.

116. Ibid.

117. Ashley Lutz, "These 6 Corporations Control 90% of the Media in America," Insider Inc., June 14, 2012, https://www.businessinsider.com/these-6-corporations-control-90-of-the-media-in-america-2012-6.

118. Porter, True to Life, 1–6, 107.

119. "Roy Moore Spokeswoman's Interview With Anderson Cooper," YouTube, 15:50, CNN, December 6, 2017, https://www.youtube.com/watch?v=Q7E93Fe0-ow.

120. John Nolte, "Nolte: CNN Loses Nearly 50% of Primetime Audience, MSNBC Down Nearly 30%," Breitbart, April 17, 2019, https://www.breitbart.com/the-media/2019/04/17/nolte-cnn-loses-nearly-50-of-primetime-audience-msnbc-down-nearly-30/.

121. Nolte, "Nolte: CNN Loses Nearly 50% of Primetime Audience, MSNBC Down Nearly 30%."

122. Brian Flood, "Fox News Beats CNN, MSNBC Combined in Ratings, Tops All of Cable," FOX News Network, LLC., June 18, 2019, https://www.foxnews.com/entertainment/fox-news-beats-cnn-msnbc-combined-in-ratings-tops-all-of-cable.

123. Flood, "Fox News Beats CNN, MSNBC Combined in Ratings, Tops All of Cable."

124. https://www.breitbart.com/the-media/2019/12/06/bottom-falls-out-cnn-ratings-hit-3-year-low/

125. Ibid.

126. http://www.quotationspage.com/quote/33739.html

Notes

Chapter 12: Pick Up the Sword

1. "Heartbeat Bill Celebration: Knights of Columbus," YouTube, 4:25, faith2action, September 29, 2011, https://www.youtube.com/watch?v=ElRCN_rxFCU.
2. https://www.azquotes.com/quote/530616
3. Jerry Fallwell (@JerryFallwellJr), 2017, "'A mans greatness is measured not by his talent or his wealth, but by what it takes to discourage him.' Jerry Falwell Sr." June 13, 2017, 11:20 a.m., https://twitter.com/jerryfalwelljr/status/874692991453155328?lang=en.
4. Dr. and Mrs. Howard Taylor, *Hudson Taylor's Spiritual Secret* (n.p.: Incense House Publishing, 2013).
5. Dietrich Bonhoeffer, *The Cost of Discipleship* (New York: Touchstone, 1995), 44
6. "Dangers of the New Century," The Homiletic Review 44 (July–December 1902): 382, https://books.google.com/books?id=qUJQAQAAMAAJ&pg; "William Booth Quotes," Goodreads, Inc., October 2, 2019, https://www.goodreads.com/quotes/291048-the-chief-danger-that-confronts-the-coming-century-will-be.
7. Bobby Conner, "The Secret to True Boldness," Eagles View Ministries, March 8, 2018, https://www.bobbyconner.org/articles/The-Secret-to-True-Boldness.
8. https://everydaypower.com/dave-ramsey-quotes/
9. https://www.abbyjohnson.org/abbyjohnson/2019/3/29/transcript-abby-johnson-sb9-testimony-kentuck
10. https://afomail.net/?_task=mail&_caps=pdf%3D1%2Cflash%3D1%2Ctif%3D0&_uid=41148&_mbox=INBOX&_search=0d3a5b7f49b4b0a5642a1a7d9afd8524&_action=show
11. https://www.cleveland.com/open/2019/04/ohio-house-passes-heartbeat-abortion-ban.html
12. https://www.breitbart.com/politics/2019/04/11/ohio-gov-mike-dewine-signs-heartbeat-abortion-bill-into-law/
13. https://www.lifesitenews.com/news/trump-makes-roe-anniversary-sanctity-of-life-day-we-will-never-tire-of-defending-innocent-life
14. https://www.lifesitenews.com/news/full-text-trumps-2020-march-for-life-speech

Epilogue: Take the Land

1. https://www.azquotes.com/quote/872037
2. https://billygraham.org/answer/did-jesus-ever-say-anything-about-hell-i-dont-believe-in-hell-myself/
3. https://www.azquotes.com/quote/757359
4. https://www.britannica.com/topic/NARAL-Pro-Choice-America
5. https://www.dallasnews.com/news/dallas/2017/02/19/norma-mccorveys-journey-roe-v-wade-plaintiff-anti-abortion-activist-words
6. https://www.youtube.com/watch?v=T_MUUvcvjEg
7. https://www.lifenews.com/2014/09/30/sandra-cano-doe-of-doe-v-bolton-abortion-case-passes-away/
8. https://www.lifenews.com/2018/01/08/this-former-abortion-activist-claimed-1-million-women-died-in-back-alley-abortions-then-he-admitted-he-lied/

9. https://www.bmj.com/rapid-response/2011/11/03/how-abortion-movement-started-deceit-and-lies-dr-nathanson

10. https://www.priestsforlife.org/testimonies/1130-testimony-of-dr-bernard-nathanson-co-founder-of-naral-

11. https://www.goodreads.com/quotes/574599-salvation-is-not-a-reward-for-the-righteous-it-is

12. https://www.azquotes.com/author/33490-Reinhard_Bonnke

13. https://fbcclarendon.com/salvation_15326

14. http://brownsvillebaptist.com/how_to_be_saved

15. https://www.azquotes.com/quote/954246

16. https://jesus-is-savior.com/Believer's%20Corner/promises.htm

17. https://bethelmusic.com/blog/bill-johnson-quotes/

18. file:///C:/Users/Janet/AppData/Local/Temp/Understanding%20the%20Trinity%20-%20D-1.%20James%20Kennedy,%20Ph.D_.epub

19. https://www.azquotes.com/quote/855094

20. https://www.snopes.com/fact-check/stalin-vote-count-quote/

21. https://www.nationalreview.com/2017/08/election-fraud-registered-voters-outnumber-eligible-voters-462-counties/

22. https://www.forbes.com/sites/rebeccabellan/2020/02/03/twitter-bans-zerohedge-for-publishing-coronavirus-conspiracy-theory-doxxing-chinese-doctor/#254810871b30

23. https://www.zerohedge.com/news/2019-03-11/facebook-bans-zero-hedge

24. https://www.zerohedge.com/news/2016-10-24/concern-grows-over-soros-linked-voting-machines

25. https://thehill.com/policy/cybersecurity/222470-states-ditch-electronic-voting-machines

26. https://www.romper.com/p/which-states-require-a-voter-id-there-are-32-states-where-you-cant-vote-without-one-19105

27. https://www.realclearpolitics.com/articles/2019/07/13/who_will_clean_up_americas_voter_rolls_140777.html

28. https://www.washingtontimes.com/news/2009/aug/30/home-schooling-outstanding-results-national-tests/

29. https://www.washingtontimes.com/news/2009/aug/30/home-schooling-outstanding-results-national-tests/

30. https://www.washingtontimes.com/news/2009/aug/30/home-schooling-outstanding-results-national-tests/

31. https://www.washingtontimes.com/news/2009/aug/30/home-schooling-outstanding-results-national-tests/

About Janet Porter

J anet Porter is the founder and president of Faith2Action, an organization committed to winning the cultural war of life, liberty, and the family, and the architect of the pro-life Heartbeat Bill. She is a former national director of the Center for Reclaiming America, founded by Dr. D. James Kennedy, and a former legislative director of Ohio Right to Life, where she successfully lobbied for the passage of the nation's first ban on Partial-Birth abortion. Porter hosted a daily syndicated radio program and daily radio commentary in 300+ markets for nearly twenty years. She has appeared on numerous media outlets, including CNN, NBC, ABC, CBS, Fox News, and MSNBC. In addition to her pro-life advocacy, she produced the documentary *Light Wins: How to Overcome the Criminalization of Christianity* and is the author of five books: *The Criminalization of Christianity, True to Life, What's a Girl to Do While Waiting for Mr. Right?, Truth to Go*, and *30 Seconds to Common Sense*. She lives in Ohio with her husband, David.